Informatik-Fachberichte 189

Herausgegeben von W. Brauer
im Auftrag der Gesellschaft für Informatik (GI)

B. Wolfinger (Hrsg.)

Vernetzte und komplexe Informatik-Systeme

Industrieprogramm zur 18. Jahrestagung
der Gesellschaft für Informatik

Hamburg, 18./19. Oktober 1988

Proceedings

Springer-Verlag
Berlin Heidelberg New York
London Paris Tokyo

Herausgeber

Bernd E. Wolfinger
Fachbereich Informatik, Universität Hamburg
Bodenstedtstraße 16, 2000 Hamburg 50

CR Subject Classifications (1987): C.1-2, D.2, D.4, H.2

ISBN-13: 978-3-540-50462-7   e-ISBN-13: 978-3-642-74230-9
DOI: 10.1007/978-3-642-74230-9

2145/3140 – 543210 – Gedruckt auf säurefreiem Papier

Wenn man über eine richtige Theorie verfügt,
sie aber nur als etwas behandelt,
worüber man einmal schwatzt,
um es dann in die Schublade zu legen,
jedoch keineswegs in die Praxis umzusetzen,
dann wird diese Theorie,
so gut sie auch sein mag, bedeutungslos.

Mao Tse-tung ("Über die Praxis", Juli 1937)

<u>VORWORT</u>

Der vorliegende Tagungsband enthält die schriftlichen Ausarbeitungen zu den Vorträgen, die im Rahmen des zweitägigen Industrieprogramms der 18. Jahrestagung der Gesellschaft für Informatik (GI'88) präsentiert wurden. Dieses Industrieprogramm fand am 18./19. Oktober 1988 im Congress-Centrum Hamburg statt mit dem Ziel einer Vorstellung neuerer Produkte und Konzepte der Datenverarbeitung durch auf dem Gebiet der Informations- und Kommunikationstechnik tätige Unternehmen.

Die Mehrzahl der in den Proceedings enthaltenen Beiträge wurden in deutscher Sprache verfaßt; auf Wunsch mehrerer Autoren wurden allerdings - dem heutzutage durchaus üblichen Brauch entsprechend - auch englischsprachige Papiere akzeptiert. Der Anteil der angenommenen Beiträge, bezogen auf die eingereichten, lag bei ca. 60%, wobei innovative Arbeiten mit Praxisrelevanz bevorzugt berücksichtigt wurden.

Bei der Auswahl der Beiträge zum Industrieprogramm wurde im übrigen versucht, so weit wie möglich dem Leitthema "Vernetzte und komplexe Informatik-Systeme" der GI'88 gerecht zu werden. Eine hinreichend starke thematische Bündelung der Vorträge wurde durch eine Beschränkung auf die vier folgenden Themenschwerpunkte erreicht:

* Innovative Rechnerarchitekturen
* Kommunikationssysteme und verteilte Systeme
* Datenbanken und Informationssysteme
* Programmierung, Software Engineering und Mensch-Maschine-Kommunikation

Diese Themenschwerpunkte resultieren insbesondere aus dem Wunsch, auch eine gewisse Überlappung mit einigen zentralen Themen von Fachgesprächen der GI'88 zu erreichen. Auf diese Weise wurde den interessierten Unternehmen die Gelegenheit gegeben, bei einem Fachgespräch über eher forschungsorientierte Arbeiten zu berichten und diese Beiträge durch die Darstellung von eher entwicklungsorientierten Resultaten im Rahmen des Industrieprogramms zu komplettieren.

Die Themenschwerpunkte wurden auf sechs Sitzungen abgebildet, deren Inhalte in der Folge kurz zusammengefaßt werden sollen:

- Die Vorträge der Sitzung "Innovative Rechnerarchitekturen" reichen von Beispielen für die Ausnutzung der technologischen Fortschritte (VLSI-Architekturen) über Workstation - (PRISM) und Supercomputer-Architekturen (ETA 10) bis hin zu der Erprobung relativ neuer Operationsprinzipien für Rechensysteme (Datenflußrechner).

- "Kommunikationssysteme und verteilte Systeme I" beinhaltet existierende Kommunikationshard- und -software bzw. Kommunikationssystem-/Rechnernetzarchitekturen (CDCNET, Tina, Vtx).

- "Kommunikationssysteme und verteilte Systeme II" präsentiert eine Reihe von Vorschlägen zur Realisierung verteilter Betriebssysteme (CSA, DACNOS, NCS).

- Die in der Sitzung "Datenbanken und Informationssysteme" vorgestellten Datenbanklösungen der Industrie reichen von Datenbankkonzepten (z.B. für einen Software-Dictionary) über existierende Retrievalsysteme (TAURUS, GOLEM) und verteilte Datenbanken bis hin zu Datenbankanwendungen (z.B. in der Montageplanung).

- "Programmierung, Software Engineering und Mensch-Maschine-Kommunikation I" ist dem Thema Softwareentwicklung für verteilte Systeme gewidmet, wobei sowohl Methoden als auch Werkzeuge dargestellt werden (u.a. ANIMOS, DOCASE, Speedbuilder).

- Das Spektrum der Sitzung "Programmierung, Software Engineering und Mensch-Maschine-Kommunikation II" ist hingegen etwas breiter; diese Sitzung enthält Beiträge mit Bezug zur Projektierung, zum Einsatz und zur Analyse komplexer Software - bzw. Datenverarbeitungssysteme (u. a. die Informationsflußanalyse-Methode zur Systemanalyse, PPS3 zur Projektplanung und -steuerung sowie das User-Interface-Management-System THESEUS).

Mein besonderer Dank gilt den Vortragenden für die (weitgehend) termingerechte Erstellung ihrer Beiträge sowie den Sitzungsleitern, die - aus Gründen der Objektivität - allesamt aus dem Hochschulsektor gewählt wurden. Auch die Unterstützung durch Frau U. Wosegien bei der Aufbereitung der eingereichten Manuskripte für die druckfertigen Proceedings verdient lobende Erwähnung. Des weiteren sei den Firmen Apollo Domain Computer, Digital Equipment, IBM Deutschland, Philips sowie Stollmann für die freundliche Unterstützung bei der Finanzierung des vorliegenden Tagungsbandes sehr herzlich gedankt.

Es ist zu wünschen, daß das beträchtliche Engagement all dieser Personen und Institutionen dazu führt, daß auch bei der 18. Jahrestagung der GI wiederum für die Industrie ein adäquates Forum geschaffen werden konnte zur Präsentation praxisrelevanter Arbeiten mit Innovationscharakter.

Hamburg, im Oktober 1988   Bernd Wolfinger

VLSI-/370 Microprocessor Overview

Helmut Painke

IBM Laboratories
Schoenaicher Str. 220
7030 Boeblingen, West Germany

This paper gives an overview of a CMOS microprocessor implementing the IBM /370 mainframe architecture. It focuses on the design principles used and the methodology employed in the design of that unit.

Introduction

With steadily increasing circuit density on CMOS chips the time has finally come to put a mainframe architecture on a CMOS chip. As /370 is the most widely used mainframe architecture it was the natural candidate for such an implementation. This paper describes the design principles and the implementation strategy that led to the VLSI-/370 Microprocessor chipset. It serves as an introduction to the six papers referenced under {1} thru {6} which expand on the technology used, the design language employed, the various tools for logic design, delay optimization and physical design, and the verification process and experience.

The basic design goals for the VLSI-/370 Microprocessor were:

- exploit the latest CMOS technology in order to drastically increase mainframe CPU density and reduce power requirements.
- shorten the design cycle by using design tools to convert a high level design description into the actual chip image.
- ensure design integrity thru the use of before mentioned design tools and thorough verification by logic simulation.

Processor Description

To minimize the design risk we chose a proven mainframe design (the 9377-90, the high end of the 9370 line) as the base, modifying the design where necessary to reflect the partitioning constraints of the CMOS chips. The main characteristics of the processor are as follows:

- full /370 compatibility, no subsetting. Runs existing operating systems (VM/SP, VSE/SP, IX/370)
- performance critical instructions (70) directly executed in hardware, rest microcoded
- 2 byte wide microinstruction set
- 4 byte dataflow
- 3 stage pipelining
- full /370 timer facilities
- 8 kB cache, 4 way set associative
- 4 kB key store for storage protection keys
- parity checking in dataflow, ECC in main memory
- floating point support
- various cycle time options (100 ns, 80 ns, 62.5 ns)

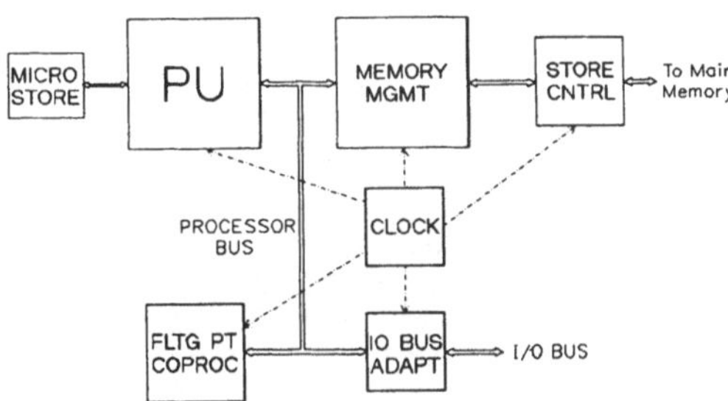

Fig. 1: VLSI-/370 Microprocessor Chip Set

Fig. 1 shows the complete chip set. The functions and characteristics of the individual chips are:

1. PU
   - 4 byte dataflow
   - 3 deep pipelining
   - 48 fullwords 3-port DLS (Data Local Store)
   - /370 timers
   - 12.7 x 12.7 mm
   - 60 k cells + DLS
   - 158 signal I/O
   - 1.8 W

Fig. 2 shows the PU chip image.

Fig. 3: Memory Management Chip Image

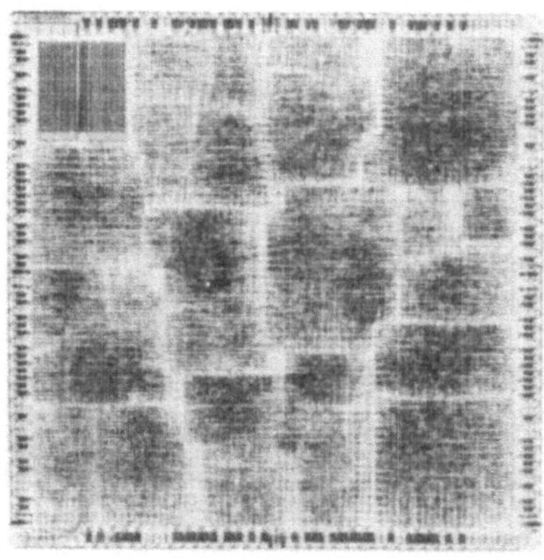

Fig. 2: PU Chip Image

2. MEMORY MANAGEMENT
   - 8 kB cache, 4 way set associative   24 ns acc
   - cache directory 4 x 32 x 17   15 ns acc
   - TLB   2 x 32 x 34   15 ns acc
   - 4 kB key store   20 ns acc
   - 12.7 x 12.7 mm
   - 25 k cells + 110 k bits
   - 143 signal I/O
   - 1.8 W

Fig. 3 shows the chip image

3. STORE CNTRL
   - memory access control
   - memory interleave
   - scrub feature to fix soft fails
   - redundant bit control
   - memory initialization
   - partial store control
   - ECC - single error correction, double error detection
   - 8.6 x 8.6 mm
   - 17 k cells
   - 161 signal I/O
   - 1.0 W

4. CLOCK
   - 52 clock generators
   - programmable (cycle, pulse width, phase)
   - programmed by Power On Reset, shift chains, or external ROM
   - system Power On Reset control
   - run control
   - clock checking
   - 7.5 x 7.5 mm
   - 17 k cells
   - 166 signal I/O
   - 1.0 W

5. I/O BUS ADAPTER
   - adapter between processor bus and up to 2 I/O buses
   - protocol conversion
   - 64 B buffer for speed matching
   - 7.5 x 7.5 mm
   - 17 k cells
   - 165 signal I/O
   - 1.5 W

6. FLOATING POINT COPROCESSOR (optional)
  - all /370 floating point instructions
  - 6 x 64 bit floating point registers
  - 9 bit exponent ALU
  - 62 bit fraction ALU
  - 62 bit shift unit
  - 8 x 56 bit multiplier
  - 9.4 x 9.4 mm
  - 23 k cells
  - 94 signal I/O
  - 1.0 W

7. MICRO STORE
  - 8 k x 18 array chip
  - dual chip module
  - 30 ns access
  - 7.25 x 6.3 mm
  - 144 k bits
  - 0.5 W

Fig. 4 shows the entire processor card.

Fig. 4: Processor Card

Design Methodology

Design Description and Compilation

One of the basic design principles was to use a high
level language description of the whole processor
throughout thus providing full syntax checking of the
input and to leave the actual circuit implementation
to automated tools, thereby eliminating a lot of trivial
errors that tend to occur on gate level input systems,
be they graphic or textual. The design language and
the compiler used to generate the technology dependent gate logic are described in separate papers
{2, 3}. Even in those rare instances where we chose
to specify the detailed circuit implementation of a
specific function (e.g. the ALU) we stayed inside the
language envelope using assembler like macro statements, but never leaving the one cohesive environment. This was by no means an easy, painless task.
Though most of the tools had been developed before,
the unique requirements of a high performance
processor design, a new technology target and, above
all, the sheer mass of data associated with a design
of that size proved to stress those tools to the limit
and constantly forced us to upgrade and extend them
in parallel to doing the actual design.

On the other hand this strategy allowed us to largely
separate the logic design from the physical implementation. This was particularly important as we
were relying on the most advanced CMOS technology which meant that in the beginning the technology
was still in a definition stage and evolved as the design got along. Changes in technology parameters
which are inevitable under those circumstances could
thus be captured at the tool level rather than surfacing at the logic design level. If, for instance, the speed
ratio between NAND and NOR gates changed the
compiler could reflect this in its strategy without the
logic designer being aware of it.

Partitioning

Of course in a VLSI environment the logic designer
can never be completely disengaged from physical
considerations. Partitioning, above all else, is of
prime importance at those integration levels. Com-
pared to less dense technologies, and especially to the
bipolar technology of the precursor system, the off
chip driver delay is dramatically different from the
on chip circuit delay, the ratio between those two
approaching an order of magnitude. Fitting the major units of a system to chip boundaries is, therefore,
the first step in defining the internal structure of that
system. This encompasses the definition of bus systems (with their associated protocols), the use of
internal arrays for speed matching and buffering (e.g.
instruction buffer), tradeoffs between the length of a
data transfer and the overhead associated with each
transfer, and the like. And even on the chip global

wiring congestion enforces conscientious use of bussing to reduce the number of wires that connect the various subunits. An absolute prerequisite for a decent VLSI partitioning is obviously the ability to fairly liberally mix logic circuits with arrays of any size and organization on the same chip. This led to the selection of the master image concept described in more detail in paper {1}.

Once the partitioning is done and the global structure is defined, detailed design can proceed on a fairly high level of textual description rather disconnected from technology evolution and chip image changes.

Physical Design

Another benefit of the master image concept is that it allows layout and wiring to use tools that were originally developed for masterslice chips. Very sophisticated placement and wiring algorithms and a mature set of programs were thus available. Nevertheless the sheer amount of design data enforced a hierarchical approach splitting the design database into several functional units that could be dealt with separately. The methodology used to determine the inter unit wiring and reflect it in floorplanning as well as the total approach used in placement and wiring is described in a separate paper {5}.

Simulation

There are two challenges to any processor design:

- to get the design logically correct according to the specifications and

- to achieve the shortest cycle time possible under the technology constraints.

Having a fairly high level structural description of the design as the only source for the implementation is certainly a big help towards achieving the first goal as it provides an excellent safeguard against all kinds of trivial errors at data entry time and allows for a multitude of consistency and rules checks. Unfortunately this does not safeguard against all logic errors as the logic description is on the structural level, not on a specification level. But even if a fully automated path from specification to gate level implementation would be available this would still leave us with the problem that specifications are seldom complete in the beginning and often change very late in the design cycle. This brings up the issue of incremental local changes which are hard to cope with in any automated design system. Furthermore, if the design tools are improved in parallel with the design the possibility of compilation errors cannot be disregarded with certainty. This forced us to resort to a supplementary strategy for design verification: logic simulation. With the size and complexity of our design the elimination of design errors that are a

showstopper in the debug phase can be quite an elaborate and resource consuming task as paper {6} shows.

An essential feature of our methodology was the ability to run mixed level simulation, i.e. initially only part of the design was available at the RT level description with the missing parts filled in by very high level behavioral models. This allowed us to start simulation already very early on a partial design and fill in the missing parts gradually. This overlap of design and verification was essential to achieving a short design cycle.

Simulation is an iterative process, with the 'simpler' errors surfacing very soon and the trickier ones showing up pretty late in the game when the test cases that are run on the model of the design get more and more sophisticated. Those late design changes, on the other hand, usually require very few locally contained modifications that just affect a few circuits and wires. To reduce turnaround time for those late changes where quick reaction is essential to the overall schedule we had some spare gates allocated dispersed over the whole chip. This strategy enabled us to make small wiring changes on chips that had been completed up to first level wiring thus cutting the implementation time for those changes to a mere fraction of what the production of a whole new chip would have taken.

Delay Optimization

Achieving the cycle time objective usually forces the logic designer to tune his design closely to the technology parameters of the individual gates and to reflect the pathlength between registers in his logic design. Both constraints are highly undesirable as they tie the design closely to the technology gyrations and burden the designer with details which keep him from concentrating on his primary job: doing a logically correct design. Since we were using a compiler anyway to generate the implementation we decided to augment our tool set with a delay calculator that provided the following functions: calculate the delay of all logic paths of a compiled design dependent on technology parameters and placement assumptions, determine the critical paths, compare them against predetermined boundaries, and feed the result back into the optimizing phase of the compiler {4}. This allowed the designer to focus his attention on the few cases where initial implementation and delay objectives were so far apart that the compiler was not able to resolve the conflicting requirements without a circuit explosion due to massive parallelism. With the extensive diagnostics available with the delay calculator the designer has then all the information necessary to fix the problem by changing the design description in an appropriate way.

Clock Design

As those portions of the system that run synchronously usually span several chips the design of the clocking system deserves special attention. If clock signals are distributed over several chips the individual chips may be drastically different with regard to process tolerances, thus the same clock signal may arrive at the using logic with quite a wide spread, referred to as clock skew. Since racefree operation requires that individual clocks must not overlap sufficient gaps must be provided to account for the clocking skew. On the other hand, these gaps, in most instances, constitute unproductive time that is lost for logic evaluation. At cycle times below 100 ns clock skews may increase the cycle by up to 10 % thus reducing processor performance accordingly. Controlled clock wiring between chips, special clock drivers and a careful selected topology for clock wiring on chip help reduce the overall clock skew.

Another problem in the design of the clocking system is late availability of exact clocking specs especially for embedded arrays when the technology is evolving in parallel to the logic design. The solution in this case was to make the clock fully programmable with all leading and trailing edges adjustable in the nanosecond range. The actual program is loadable by shifting in a bitpattern. At a very late stage in the development phase several such programs, covering a range of different applications and selectable by module pin tiedown, can be fixed in the final metal layer.

References

{1} H. Schettler, "VLSI-/370 Microprocessor Chip Technology", EUROMICRO 88, Zurich, Sept. 88

{2} W. Roesner, "The Logic Design Language and Verification Environment for the VLSI-/370 Microprocessor", EUROMICRO 88, Zurich, Sept. 88

{3} B. Kick, "Logic Synthesis in the Design of the VLSI-/370 Microprocessor", EUROMICRO 88, Zurich, Sept. 88

{4} S. Heinkele, "Timing Verification for the VLSI-/370 Microprocessor", EUROMICRO 88, Zurich, Sept. 88

{5} U. Schulz, "Hierarchical Physical Design for the VLSI-/370 Microprocessor", EUROMICRO 88, Zurich, Sept. 88

{6} H. Gerst, "VLSI-/370 Microprocessor Verification", EUROMICRO 88, Zurich, Sept. 88

The Stollmann Data Flow Machine

Michael Jöhnk, Ute Schürfeld
Stollmann GmbH *)
Max-Brauer-Allee 81
D-2000 Hamburg 50

Abstract

Most of the data flow architectures proposed in the last years aim at number crunching, which naturally seems to imply fine grain paralellism. Just so fine grain seems to lead naturally to (expensive) special hardware. Our aim is to adapt the data flow concept to commercial applications as for example from the database field. These applications more naturally lead to symbolic crunching and coarse respectively variable grain. For this reason and w.r.t. market acceptance we built a machine using off-the-shelf hardware and lifted up the data flow mechanism from hardware to software level. To avoid the classical bottleneck of "firing" we introduced parallel firing.

The dataflow mechanism is implemented on a shared memory architecture. The chosen hardware configuration is based on four processor boards – each equipped with a microprocessor and 4 MByte dual ported RAM – connected to a VMEbus. The host processor runs the UNIX V.3 operating system whereas the other three nodes run SRTX, a realtime operating system kernel. A first prototype will run in October '88.

Subjects of investigation on the prototype will be among others the correct choice of grain size, the appropriate ratio of firing control units and execution units and questions related to the topic of load balance.

1. Introduction

For a long time the principles of computer architecture design have largely remained static, based on von Neumann principles. These include a single computing element, a linear organization of fixed-size memory cells, a one-level address space of cells, a low-level machine language and at least a sequential, centralized control of computation.

The desire to utilize concurrency to increase computer performance based on the continuing demand from areas such as weather forecasting, wind tunnel simulation etc., the desire to exploit very large scale integration technique and thirdly the mismatch between the various principles of new classes of high level languages (e.g. functional) and those of von Neumann computer tending to inefficient implementations may be considered as the three basic driving forces for the development of novel computer architectures based on new "naturally" parallel organizations for computations during the last 10 to 15 years

*) This work is partly funded by ESPRIT project 415

Beside a lot of demand driven parallel architectures a broad range of approaches to parallelism are based on the pioneering work on dataflow by Rodriguez [11], Adams [1], Dennis [4] [5]. Whereas the main characteristics of the von Neumann model are a global updatable memory and a single program counter the dataflow model has neither of these.

Firstly, the dataflow model deals only with values i.e. the concept of a variable (name of a value container the value of which may be manipulated) is not known. Secondly, the dataflow model has nothing like an instruction counter : an instruction is enabled for execution if all the required input values are available. Enabled instructions consume input values for execution and produce output values which are sent to other instructions which wait for these values. In other words, the driving force of computation is the availability of data. An instruction in data flow has no side effects and there exist no sequencing constraints in a dataflow program other than the ones imposed by data dependencies. Thus, in principle, it is possible to expose all of the parallelism visible in a dataflow program.

Since the pioneering work on dataflow a large number of dataflow computer architectures have been proposed and some of them even built for example the MIT Dataflow Computer, the Distributed Data Processor (DDP) of Texas Instruments, the Data-Driven Machine #1 (DDM1) developed at Burroughs Interactive Research Center and later continued at the University of Utah, the Irvine dataflow machine (Id) originated at the University of California at Irvine and continued at MIT, the Manchester Data Flow Computer at Manchester University, the LAU System at the CERT Laboratory in Toulouse, the Newcastle Data-Control Flow Computer and a lot more. A good overview of the differing concepts in these dataflow projects may be found in [12].

Most of the mentioned dataflow architectures were developed with the idea in mind to run applications like weather forecasting, wind tunnel simulations etc. which naturally lead to the problem of number chrunching. And number crunching again seems naturally to lead to fine grain parallelism i.e. the processes which may be executed in parallel are very small, about the size of an individual machine operation in conventional computers.

To be able to exploit all parallelism at fine grain level the mechanism which determines at runtime which instructions can be executed concurrently has to be extremely quick to avoid that the processing elements simply executing these instructions but nothing else run out of work. Therefore in the above approaches (expensive) special hardware has to be provided to assure this.

In contrast to this in ESPRIT 415-E project at Stollmann GmbH the area of commercial applications is considered. It is intended to build a general purpose dataflow machine suited for running arbitrary commercial applications. The chosen example for studies which promises a worthwhile adaption of the dataflow concept is the database area (and for the future the simulation of Petri Nets used for describing the behaviour of architectures).

The commercial applications more naturally lead to symbolic crunching than number crunching. Some kind of "atomic instruction" w.r.t. the database application for example might be manipulations on tuples of relations. Other applications may lead to other application dependent natural "atomic instructions". These symbolic manipulating instructions although w.r.t. the application considered as some kind of "finest grain instruction" is of much coarser grain than an individual machine operation in conventional computers. As well there may be differing application dependent grain sizes side by side. For example manipulations on triples may be of varying granularity.

Firstly we provided load distribution and balancing mechanisms to support variable coarser grain size and secondly the concept of user-defined instructions which allows to augment the basic instruction set by application specific instructions.

Both the support of variable grain and the concept of user-defined instructions imply to deviate from the special hardware approach. And there is a second reason to do this. Because of the major hardware effort very few real machines have been built yet. Thinking about market acceptance it is of major importance to built a machine at minimal expense and with off-the-shelf hardware. In our case we use 68020 processors communicating via a VMEbus. The use of off-the-shelf hardware implies that we lift up the control mechanism which exploits parallel executable instructions at runtime, the units executing instructions as the communication between these units onto software level. This lifting up of the dataflow mechanism onto software level additionally allows it to easily reconfigurate the dataflow machine to meet application dependent requirements.

In the following chapters we first describe the Stollmann Data Flow Machine and the planned application in more detail. In the subsequent chapter we describe a first version of the prototype which is planned to run in October '88. For expansion considerations we refer to [9].

2. The Stollmann Data Flow Machine (SDFM)

In this chapter we roughly outline the dataflow approach we have chosen and the application investigated. A more detailed description of the Stollmann Data Flow Machine SDFM can be found in [10], [11].

2.1 The SDFM-Model

Programs executed on the SDFM are written in an assembler like basic language developed at Stollmann. A program in this basic language is nothing else but a textual representation of a data flow graph.

The basic instruction set contains beside simple instructions, data manipulation instructions working on structured datatypes, the functions-invocation-instruction and RESTART-instruction to be able to replicate code during runtime The basic instruction set may be enlarged by each kind of application dependent instruction by making use of the CALL-construct to incooperate user-defined instructions.

The SDFM executing programs written in this SDFM basic language is designed with respect to the following paradigms:

–	control paradigm:	Each instruction is executed exactly once.
–	operand paradigm:	Each operand is self describing.
–	instruction paradigm:	Input operands are part of an instruction.

The machine consists of three different types of functional units:

–	Execution units (EU):	They perform the execution of the basic instructions.
–	Firing Control Units (FC):	They distribute the program for execution by detecting those instructions of which all input operands are available and firing them for execution.
–	Administration Units (AU):	They support the other units whenever help from the underlying operating system is necessary as may be in the case of function invocation or I/O. Additionally they are partly responsible for error detection / handling.

All communication between the functional units takes place via so called "buckets" consisting simply of two types of queues differing in the kind of allowed access.

We first describe how firing controls and execution units cooperate via bucket-communication for program execution. Figure 1 below summarizes the basic mechanism.

Firing control units as execution units are augmented by some "private home buckets". "Private" is meant w.r.t. access rights. The "owning" processing unit has exclusive read access to one of the bucket-queues (expedited entry, FIFO access) and a preferred read access to the other bucket-queue (normal entry, FIFO access). The reason for two types of queues supplying the units is that at first the expedited entry yields the possibility to force locality w.r.t. memory accesses and secondly to handle error situations.

Firing control units are supplied by o-buckets (operand-bucket) which queue operand words representing already available operand values.

The o-bucket entry contains information about

- to which instantiation of which function the operand belongs,
- to which input port of which instruction in this function instantiation it belongs and
- the operand value itself if small enough or an address where to find it.

o-bucket entry:

runtime part address	instruction number	operand number	operand value or address

We remark here that as a consequence of the variable / coarse grain approach no longer data themselves are sent between the units but representatives.

A firing control reads an entry from its o-bucket (first scanning the expedited entry, if this empty, the normal entry and if both are empty foreign buckets following some search strategy). With the information found in the o-bucket entry it updates the runtime part i.e. bookkeeps the availability of the corresponding operand and checks whether the instruction it belongs to has become fireable because all input operands now are available. If this is not the case it reads the next o-bucket entry. Otherwise it prepares a firing word containing information about

– which instruction is executable and

– where to find all information for execution.

firing word or i-bucket entry:

runtime part address	instruction number

The firing word is written into the i-bucket (instruction bucket) of an execution unit. Again the variable / coarse grain approach implies not to send the instruction and its input data itself but a representative.

An execution unit reads an i-bucket entry from its bucket (firstly scanning the expedited entry, then the normal and if both are empty foreign buckets following some search strategy)..

With the information of the firing word it fetches the input operands, executes the instruction and prepares for each produced output operand and each successor instruction waiting for this value an operand value. The prepared operand words then are written into the o-buckets of the firing controls. And the firing execution cycle starts again.

Sometimes the execution of an instruction needs help from the underlying host operating systems for example in the case of function invocation or I/O. In this case the execution unit informs the administration unit by writing the firing-word it is not able to handle itself into the a-bucket (administration bucket) of the administration unit. This supplies the necessary suppport by interacting with the underlying host operating system and then writes the firing word again into the i-bucket of an execution unit.

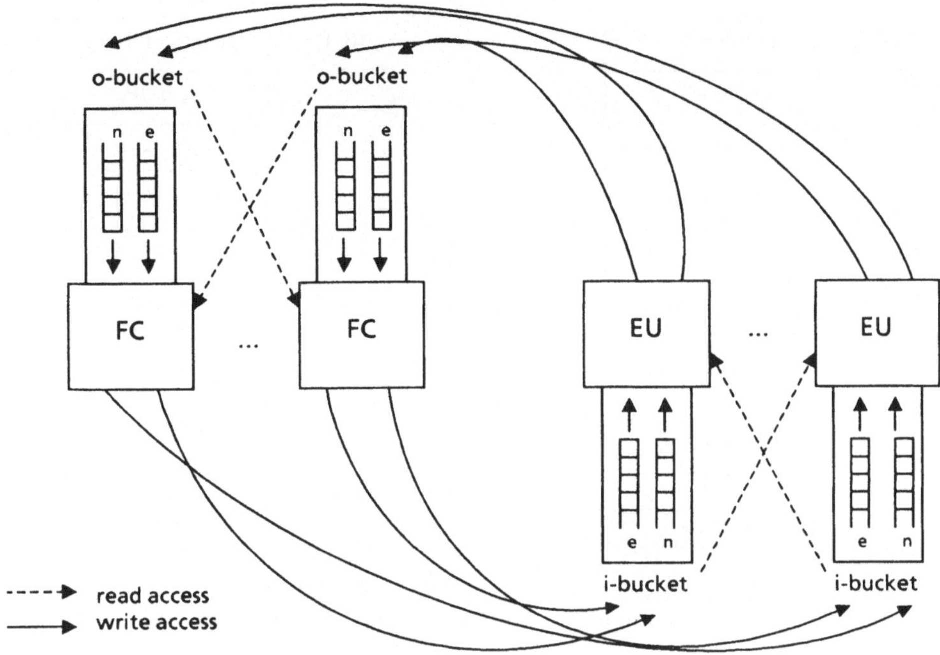

Figure 1: Basic mechanism of program execution

The functional units are supported by two types of underlying data structures:

°   Read Only Part (ROP) which may be also called the SDFM object code corresponding to an SDFM basic language program.

°   Runtime Update Part (RUP) which is the administrative structure for bookkeeping status information on progress of computation

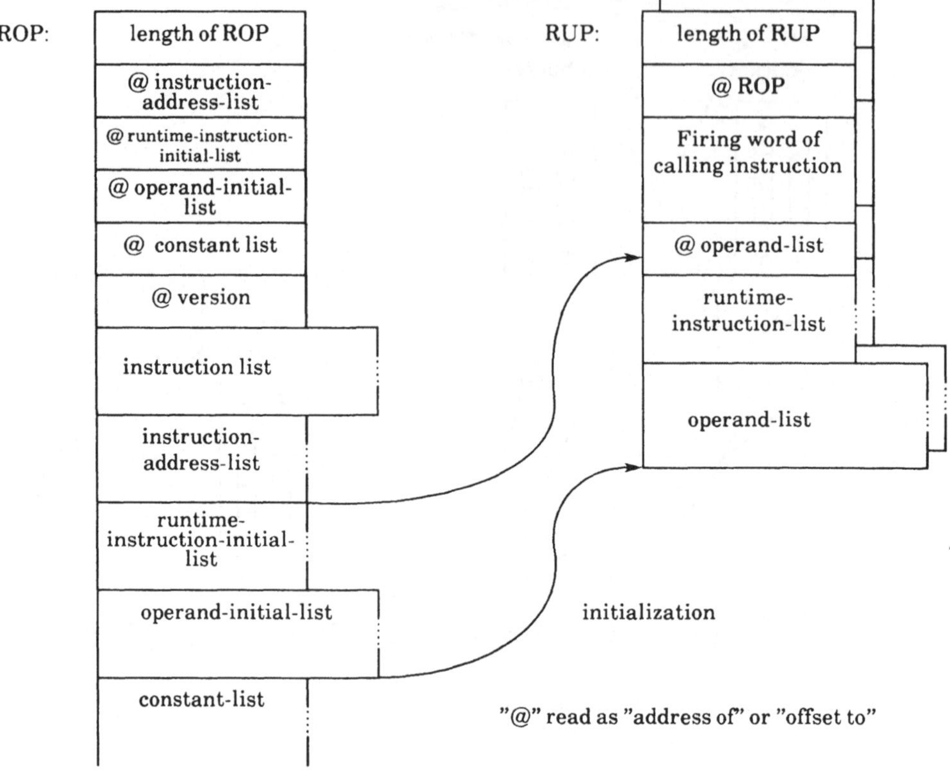

Figure 2: Basic Control Structures of the SDFM

A detailed description of these structures and how the units make use of them may be found in [10].

Logically the SDFM works on a globally addressable memory which may be subdivided in three parts:

- program memory containing ROP's and a ROP-load table
- runtime part containing RUPs
- data memory storing the operand values.

Although from the logically point of view there exists a homogeneous global address space, it physically consists of many parts which may be associated with the functional units. This implies that there exist local ("on-board", quick) and non-local ("non-on-board", slower) memory accesses.

To reduce the number of non-local memory accesses the memory parts described are distributed basically as follows:

- ROPs are stored on memory parts associated with execution units
- RUPs are stored on memory parts associated with firing control units
- data are distributed on memory parts associated with execution units.

With respect to locality properties the above firing-execution cycle may be enlarged with a strategy how to distribute firing words between execution units and operand words between firing controls to minimize non-on-board slow memory accesses:

- A firing word resp. the corresponding instruction is allocated to the execution unit holding most of the input data of the instruction.
- Data (memory operands) are stored where they are produced.
- An operand word is allocated to the firing control which holds the RUP it belongs to.

It may be that this strategy from time to time does not yield load balance. There are two mechanisms handling this situation. At first we restrict the bucket size. If a firing control wants to allocate an instruction to an execution unit already overwhelmed by work this is detected because the corresponding bucket is full and the firing control tries to allocate the instruction to another execution unit. Secondly it is possible for the idle processor to "attract" work (**task attraction**) from other units of the same type by reading bucket entries from foreign buckets (from the normal entry in FIFO manner). With these two mechanisms it is possible to counteract against unbalanced system operation introduced by a distribution strategy aiming on locality.

2.2. Considered Application

The application we have studied in some detail to run on our dataflow machine stems from the database area. More precisely we study the parallel evaluation of queries on a relational database in a dataflow manner.

A scenario we have in mind is that of a conventional centralized relational database system using SDFM as a co-computer for query evaluation.

The high level language thought of is a relational query language (for example standard SQL). A query is compiled to a relational query tree the nodes of which are marked by the five basic relational algebra operations.

This query tree is compiled to a dataflow program in the basic dataflow language of the SDFM augmented essentially by five user-defined instructions corresponding to the basic relational algebra operations RESTRICT, PROJECT, UNION, DIFFERENCE, PRODUCT.

To reduce data transfer to the dataflow machine it is worthwhile to split RESTRICT operations at the leaves of the query tree into one part which is evaluated using classical filtering techniques on base relations and a second part computed in a dataflow manner.

From the conceptional point of view we introduce more parallelism (i.e. more than already visible in the query tree) into the evaluation of queries by splitting each relational algebra operation working on complete relations into many instantiations of this operation on appropriate combinations of equal size submits (packages) of relations. Schematically this is summarized in the figure 3 below.

It has to be assured that appropriate "package instructions" are instantiated, the "package instructions" in total will yield to the same result as the corresponding relational algebra operation on complete relations and that it is possible to detect termination i.e. determine whether all packages of the input relations are handled.

Thus with exploitation of more parallelism administration overhead is introduced which leads to the conjecture that package size has to be large perhaps approximately the average size of relations divided by the number of processors.

Further details w.r.t. the database application can be found in [10].

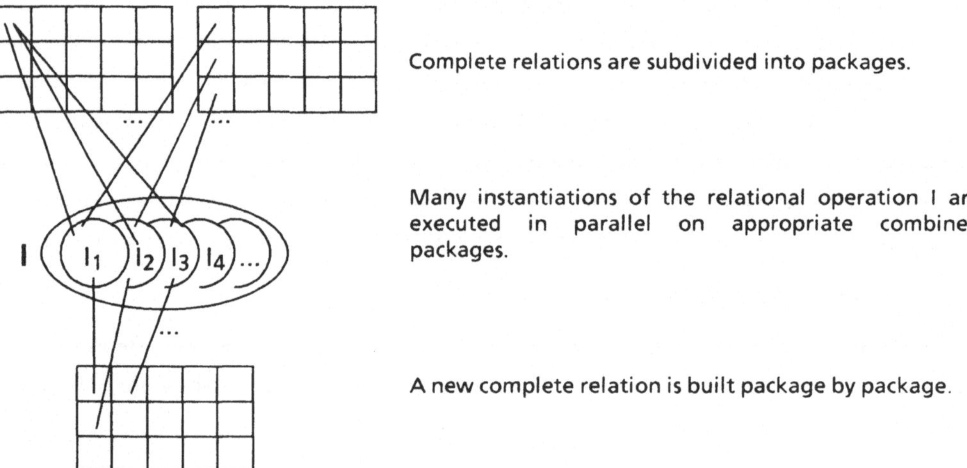

Complete relations are subdivided into packages.

Many instantiations of the relational operation I are executed in parallel on appropriate combined packages.

A new complete relation is built package by package.

Figure 3: Splitting of relational operations

3. Mapping of the dataflow model onto the prototype

We are going to build a prototype, which realizes the principles of our dataflow model. This approach allows investigations on main factors affecting the execution of dataflow programs.

In the following the prototype and the implementation of our dataflow model are outlined. For more details see [9].

3.1 Hardware configuration of the prototype

We are using a multiprocessing system consisting of off-the-shelf components. The main part of our system are four processor boards connected to a VMEbus. One processor board serves as a host and three processor boards are used as processing nodes.

The VMEbus is a 32 bit wide parallel bus supporting modern 32 bit microprocessor architectures, in particular microprocessors of the 680x0 family of Motorola.

The VMEbus is divided into four independent subsystems. The data transfer bus contains all data and address lines as well as control lines for executing an asynchronous bus protocol. Byte, word and longword data transfers are possible. Additional address modifier lines realize a comfortable concept for managing addresses as decoding different address ranges or realizing privileged memory accesses. Arbitration of access to the data transfer bus takes place by using four independent request lines of different priority, which are building the arbitration bus.

Additionally there is installed a daisy chaining mechanism on all priority levels allowing to connect more than four bus masters to the system. Furthermore the VMEbus is provided with seven interrupt request lines (Interrupt Bus) and auxiliary lines for power supply, systemclock and system reset.

A local 32 bit extension of the VMEbus, called VME-Subsystem-Bus, serves to improve operation conditions in a multiprocessor environment. It is possible to connect additional memory or I/O modules to processor boards via the VME-Subsystem-Bus.

The processors boards are equipped with a Motorola 68020 processor and 4 Megabyte dual ported memory. The memory is accessible from the local CPU or from external modules via VMEbus addresses, which are admitting a global address space. The host processor is running UNIX V.3.

Hence, the corresponding processor board contains a Paged Memory Management Unit (PMMU) to meet the virtual memory requirements of UNIX.

The 68020 processors are 32 bit microprocessors based on 68000 and 68010. The increased processing speed is achieved by a fast cache memory, pipelined instruction execution, the internal 32 bit design of the ALU and the 16 MHz clock. The 68020 supports higher programming languages like C or PASCAL by means of an extended set of addressing modes.

The complete configuration of our prototype is depicted as follows.

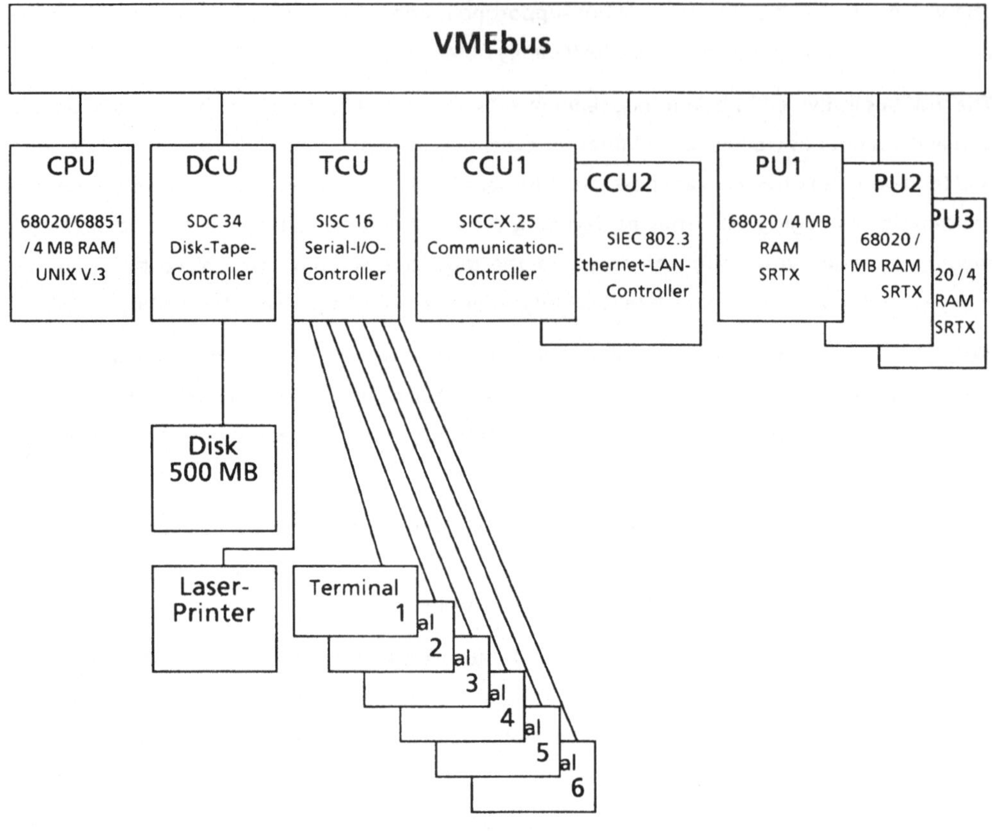

Figure 4: Hardware Configuration of the Prototype

3.2 The Operating System Configuration

While the host operating system is UNIX, the operating system running on all processing nodes is SRTX (Stollmann Real Time Executive), a realtime operating system with priority controlled or time sliced scheduling.

SRTX also is developed for 680x0 microprocessors and provides the functionality of VRTX (Ready & Hunter) extended by means of communication facilities supporting multiprocessor system programming. SRTX functions are called via C subprogram calls. The subprograms are linked to the user's program directly from a C library. Application programs are written in C and compiled under UNIX, linked together using the special SRTX library and downloaded to the target processing board.

Basically, SRTX is hardware independent. It is adapted to a special hardware via user written driver routines, called "user exits".

Memory management will be done by SRTX on two levels. On the first level there exist memory segments called buffers. Buffers of equal size are grouped in so called partitions. On the second level partitions, containing buffers of different size, are joined in pools. A process can request memory from a pool, whereupon SRTX will satisfy the request with a suitable buffer or from a partition, whereupon SRTX will deliver a free buffer of that partition.

To obtain an operating system configuration which meets the requirements of our dataflow model a new layer is added to the existing operating system called SMOCS. One may remind that the program execution by the functional units is supported by several data structures which have to be global accessable by all units. Furthermore the task attraction principle implies all operand values have to be global accessible too. To meet this requirement SMOCS provides a SRTX like memory management on global semaphore protected memory resources, which allows to request and release "non-on-board" memory.

The implementation of the above-mentioned bucket communication among the unit implies the necessity of a new queue type not provided by SRTX which – as global resource – is also semaphore protected.

3.3 Mapping of the dataflow model

The mapping of the virtual machine we described above onto the hardware configuration is straight forward. Each functional unit is modeled as process scheduled by one of the node operating systems. As SRTX is not capable of disk I/O yet the administration unit has to be modeled as UNIX process. Firing controls and execution units will be realized as SRTX processes. Several mappings of varying numbers of the three types of processes are imaginable and will be subject of investigation.

There will be the following implementation layers. Based on the node operating systems we have the SMOCS layer providing a protected management of global resources as well as the new queue type. On top of the SMOCS layer we will implement the bucket communication. It should be mentioned that the default bucket access strategies aim on locality w.r.t. memory accesses.

At least the data flow mechanism as described previously is realized by modeling the functional units as UNIX resp. SRTX processes which make use of this bucket communication and the SMOCS functions for protected management of global resources.

3.4 Investigations on our prototype

A first version of our prototype will be implemented in October, 1988.

We plan to answer the following questions concerning our data flow approach by performing experiments with the prototype.

The administration of parallel execution requires some computation overhead. Fine grain operations allow high parallelism, but cause considerable overhead, coarse grain operations lead to lower parallelism, but decrease the fraction of overhead. Thus a trade-off exists between the degree of parallelism and the overhead. We will measure the overhead necessary for the execution of operations in order to determine the optimal grain size.

Another question concernes the number of firing controls. We have to find out, how many firing controls are appropriate to prevent the firing mechanism being the bottleneck.

The number of execution units will be varied in order to investigate its impact on the speed-up of the system. It also seems to be necessary to compare execution times of dataflow programs to those of sequential programs doing the same tasks.

There is also a trade-off between locality of execution (minimizing non-on-board slow memory accesses) and load balance.

If execution takes place strictly locally, one processing node may be overwhelmed by instructions while the others remain idle.

Hence, the task attraction principle has been introduced in order to fetch instructions from other nodes if a node is idle. The bucket size may additionally affect the degree of locality. If a particular bucket is full, the firing control puts the instruction identifier into another bucket, which may reside on a node, that is not local to the operands. If the bucket size is too large, it does not have any effect to the locality of execution and hence, cannot contribute to load balance, if it is too small, the firing control is mainly engaged with selecting an appropriate bucket. Hence, we have to determine a suitable bucket size.

A point related to the load balancing problem is the program length. Obviously, a good load balancing of execution units needs time. The first period of program execution is characterized by dynamically changing load of execution units. Therefore, programs must have a specific length to allow the system turning to a balanced state.

Last, but not least we have to analyse the bottlenecks existing on the hardware level. Will the bus limit the performance because of too many data transfers or the host because of performing a lot of I/O operations?

Acknowledgements

The work presented in this paper is due to the efforts of the team of the ESPRIT-415-E project momentary consisting of: Peter Friedrich, Elvira Glück-Hiltrop, Thomas Jipp, Michael Jöhnk, Peter Kalmer, Frank Rolf, Mathias Ramlow, Ute Schürfeld, Werner Zucker.

References

[1]   Adams, D.A.: A Computation Model with Data Flow Sequencing;Technical Report CS 117, School of Humanities and Sciences, Stanford University, Stanford, Calif.; 1968.

[2]   Boral, H., Dewitt, D.J.: Design Considerations for Data Flow Machines; Proceedings of 1980 International Conference on Management of Data, ACM-SIGMOD; 1980.

[3]   Boral, H., Dewitt, D.J.: Applying Data Flow Techniques to Data Base Machines; Computer IEEE; 1982.

[4]   Dennis, J.B.: First Version of Data Flow Procedure Language; in Programming Symp.: Proc.Colloque sur la Programation, (Paris, France, Apr.74), Robinet, B. (Ed.) Lecture notes in computer science, vol. 19, Springer-Verlag, New York; 1974.

[5]   Dennis, J.B. , Misunas, D.P.:A Computer Architecture for Highly Parallel Signal Processing; in Proc.1974 Nat. Computer Conf. AFIPS Press, Arlington, Va.; 1974.

[6]   DeWitt, D.J., et al.: GAMMA - A High Performance Data Flow Database Machine; Proceeding of 12th International Conference on Very Large Data Basics; 1986.

[7]   Eich, M.H., Wells, D.L.: Database Concurrently Control Using Data Flow Graphs; ACM Transactions on Database Systems, Vol. 13, No. 2; 1988.

[8]   Gurd, J.: Data Flow Computers and Languages; ESPRIT Summer School on Future Parallel Computers; 1986.

[9]   Glück-Hiltrop, E., Jöhnk, M., Kalmer, P., Ramlow, M., Schürfeld, U., Rolf, F.; Expansion Considerations; ESP-415E-STO-032, Deliverable 5 of Stollmann GmbH in ESPRIT Project 415,Stollmann GmbH, Hamburg; 1988.

[10]   Jipp, T., Friedrich, P., Oldach, H. , Fuhlrott, O., Sievers, M.: Definition of Principles and Basic Language; ESP-415E-STO-022, Deliverable 4 of Stollmann GmbH in ESPRIT Project 415, Stollmann GmbH, Hamburg; 1987.

[11]   Rodriguez, J.E:A Graph Model for Parallel Computation; MIT Technical Report TR-64, Laboratory for Computer Science, MIT, Cambridge, Mass.; 1969.

[12]   Treleaven, P.C., Brownbridge, D.R., Hopkins, R.P.: Data Driven and Demand Driven Computer Architectures; Computing Surveys, Vol.14, No.1; 1982.

[13]   von Bültzingloewen, G., Dittrich, K.R., Iochpe, C., Liedtke, R.-P., Lockemann, P.C., Schryro, M.: KARDAMOM - A Dataflow Database Machine For Real-Time Application; SIGMOD RECORD, Vol. 17, No. 1; 1988.

[14]   von Bültzingloewen, G., Liedtke, R.-P., Dittrichs, K.R.: Set-Oriented Memory Management In a Multiprocessor Database Machine; Proceedings of 5th International Workshop on Database Machines; 1987.

[15]   Zucker, W., Glück-Hiltrop, E., Jipp, T., Rennhak, B., Schäffler, G.: Selection and Determination of the Class of Applications; ESP-415E-STO-014, Deliverable of Stollmann GmbH in ESPRIT Project 415, Stollmann GmbH, Hamburg, 1986.

PARALLELVERARBEITUNG MIT DER

ETA 10

RECHNERSERIE

Wolfgang Bez

CONTROL DATA GMBH

Die ETA 10 Rechnerserie von CONTROL DATA erschließt ein neues Feld der Parallelverarbeitung. Bis zu 8 autonome Rechner sind über ein "Shared Memory" gekoppelt und können synchron ein Benutzerprogramm bearbeiten. Jeder Rechner verfügt über parallele Funktionseinheiten für Verarbeitung von Skalaren und Vektoren sowie über einen eigenen lokalen Speicher. Durch Kombination von Mikroparallelität von Funktionseinheiten innerhalb einer CPU und Makroparallelität mehrerer CPUs erreicht das ETA 10 System eine bedeutende Leistungssteigerung gegenüber rein serieller Verarbeitung und reiner Vektorverarbeitung. Der Compiler erreicht einen hohen Grad der Autovektorisierung und unterstützt automatische Parallelverarbeitung.

EINLEITUNG

Parallelverarbeitung ist heute Bestandteil eines jeden technisch-wissenschaftlichen Rechners. Ein Höchstleistungsrechner zeichnet sich durch eine besondere Ausgewogenheit des Entwurfs aus. Komplexität des Instruktionssatzes versus niedrige Zykluszeit, kurze Startupzeit versus hohe Vektorleistung, Mikroparallelität der Funktionseinheiten versus Makroparallelität mehrerer Prozessoren und schließlich die Ausführung des Systemkonzepts in der richtigen Hardwaretechnologie, all dies sind Entscheidungen, die dem Entwicklungsteam ein hohes Maß an Intuition abverlangen und die letztlich die Leistung des Systems ausmachen. Nicht zuletzt hängt der Erfolg eines Systemkonzepts auch vom Stand der Softwareentwicklung ab. Während zu Beginn der 80er Jahre Systeme mit geringer Hardwareparallelität, einfachem Instruktionssatz und daraus resultierender kurzer Taktzeit bei Anwendungen mit geringem Vektorisierungsgrad erfolgreich waren, sind automatische Vektorisierer einerseits und die Umstrukturierung von Anwendungspaketen für Vektorrechner andererseits heute soweit fortgeschritten, daß ein Systemkonzept mit höheren Vektorisierungseigenschaften den besseren Erfolg verspricht. Die ETA 10 Rechnerserie von CONTROL DATA setzt in einer solchen Rechnerlandschaft neue Zeichen. Ein Mehrprozessorsystem mit loser Kopplung über Shared Memory, Einzelprozessorleistungen im Bereich GFLOP/s, die Verbindung von virtueller Speicherarchitektur mit hoher Vektorleistung und - als Krönung des Konzepts - die Ausführung eines Höchstleistungsrechners mit Taktfrequenzen bei 100 bis 200 MHz in CMOS Technologie, all dies sind Merkmale, die ETA 10 Rechner zu Meilensteinen der Rechnerentwicklung machen.

SPEICHERARCHITEKTUR

Das herausragende Kennzeichen eines Mehrprozessorsystems ist die Anordnung seiner Speicher. Man kann unterscheiden zwischen Prozessoren (CPUs), die über einen gemeinsamen Speicher verfügen und autarken Rechnern (CPU plus Speicher), die über ein Kommunikationsnetz Daten austauschen. Die meisten heute erhältlichen Rechnersysteme fallen in eine der beiden Kategorien. Die ETA 10 Rechnerserie verbindet beide Möglichkeiten, indem autarke Rechner (CPU plus lokaler Speicher) auf einen gemeinsamen Speicher (Shared Memory) zugreifen können. Neben dieser losen Kopplung sind die CPUs eng gekoppelt über einen Kommunikationsspeicher, der zur Ablage von Synchronisationsvariablen dient. Dies ist in Bild 1 dargestellt. Die lose Kopplung über Shared Memory

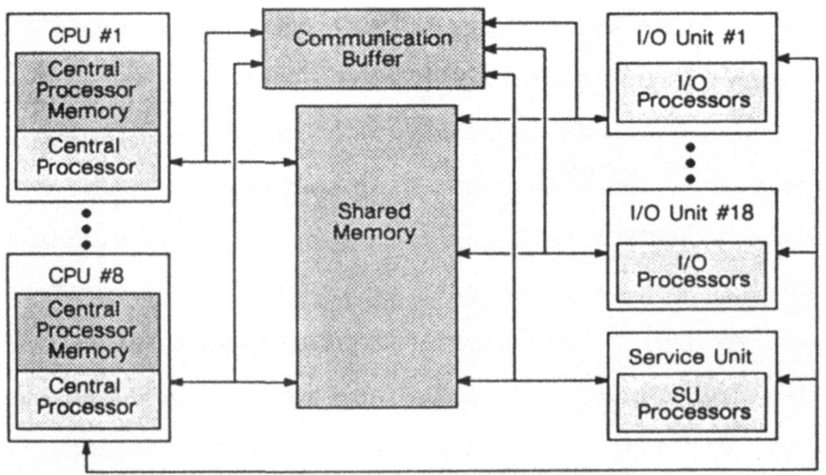

vermeidet einen Nachteil, der Systmen mit enger Kopplung über einen gemeinsamen Speicher sonst immanent ist. Greifen mehrere CPUs auf einen gemeinsamen Speicher zu, so werden dadurch selbst im asynchronen Betrieb unnötige Bankkonflikte erzeugt. Die betroffene CPU kann keine weitere Instruktion ausführen bis die angesprochene Speicherbank wieder frei ist, die CPU steht. Dies bedeutet einen ernsthaften Engpass einer solchen Architektur. Ist n die Anzahl der Prozessoren in einem solchen Mehrprozessorsystem und b die Anzahl der unabhängigen Speicherbänke, so steigt die Anzahl aller möglichen Speicherzugriffe mit der Potenz $b**n$, während die Anzahl der konfliktfreien Speicherzugriffe nur mit der Kombination n aus b, also wesentlich langsamer wächst. Schon für wenige Prozessoren (z.B. n=16) ist deshalb eine enorme Anzahl von Speicherbänken (z.B. b=8192) notwendig, um ein noch vertretbares Verhältnis von konfliktfreien Speicherzugriffen zu erhalten.

Dieser wesentliche Nachteil des gemeinsamen Speichers tritt bei der ETA 10 Architektur nicht auf. Speicherzugriffe auf Shared Memory können nämlich asynchron ablaufen, also ohne Unterbrechung der CPU. Die ETA 10 CPU kann somit Instruktionen ausführen während sie auf Operanden aus dem Shared Memory wartet. Durch den großen lokalen Speicher (32 MByte) können diese Instruktionen Teil des Programmes sein, das den Shared Memory Transfer initiiert hat, oder das Betriebssystem kann während dieser Zeit ein anderes Programm bedienen, das im lokalen Speicher auf die Ausführung wartet. Durch den Wegfall von Bankkonflikten mit den verbundenen Wartezeiten für die CPUs ist die Durchsatzleistung eines ETA 10 Systems gegenüber Mehrprozessorsystemen mit gemeinsamem Speicher beträchtlich höher.

MIKROPARALLELITÄT UND MAKROPARALLELITÄT

Das ETA 10 System erhält seine Leistungsfähigkeit durch ein hohes Maß an Parallelverarbeitung bei niedrigen Rechnertaktzeiten. Es sind drei Ebenen der Parallelität zu unterscheiden: Vektorverarbeitung, also Parallelität innerhalb von Funktionseinheiten, paralelle Funktionseinheiten innerhalb einer CPU und Parallelverarbeitung auf verschiedenen CPUs. Im letzteren Fall muß dann noch die Unterscheidung zwischen asynchronem Betrieb (Multiprogramming) und synchronem Betrieb (Multitasking) auf mehreren CPUs gemacht werden. Die ETA 10 Rechner machen von allen drei Ebenen der Parallelverarbeitung Gebrauch.

VEKTORVERARBEITUNG

Vektorverarbeitung steht im Mittelpunkt des Entwurfs einer einzelnen CPU. Neben der üblichen Vektorisierung von arithmetischen Operationen, auf die hier nicht näher eingegangen wird /1/, gibt es auch Vektorinstruktionen für logische Verarbeitung (Bitvektoren). Bitvektoren werden einerseits eingesetzt um den Wert von logischen Variablen zu berechnen, beispielsweise in dem Ausdruck

$$BIT(1{:}N) = X(1{:}N) \ . \ LT \ . \ Y(1{:}N)$$

Dem Vektor BIT (der Länge N Bit) wird dabei dort der Wert 1 zugewiesen, wo der Vektor X (der Länge N Worte) kleiner als Y ist. Bitvektoren werden andererseits eingesetzt um Verzweigungen zu vektorisieren, also um arithmetische Vektoroperationen zu steuern.

Beispielsweise kann die skalare Verzweigung

```
      DO  1 I = 1,N
    1 IF ( X(I) . LT . Y(I) )   X(I) = 0.
```

durch den Vektorbefehl

```
      WHERE ( BIT(1:N) )      X(1:N) = 0.
```

ersetzt werden. Der Vektor X wird in diesem Beispiel dort Null gesetzt wo X kleiner als Y ist. Durch den Einsatz von Bitvektoren können auf diese Weise komplizierte skalare Ausdrücke mit einem einzigen Vektorbefehl ausgeführt werden. Logische Operationen werden mit einer Geschwindigkeit von 16 Resultaten pro Takt ausgeführt. Damit erhalten gerade solche Programmteile eine besonders große Beschleunigung, die auf Vektorrechnern mit einfacherem Befehlssatz nicht zu vektorisieren sind.

PARALLELE FUNKTIONSEINHEITEN

Innerhalb einer CPU verfügt die ETA 10 über eine Vielzahl von parallelen Funktionseinheiten. Eine vereinfachte Darstellung einer CPU ist in Bild 2 gezeigt.
Der Skalarprozessor kann parallel arithmetische Operationen wie Add, Multiply oder Divide sowie logische Operationen ausführen, wiederum parallel dazu können im Vektorprozessor arithmetische oder logische Operationen abgearbeitet werden. Die arithmetischen Pipelines im Vektorprozesor sind doppelt vorhanden und können durch chaining bis zu 8 Operationen pro Takt ausführen. Durch die verschiedenen Funktionseinheiten werden einzelne Anweisungen in einem Programm parallel abgearbeitet. Diese Mikroparallelität in

einem Programm wird durch den Compiler und direkt die Hardware automatisch ausgenützt und führt zu einer deutlichen Leistungsverbesserung gegenüber rein serieller Verarbeitung. Im Gegensatz zu Microtasking /2/, also der parallelen Bearbeitung einzelner Programmanweisungen auf verschiedenen CPUs, benötigt diese Art der Mikroparallelität keinen Synchronisationsoverhead. Obwohl Microtasking auf dem ETA 10 System beherrscht wird, ist eine Leistungsverbesserung gegenüber der effizienteren Mikroparallelität nur in wenigen Fällen möglich.

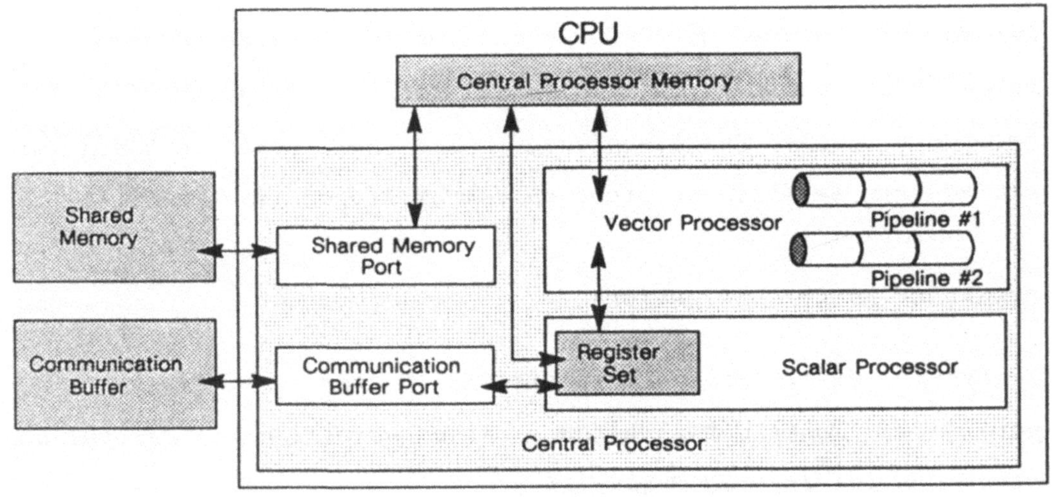

MULTITASKING

Trotzdem spielt die synchrone Bearbeitung eines Benutzerprogrammes auf mehreren CPUs (Multitasking) in der ETA 10 Architektur eine bedeutende Rolle. Allerdings wird man in aller Regel makroskopische Programmteile auf verschiedene CPUs verteilen. Makroskopisch betrifft in diesem Fall jedoch weniger die Größe der

Programmsegmente sondern hauptsächlich die Größe der Datensegmente, die parallel verarbeitet werden sollen. Die Unterscheidung von Microtasking, also der parallelen Bearbeitung kleiner Programmsegmente, z.B. einzelner Vektorinstruktionen, und Macrotasking /2/, der parallelen Verarbeitung großer Programmsegmente, z.B. Unterprogramme, ist dagegen für die ETA 10 wenig hilfreich. Dafür ist die Lokalität einer Task ein wichtiges Kriterium. Lokalität ist dabei das Verhältnis der Zeit, die für den Datenaustausch zwischen Shared Memory und Local Memory benötigt wird, zu der Zeit, die für die Berechnung auf einer CPU verbraucht wird. Wenn dieses Verhältnis einen Faktor von etwa 30 überschreitet, ist Multitasking auf der ETA 10 erfolgreich /3/. Es muß unterstrichen werden, daß der Lokalitätsparameter nicht ein Kennzeichen der ETA 10 ist, sondern für alle Systeme, die Multitasking erlauben, große Wichtigkeit hat. Allerdings tritt er bei Multiprozessorsystemen mit gemeinsamem Speicher weniger explizit auf. In derartigen Systemen führt geringe Lokalität zu einem starken Anwachsen von Speicherkonflikten, ein Verhalten, das der Benutzer i.a. nicht ausdrücklich steuern kann.

Die Forderung nach ausreichender Lokalität schränkt ein vollkommen automatisches, ausschließlich vom Compiler gesteuertes Multitasking ein. In aller Regel wird man genügend lokale Tasks dann erzeugen können, wenn man weit außen liegende Schleifen auf verschiedene Prozessoren verteilt. In solchen Schleifen werden dann jedoch häufig schwer auflösbare Rekursionen oder auch Unterprogrammaufrufe auftreten, die nur einer globalen Optimierung zugänglich sind. Compiler mit programmübergreifenden Optimierungsstrategien sind jedoch erst am Anfang der Entwicklung.

Multitasking auf der ETA 10 wird deshalb vom Benutzer mit Compilerdirektiven gesteuert. Dies erlaubt dem Programmierer eine globale Parallelisierung ohne die Portabilität seines Codes anzutasten. Aufgrund dieser Anweisungen erzeugt dann der Compiler automatisch Aufrufe an die Multitasking Library und nimmt dem Benutzer die Verwaltung des Mehrprozessorsystems ab. Die Direktiven sind einfach zu handhaben und von der Syntax weitestgehend selbsterläuternd /4/.

Multitasking wird auf diese Weise zu einem einfachen Werkzeug, das die Leistung eines ETA 10 Systems in den Bereich GFLOP/s ausweitet /5/ und das in vielen Anwendungspaketen Eingang finden wird.

LITERATUR

*/1/ ETA 10 Systems Overview: ETA System V,
ETA Systems Inc. PUB-1232*

*ETA 10 Systems Reference Manual,
ETA Systems Inc. PUB-1005*

*/2/ CRAY-2 Multitasking Programmer's Manual
CRAY Research Inc. SN-2026*

*/3/ Cliff Arnold, Multitasking Library ERS,
ETA Systems Inc. Internal Documentation*

*/4/ ETA 10 Systems Multitasking Library
User's Guide and Reference Manual
ETA Systems Inc. PUB-1120*

*/5/ Denis Duke, Daan Sandee, PIK Sonderheft 1,
Supercomputer '88*

PRISM – ein neues Rechnerkonzept

Thomas Mundt
Apollo Domain Computer GmbH
Borsteler Chaussee 85–99a/Hs 6
2000 Hamburg 61
Tel.: 040/510021

Einleitung

Die Firma Apollo Computer Inc. in USA hat während der vergangenen Jahre eine 64-Bit-orientierte Rechnerarchitektur, die als Grundlage für eine neue Computergeneration der 90er Jahre Verwendung finden soll, komplett selbst entwickelt. Diese Rechnerarchitektur erhielt den Namen PRISM (Parallel Reduced Instruction Set Multiprocessing). PRISM beinhaltet sowohl neue Hardware- als auch Software-Ideen. Zur Hardware gehört dabei ein Prozessor, der sowohl eine Einheit zur Bearbeitung von Integer-Instruktionen als auch eine weitere zur Abhandlung von Floatingpoint-Anweisungen enthält. Auf diese Weise kann die parallele Ausführung von mehreren Assembler-Anweisungen in einem Maschinentakt erreicht werden, wobei die Integer-Einheit nicht mehr dafür zuständig ist, Fließkommabefehle an die Floatingpoint-Einheit weiterzureichen. Ein neuer Systembus mit Standardanschlüssen in die Außenwelt sowie ein neues Hochgeschwindigkeitsgrafiksubsystem sind ebenso hardware-seitig Bestandteil des PRISM-Gedankens wie die Möglichkeit, Teile von Dateien parallel auf Massenspeichern unterzubringen (Disk Striping). Um PRISM auszunutzen, unterstützen software-seitig neue Compiler die Fähigkeiten der Hardware. Neben der Parallelität auf einem Prozessor können mehrere CPUs gleichberechtigt parallel am Systembus betrieben werden.

Die erste Maschine, die bei Apollo konkret nach PRISM gebaut wird, trägt die Bezeichnung DN 10000. Daher wird an dieser Stelle, wenn es sinnvoll erscheint, auf diese Maschine Bezug genommen. Allerdings sei darauf verwiesen, daß die mit der DN 10000 erreichten Leistungsdaten die einer ersten Implementation der PRISM-Architektur darstellen. Diese Daten dürfen daher nicht mit PRISM gleichgesetzt werden. Mit dieser Maschine sind noch lange nicht die Werte erreicht, die man mit der neuen Architekur im Laufe der Zukunft zu erreichen erwartet.

RISC

Wie der Name sagt, bildet der Gedanke an einen reduzierten Befehlsvorrat eine Basis bei PRISM ähnlich wie es mit der RISC-Architektur (Reduced Instruction Set Computer) von einigen Rechnernherstellern vorgestellt wurde, nur sollen die Nachteile, die bei RISC durch das Fehlen von komfortablen Kommandos entstehen, vermieden werden.

Der Gedanke, der zur RISC-Architektur führte, war folgender: herkömmliche CPUs besitzen inzwischen sehr komplexe Befehle. Diese Befehle sind zwar leistungsfähig, bewirken auf der anderen Seite aber einen hohen Verwaltungsüberhang, der Zeitverluste bei der Ausführung aller Instruktionen bedeutet. Diese komplexen Anweisungen werden, so hat die Praxis gezeigt, nur selten benutzt. Somit sind der Verwaltungsüberhang und die damit verbundenen Zeitverluste in den meisten Anwendungen nicht gerechtfertigt.

Wenn man nun eine CPU aller komplexen Befehle und somit des – aus Sicht derjenigen, die überwiegend Verwendung finden – Verwaltungsüberhangs entledigt, wird der Aufbau der CPU vereinfacht und die verbleibenden Befehle können sehr viel schneller als in einer CISC-CPU (Complex Instruction Set CPU) ausgeführt werden. Dem Vorteil der schnelleren Entschlüsselung und Ausführung fielen Anweisungen zum Opfer, die dem Programmierer das Leben erleichtern wie z.B. komfortable Adressierungsmöglichkeiten. In der CISC-Architektur komfortable Befehle müssen bei Abbildung auf die RISC-Architektur durch eine große Anzahl einfacher Anweisungen erzeugt werden. Dadurch kann der ausführbare Code in Binärdateien sehr viel umfangreicher als in 'CISC-Dateien' sein. Dadurch wird letztendlich, bezogen auf eine Anwendung, nicht immer die Leistung erreicht, die man aufgrund schnellerer Abarbeitung der einzelnen Befehle erwarten sollte.

PRISM

Bei der PRISM-Architektur wurde wie bei RISC davon ausgegangen, ausführbare Befehle soweit zu vereinfachen, daß sie mit möglichst wenigen CPU-Takten verarbeitet werden können, wobei der Befehlsvorrat selbst nicht notwendigerweise eingeschränkt werden sollte. So existieren für eine PRISM-CPU z.Z. 107 Befehle, die bis auf drei Ausnahmen alle in einem einzigen CPU-Takt ausgeführt werden können. Das gilt auch für LOAD-/ STORE-Anweisungen, die zwangsläufig oft in Programmen benötigt werden und bei herkömmlichen RISC-CPUs bis zu acht Takte lang sein können. Floatingpoint- und Integer-Division sowie die Wurzel aus einer Fließkommazahl benötigen bei PRISM mehr als einen CPU-Takt. PRISM bietet weiterhin komfortable Adressierungsmöglichkeiten, Floatingpoint-Anweisungen und spezielle Grafik-Befehle. Alle Anweisungen gelangen ohne Umsetzung in einen internen Microcode zur Ausführung, sind von einheitlicher Struktur und 32 Bit lang. Davon weichen lediglich drei Ausnahmen ab .

Eine PRISM-CPU (Bild 1) ist dafür ausgelegt, bis zu drei Anweisungen in einem Maschinentakt zu laden bzw. in einem Takt auszuführen. Dabei ist sie grundsätzlich 64-Bit orientiert, kann also generell zwei Anweisungen aus einem Cache entgegennehmen. Weiterhin ist die CPU aus einer Integer-Prozessoreinheit und einer Floatingpoint-Prozessoreinheit zusammengesetzt. Die Floatingpoint-Einheit ist in der Lage, zwei Anweisungen nach IEEE 754 mit doppelter Genauigkeit gleichzeitig auszuführen, nämlich eine FP-Multiplikation und eine FP-Addition. Da im Befehlsvorrat sogenannte 'Compound Instructions', die eine FP-Multiplikation und eine FP-Addition enthalten, vorhanden sind, können im günstigsten Fall eine Integer- und zwei Floatingpoint-Anweisungen in einem CPU-Takt ausgeführt werden.

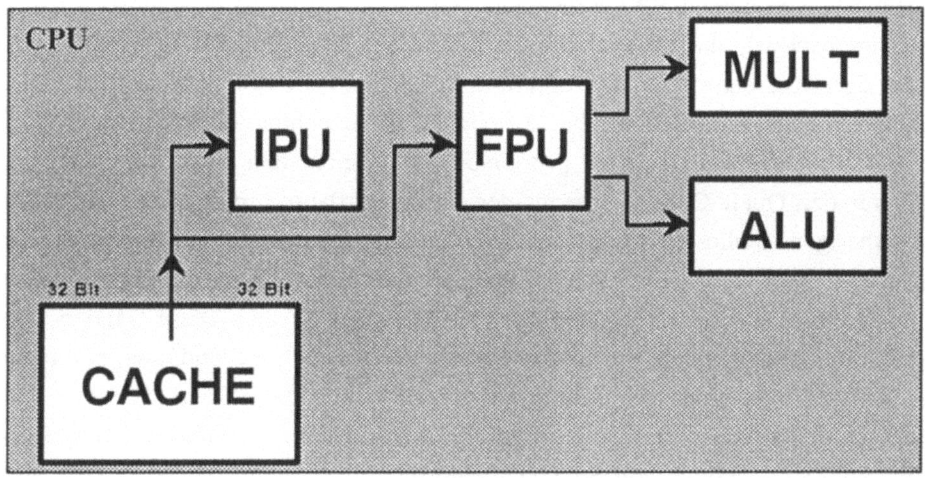

Bild 1

Berechnungen werden von der Integer-Einheit in 32 32-Bit-Registern, von der Floatingpoint-Einheit in 64 32-Bit- oder 32 64-Bit-Registern bewerkstelligt.

In der DN 10000 besitzt jeder Prozessor einen 128 KByte großen Instruktions-Cache sowie einen 64 KByte großen Daten-Cache mit 64 KByte großer Adreßkonvertierungstabelle. Es handelt sich dabei um Caches mit virtueller Adressierung und zusätzlichen Informationen über die physikalischen Adressen der abgelegten Daten. Beide Caches sind 64 Bit breit und als 'write through cache' realisiert, womit sichergestellt ist, daß alle Modifikationen, die im Cache vorgenommen werden, bis in den Hauptspeicher durchgereicht werden. Die Gültigkeit der Cache-Inhalte wird dabei ständig von einer speziellen VLSI ASIC Hardware überwacht und sichergestellt.

Compiler

Das PRISM-Konzept soll also eine Möglichkeit anbieten, die für die schnelle Verarbeitung von fließkommaintensiven Berechnungen geeignet ist. Zugehörige Compiler, die mit Hilfe von Datenflußanalyse (Bild 2) prüfen, wann Berechnungsergebnisse im Programm gefordert sind, unterstützen die Fähigkeiten der CPU. Der Datenflußanalyse folgt ein sogenanntes 'Scheduling', wobei die Abfolge der Instruktionen für die CPU festgelegt wird (Bild 3). Aufgrund der Analyse und bei entsprechender Optimierungsstufe können FP-Anweisungen, die an unterschiedlichen Stellen im Programm auftauchen, zu 'Compound Instructions' zusammengefaßt werden. Die Compiler werden dabei noch unterstützt von einer 'Wissensbasis', die als optimal bekannte Strukturen enthält. Es ist natürlich das Ziel, bei der Übersetzung eines Programms möglichst viele 'Compound Instructions' zu erzeugen. Im Schnitt werden bei heute üblichen FP-Benchmarks (Whetstones, Linpack) auf diese Weise 1.3 Anweisungen pro CPU-Takt erreicht und zwar, ohne daß ein Programmierer den Quell-Code in irgendeiner Weise bearbeiten muß, wenn das Programm in der bisherigen Apollo-Welt lauffähig war. Um ein gewisses Maß an Binärkompatibilität zur bisherigen (und künftigen) 680x0er Welt bei Apollo zu erreichen, können 'Compound Executable Object Types' als ausführbarer Code erzeugt werden. Diese Dateien enthalten ausführbaren Code für beide Prozessor-Typen und sind entsprechend lang, entbinden den Anwender jedoch in einer gemischten Umgebung von der Notwendigkeit des Wissens, welche Datei auf welcher Maschine ausgeführt werden kann. Ansonsten ist sichergestellt, daß die PRISM-Umgebung voll Sourcecode-Kompatibel zur 680x0-Umgebung ist.

Um zu zeigen, wie der Parallelbetrieb auf einer CPU erreicht wird, soll hier ein kleines Beispiel anhand eines Polynoms aufgezeigt werden. Ausgegangen wird von einem Polynom 9. Grades

$$4x^9 + 92x^7 + 580x^5 + 824x^3 + 336x$$

Das kann vom Programmierer geschrieben werden

```
        Z = X * X
      ZSQ = Z * Z
ERGEBNIS =
      (ZSQ + 14.0 * Z + 12) * 4.0 * X * (ZSQ + 9.0 * Z + 7.0)
```

Grafisch sieht die daraus resultierende Datenflußanalyse des Compilers aus wie folgt

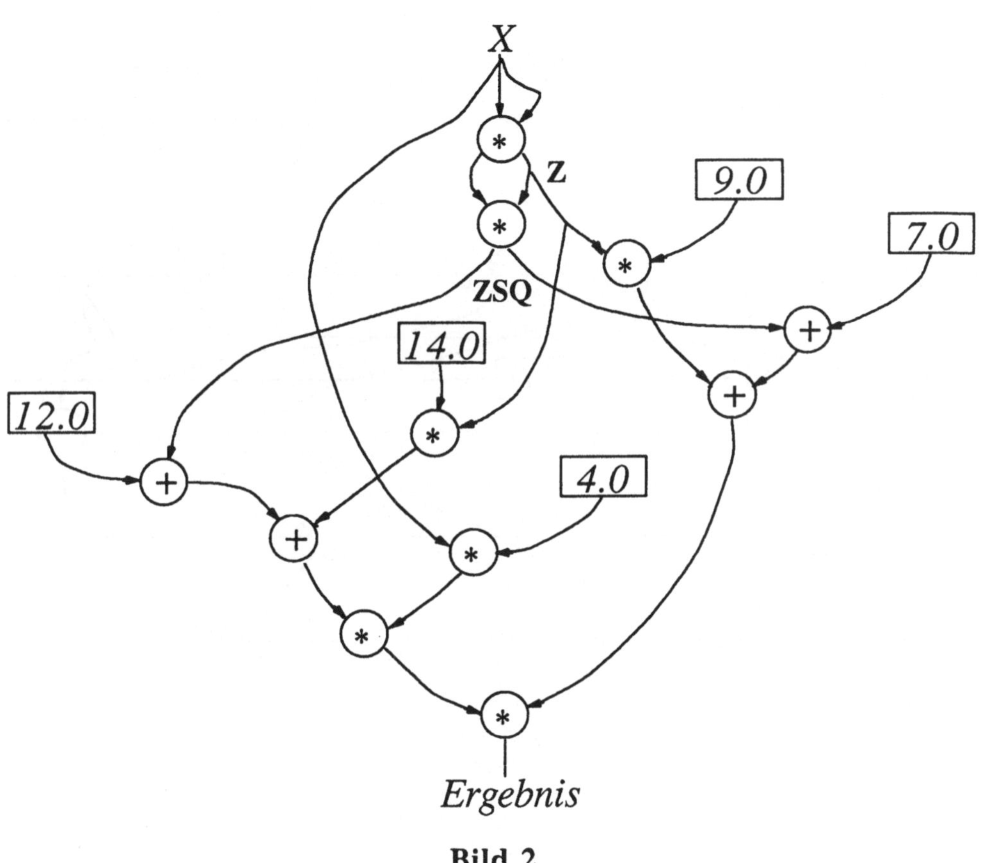

Bild 2

Aus dieser Datenflußanalyse entsteht folgende 'scheduled graph' genannte Abbildung

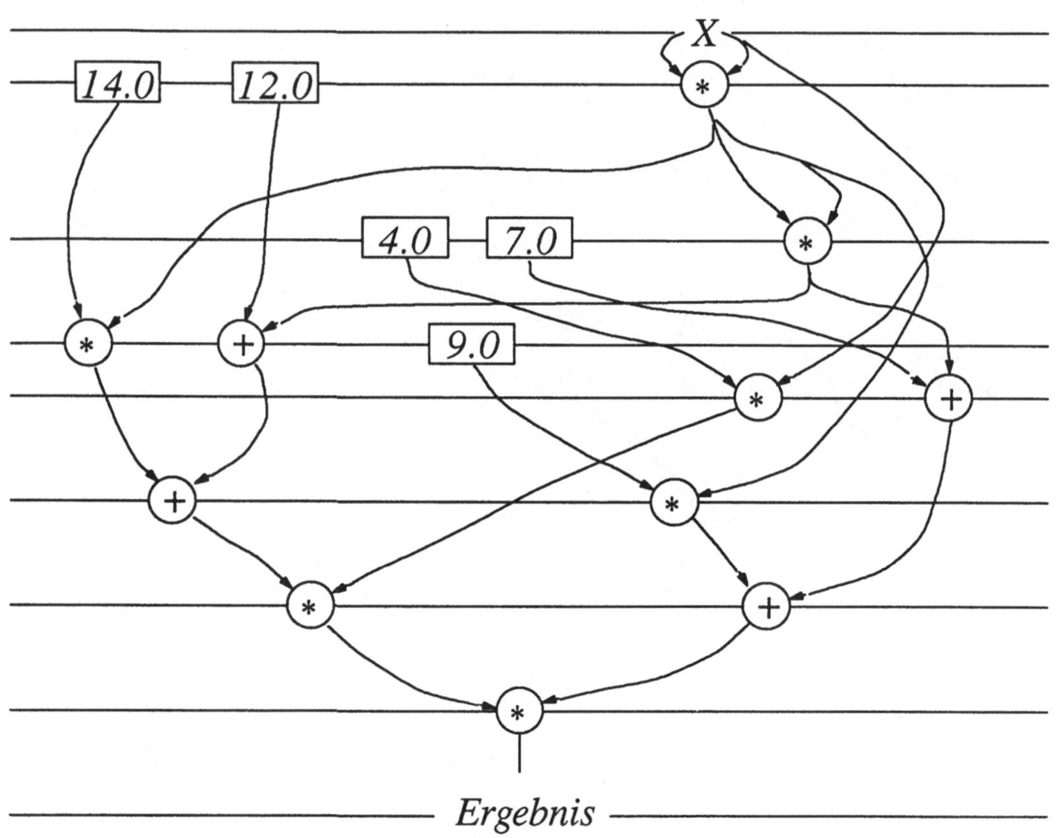

Bild 3

Daraus wiederum wird folgender Assembler–Code erzeugt:

```
Integer Pipeline                 Mult. Pipeline           ALU Pipeline

LOADS C(12.0,14.0),(S0,S1)   MULS    X, X,Z
LOADS C( 4.0, 7.0),(S8,S9)   MULS    Z, Z,ZSQ
LOADS C( 9.0)        ,S11     MULS    S1, Z,S1         ADDS ZSQ,S0
                             MULS    X,S8,S5          ADDS  S9,ZSQ
                             MULS    S11, Z,S6        ADDS  S0,S1
                             MULS    S5,S1,S7         ADDS ZSQ,S6
                             MULS    S6,S7,ERGEBNIS
```

So ist in diesem Falle durch die parallele Arbeitsweise der CPU zu erreichen, daß vierzehn Anweisungen in nur sieben Maschinentakten ausgeführt werden.

Parallele Prozessoren

Neben der Möglichkeit, mehrere Instruktionen in einem Maschinentakt auszuführen, sieht die PRISM–Architektur vor, mehrere Prozessoren gleichberechtigt parallel auf dem Systembus zu betreiben, um auf diese Weise mehrere Prozesse gleichzeitig zu bearbeiten. Dabei werden zur Ausführung anstehende Prozesse von einem einzigen (verteilten) Scheduler aus einer einzigen Prozeßwarteschlange auf freie CPUs verteilt. Hier ist ein großer Unterschied zur Vektor–/Parallelrechnerarchitektur zu sehen: es ist nicht Ziel wie bei dieser, einen einzigen Prozeß zu parallelisieren und auf mehrere CPUs zu verteilen, sondern es werden solche Applikationen parallel von mehreren Prozessoren bedient, die in mehrere parallele Prozesse zerlegt werden können. Diese Art der Parallelisierung kommt vielen UNIX–Applikationen entgegen. In der UNIX–Welt werden aus Vater-Prozessen heraus häufig Sohn-Prozesse durch das Kommando 'fork' erzeugt. Applikationen, die so aufgebaut sind, werden automatisch ohne Zutun des Programmierers in einer Mehrprozessorumgebung sehr viel schneller ausgeführt als in einer Einprozessorumgebung. Neben 'fork' stehen dem Entwickler weitere Werkzeuge zur Verfügung, um parallele Prozesse zu erzeugen und zu steuern.

Die DN 10000 kann maximal vier Prozessoren aufnehmen.

Die zuvor beschriebene Möglichkeit der Parallelisierung innerhalb eines Prozessors sowie die gleichzeitige Ausführung mehrerer Prozesse durch Einsatz mehrerer Prozessoren erfordert weitere Hochgeschwindigkeitskomponenten, um die Prozessoren überhaupt in ausreichendem Maße mit Daten zu versorgen. Als eine solche Komponente ist ein neuer Systembus als Transportmedium bei PRISM vorgesehen.

Systembus

Als Systembus findet in der PRISM-Architektur eine Neuentwicklung von Apollo Verwendung: der X-Bus. Dieser X-Bus ist 64 Bit breit (plus Parity), arbeitet mit einer Übertragungsrate von 150 Megabyte pro Sekunde und liefert den systemweiten Takt von ca. 18.5 MHz. Er ist Transportmedium für alle Hochgeschwindigkeitskomponenten (CPUs, Grafiksubsystem, Hauptspeicher, FDDI-Anschluß) und läßt parallele Zugriffe (z.B. Adreßanforderungen) von mehreren Prozessoren zu. Während einer Adreßanforderung ist der Bus nicht von einer CPU blockiert, d.h., zwischen Absetzen einer Adresse und Lieferung des Speicherinhalts haben andere Systemkomponenten Zugriff auf ihn. Ein 'Bus Optimizer' versucht, Zugriffe so zusammenzufassen, daß sie nach Möglichkeit 64-Bit-weise erfolgen. Werden beispielsweise in einer Schleife acht Bytes angesprochen, die unter einer Adresse zu finden sind, so werden diese Bytes gesammelt, bis sie mit einem Buszugriff in den Hauptspeicher geschrieben oder aus ihm gelesen werden können.

Die DN 10000 besitzt zusätzlich einen Diagnosebus, der von einem integrierten Diagnosesystem (Scan Path Technology) benutzt wird. Mit Hilfe dieses Diagnosesystems kann der normale Anwender die Verfügbarkeit von Systemkomponenten auf Controller-Ebene prüfen, Apollo-Serviceeinrichtungen können Tests z.T. bis auf Chip-Ebene durchführen.

Der X-Bus ist für den Anwender zum Anschluß von eigener Peripherie z.Z. noch nicht freigegeben. Als Verbindung zur Außenwelt stehen ein PC/AT-Bus sowie ein VME-Bus zur Verfügung. Die beiden Bussysteme sind über ein Adapter-Interface am X-Bus angeschlossen. Der PC/AT-Bus findet für Devices wie Grafik-, Floppy- und Cartridge-Controller Verwendung, der VME-Bus wird für Festplatten- und Netzwerk-Controller (Apollo Token Ring, Ethernet) verwendet.

Hauptspeicher

Der Hauptspeicher in der PRISM-Architektur ist so strukturiert, daß parallele Zugriffe von verschiedenen Prozessoren aus in unabhängige Speicherbänke erfolgen können. Dabei bedienen 'Module Controller' mehrere 'Memory Modules', die wiederum mehrere unabhängige Speicherbänke beinhalten. Die Memory Modulen besitzen Speicher-Warteschlangen, mit deren Hilfe zum einen die Parallelzugriffe gesteuert werden, zum anderen dafür Sorge getragen wird, daß Leseanweisungen vor Schreibanweisungen erfolgen. Der Hauptspeicher wird als 'shared memory' von allen Prozessoren benutzt.

Die DN 10000 ist mit zwei Modul-Controllern ausgestattet, die gemeinsam über einen Treiber Anschluß am X-Bus haben. Jeder Modul-Controller kann zwei Memory-Module bedienen und jedes Memory-Modul wiederum kann vier unabhängige Speicherbänke zu je acht Megabyte aufnehmen. Bei Vollausbau der Maschine kann daher 16fach 'interleaved' auf den Speicher zugegriffen werden (Bild 4). Dabei kommen 100 Nanosekunden 'static column' CMOS DRAMs als 1 Megabyte-Chips zum Einsatz. Auf diese Weise kann die Maschine von 8 MByte bis 128 MByte ausgebaut werden. Die Maschine ist dafür vorbereitet, 4 MByte-Chips aufzunehmen, sowie diese am Markt verfügbar sind, so daß dann ein Ausbau des Speichers auf 512 MByte erfolgen kann.

Der Hauptspeicher ist mit der Möglichkeit ausgestattet, 1-Bit-Fehler zu korrigieren und 2-Bit-Fehler zu erkennen (SEC-DED). Die Addressierung erfolgt physikalisch mit 30 Bit (virtuell mit 32 Bit).

Hauptspeicher–Struktur

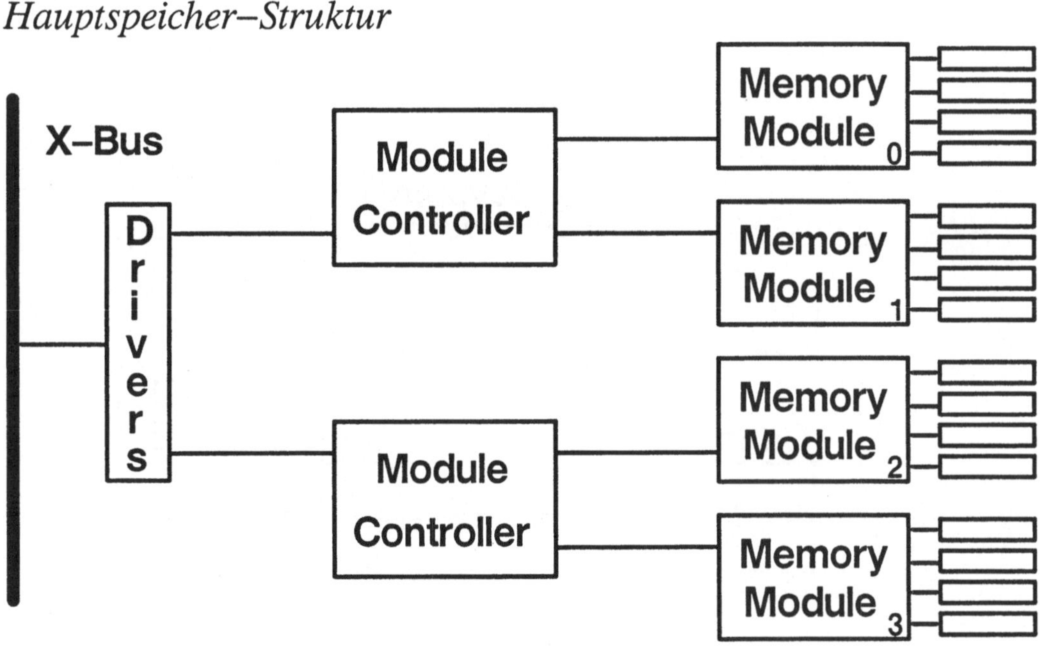

Bild 4

Massenspeicher

Unabhängig von der physikalischen Realisierung der Massenspeicher, sieht PRISM die Möglichkeit des Einsatzes von 'Disk Striping' vor (Bild 5). Disk–Striping läßt es zu, mehrere physikalisch getrennte Plattenlaufwerke dergestalt zu einer logischen Einheit zusammenzufassen, daß Teile von Dateien parallel auf die logische Platte geschrieben und ebenso wieder gelesen werden können. Dieses Verfahren erhöht den Datendurchsatz von und zu den Massenspeichern beträchtlich.

In der DN 10000 kann das Disk–Striping wahlweise über zwei oder vier Plattenlaufwerke betrieben werden. Die maximal vier Laufwerke werden von zwei Controllern bedient, die im VME–Bus stecken. Auf diese Weise ist ein Plattenspeicherausbau von 380 MByte bis ca. 3 GByte zu bewerkstelligen. Jedes Laufwerk ist in der Lage, 15 MBit Daten pro Sekunde zu übertragen, womit sich für eine Datei im Disk–Striping über vier Platten 60 MBit/sec Transferrate ergibt. So wird es möglich, auch mehrere CPUs bei Applikationen mit Schwerpunkt auf Plattenzugriffen ausreichend mit externen Daten zu versorgen.

Disk Striping

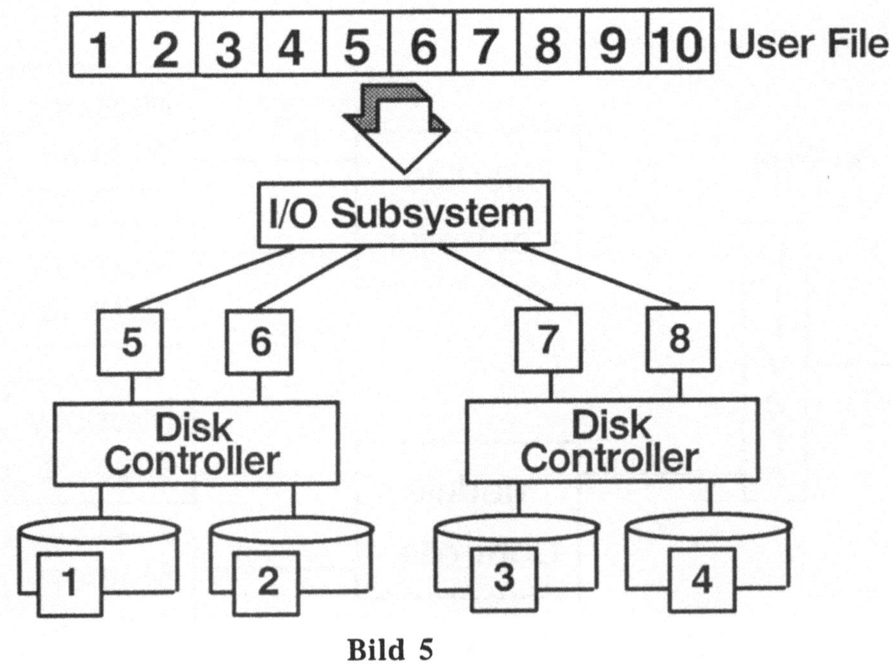

Bild 5

Grafik Subsystem

Bestandteil des PRISM-Konzeptes ist ein rasterorientiertes Hochgeschwindigkeitsgrafiksubsystem, daß aus 40 oder 80 Bitplanes bestehen kann und direkt am X-Bus angeschlossen ist. Die Verwendung der Bitplanes ist dabei in weiten Bereichen softwaremäßig für
mehrere Fenster auf dem Bildschirm konfigurierbar, so daß mehrere Grafikapplikationen
unabhängig voneinander gleichzeitig in ihrer eigenen Grafikumgebung ausgeführt werden
können. Die softwaremäßige Konfiguration beinhaltet dabei die Einstellung des Z-Buffers
in den Tiefen 16, 24 oder 32 Bit, Double Buffering, Colormap und True-Color (24 Bitplanes), Semi-True-Color (12 Bitplanes) oder False-Color (8 Bitplanes). Mit Hilfe von
CPU und vier bzw. acht parallel arbeitenden Pixelprozessoren (je nach Ausbau auf 40
bzw. 80 Bitplanes), die je zehn Bitplanes bedienen, werden so Darstellungsgeschwindig-
keiten von 700 000 2D-, 500 000 3D-Vektoren/sec, 30 000 Polygone/sec bzw. 20 bis 24
Frames/sec (Animation) erreicht. Ein sogenannter Alpha-Buffer gestatten es, Attribute an
grafische Objekte zu knüpfen. Ein solches Attribut kann eine 2D-Bitmap sein, die ein
beliebiges, vom Anwender beschriebenes Muster enthält und durch 'Texture Mapping' auf
die Oberfläche eines 3D-Modells gelegt werden kann.

Literatur

/1/   Inside a New Architecture, Apollo Computer Inc., USA
/2/   Domain Series 10000 Technical Reference Library, Vol. 1
           Processors and Instruction Set, Apollo Computer Inc., USA

Verteilte Netzwerkmoduln zur Beseitigung von Flaschenhälsen —

Illustration am Beispiel von CDCNET

Theo Weber

Control Data GmbH
Stresemannallee 30
6000 Frankfurt 70

ABSTRACT

Verteilte Netzwerke, die auf Mikroprozessoren basieren, sind
in der Lage, die Flaschenhälse zu beseitigen, die durch herkömmliche Front-End-Prozessoren (FEP) verursacht wurden.

Das Konzept der Modularität ermöglicht eine abgestufte, kosten-
günstige Netzwerklösung sowohl für Minimal-Konfigurationen als
auch für ausgedehnte große Netzwerke.

In diesem Konzept übernehmen Mikroprozessoren, die über schnelle
CPUs verfügen und die verschiedensten Anschlußmöglichkeiten bieten,
die Aufgaben der FEPs. Bei einer Anfangskonfiguration genügt es,
wenn ein oder zwei solcher Einheiten installiert werden. Mit
wachsendem Bedarf an neuen Netzwerkfunktionen können weitere Einheiten hinzugefügt werden.

Solche Einheiten sind im CDCNET von Control Data als Basis-Device-
Interfaces realisiert. Sie können durch eine große Vielfalt von
Hard- und Software-Kombinationen auf ihre jeweilige Aufgabe im
Netz maßgeschneidert werden. Zu diesen Interfaces gehört das
Mainframe-Device-Interface für die Verbindung eines CYBER-180-Rech-
ners zu einem Ethernet, weiter das Terminal-Device-Interface für den
Anschluß der Endgeräte an das Ethernet und das Network-Device-Inter-
face für die Kommunikation von CDCNET zu anderen Netzen.

Diese Hard- und Software, mit der ein CDCNET aufgebaut wird, entspricht zusätzlich noch dem 7-Schichten-Modell von OSI/ISO. Damit
ist die Zukunftssicherheit der Netzwerke gegeben.

<u>tina - ein multifunktionales ISDN-Endgerät</u>

Annette Gahn, Stollmann GmbH, Hamburg

<u>1. Einleitung</u>

ISDN mit seinen Standardisierungs- und Integrationsbestrebungen ist in der letzten Zeit in Veröffentlichungen vielfältig behandelt worden.

Welche Endgeräte können angeschlossen werden und wie sieht ein multifunktionaler ISDN-Arbeitsplatz aus?

Mit der Einführung von S-ISDN (Schmalband-ISDN) stellt man sich vor, daß die Funktionen des Arbeitsplatz-Rechners (PC oder Workstation) nicht nur um die öffentlichen Dienste Telefax, Teletex, Btx erweitert werden, sondern, daß auch das Telefon integriert wird. Der Arbeitsplatz muß die normalen Inhouse-Funktionen wie die angebotenen Dienste integrieren und abwickeln.

Die offenen multifunktionalen Arbeitsplätze sind die interessantesten Endgeräte für den Anschluß ans ISDN.

Mit der tina*-Entwicklung hat Stollmann das Telefon im PC integriert; die SØ-Schnittstelle der tina-Karte macht den PC (XT, AT) zum multifunktionalen ISDN-Endgerät.

----
tina* = telefon-integrierte-netzwerk-architektur;
       tina ist ein eingetragenes Warenzeichen der
       Stollmann GmbH

2. Schmalband-ISDN und Endgeräte

Das S-ISDN (im folgenden nur ISDN genannt) integriert mehrere
Postdienste in ein Netz über einen S∅-Anschluß.
Die bekanntesten Eigenschaften von ISDN sind die Integration von
Sprach- und Datenkommunikation, zwei 64 kbit/s-Basis-Kanäle und
ein 16 kbit/s Signalisierungskanal.

Zur Nutzung der 64 kbit/s Basiskanäle für die Dienste Teletex,
Telefax, Textfax, Sprache werden spezielle ISDN-Endgeräte
entwickelt:

Einzeldienstendgeräte,
    die nur die Nutzung eines Dienstes vorsehen, also für jeden
    Kommunikationsdienst ein Gerät - die Geräte türmen sich auf
    dem Schreibtisch, jedes Gerät hat seine Benutzeroberfläche und
    Bedienerführung.

Mehrdienstendgeräte
    fassen die Nutzung mehrerer Einzeldienste in einem Endgerät
    zusammen. Von einem Mehrdienstendgerät können über die beiden
    B-Kanäle gleichzeitig zwei Dienste abgewickelt werden, wobei
    die Verbindungen zu verschiedenen Zielen oder zum gleichen
    Ziel bestehen können.

Multifunktionale Endgeräte
    vereinen Einzeldienst- und Lokalfunktionen in einem Endgerät.
    Mit Einzeldienstfunktion ist die Nutzung der 64 kbit/s-
    (Fernmelde-)Dienste gemeint, während die Lokalfunktionen nicht
    in Verbindung mit ISDN-Diensten gesehen werden.
    Lokalfunktionen sind:
    -    Notizbuch, Kalender, Wiedervorlage, Terminverwaltung mit
        Erinnerung
    -    Nutzung der ISDN-Endgeräte für lokale Arbeiten: kopieren,
        Textverarbeitung, Datenverarbeitung (Gebührenverarbei-
        tung,...).

Terminaladapter (TA)

(ISDN-Endgeräteanpassung)

bieten die Möglichkeit, existierende Endgeräte an das ISDN anzuschließen. Die in der Datenkommunikation eingeführten Schnittstellen wie V.24 und X.21 werden von den TAs auf die ISDN-Schnittstelle umgesetzt. Mit ihnen kann nur die Datenkomponente von ISDN genutzt werden. Die Behandlung von an- und abgehenden Rufen kann vom Endgerät über V.25bis oder X.21 gesteuert werden; der TA setzt die Signalisierung auf das ISDN-D-Kanal-Protokoll um.

Solche Lösungen mögen als Übergang akzeptabel sein, können aber letztlich nicht befriedigen, da durch sie ein erheblicher quantitativer wie auch qualitativer Leistungsverlust verursacht wird;

quantitativ: die Endgeräte unterstützen 64 kbaud i.a. nicht, so daß eine rate-adaption nötig ist und der Zugang mit den üblichen Transferraten (1.2-9.6 kbaud) erfolgt;

qualitativ: die Behandlung der ISDN-Dienstsignale wird voll manuell vom Benutzer erwartet oder entfällt ganz.

Wirklich interessant sind die multifunktionalen Endgeräte, die die Dienste in die Funktionen der Arbeitsplätze integrieren und nutzbar machen.

Folgende weitere Eigenschaften des ISDN sind in diesem Zusammenhang von Interesse:

- Die Wahlinformationen und weitere Dienstsignale werden an der Teilnehmerschnittstelle in einem funktionalen Protokoll übergeben (1R6, 1TR6, DKZN1); dies ermöglicht die rechnergesteuerte Bedienung.

- ISDN kommt nicht nur durch Postanschlüsse zum Teilnehmer, sondern auch durch ISDN-fähige Nebenstellenanlagen (ISPBX), die die Postschnittstelle SØ unterstützen; darüberhinaus gibt es auch bei den privaten Schnittstellen der ISPBXen Standardisierungsbestrebungen (UpØ-Schnittstelle), die die Auswahlmöglichkeiten (Offenheit) bei Endgeräten verbessern.

3. Offene Multifunktionale Arbeitsplätze

Der Prototyp des offenen multifunktionalen Arbeitsplatzes ist der kompatible PC.
Er ist offen, denn:

- die internen Hard- und Software-Schnittstellen sind offengelegt; damit ist es möglich, neue Hard- und Software-Komponenten zu integrieren (z.B. Coprozessoren); das reicht von spezieller Peripherie über Kommunikationsanschlüsse und Anwendungssoftware bis hin zu Window-Oberflächen.

- Es gibt ein breites Angebot an Soft- und Hardware-Komponenten, mit denen der PC auf die aktuellen Bedürfnisse angepaßt werden kann (s.o.).

- Er ist preiswert, so daß er für eine Vielzahl von möglichen Anwendungen eine akzeptable Alternative darstellt.

Der Funktionalität des PCs sind fast keine Grenzen gesetzt: Neben lokalen Funktionen wie diversen Anwendungsprogrammen, Programmgeneratoren, Tabellenkalkulation, Textbearbeitung und Graphik bis hin zum Layout-System sind diverse Kommunikationsfunktionen erhältlich, die vom LAN über Hostanschlüsse wie X.25/PAD und SNA/3270 bis hin zu Postdiensten wie Btx, Teletex und demnächst auch Telefax reichen.

Ähnliches gilt auch für eine Reihe von weiteren Arbeitsplatzsystemen, aber stets mit Einschränkungen.

Sicher hat das Systemkonzept des PCs diverse Schwachstellen, die vor allem Erweiterungsversuche erheblich erschweren; dies hat der stürmischen Entwicklung der Funktionalität aber keinen Abbruch getan.

<u>4. ISDN-Nutzen für multifunktionale Arbeitsplätze</u>

Für den Anschluß von multifunktionalen Arbeitsplätzen an ISDN gibt es drei Motivationen.

a) ISDN als Datenkommunikationsnetz dem Arbeitsplatz verfügbar zu machen

b) den Arbeitsplatz als hochkomfortable Telefonbedieneinheit zu nutzen

c) beides zusammen.

Zu a) Dieser Ansatz ist selbstverständlich, da ISDN auch für Datenkommunikation genutzt wird, müssen Endgeräte angeschlossen werden. Außer der Nutzung der Postdienste können auch private Protokolle über ISDN betrieben werden, wobei u.U. Server den erforderlichen Übergang zu anderen Netzen im öffentlichen als auch lokalen Bereich herstellen können. Ein großer Nutzeffekt kann im lokalen Bereich allein die Verkabelung sein, da für die Datenübertragung über die PABX die i.A. bereits vorhandene Telefonverkabelung genutzt werden kann. Sogar LAN-Implementationen über der PABX sind möglich.

Zu b) Komfortable Telefonsoftware ist bereits für das analoge Telefonnetz entwickelt worden. ISDN bietet mit seinen vielfältigen Dienstmerkmalen und Dienstsignalen reichhaltige Möglichkeiten für computerunterstütztes Telefonieren. Durch Schnittstellen der Telefonsoftware zu Anwenderprogrammen und -datenbeständen können diese an die Telefonfunktion angebunden werden.

Zu c) Wird dieser Ansatz konsequent zu Ende gedacht, so hat der Arbeitsplatz nur eine Schnittstelle nach außen, nämlich den ISDN-Anschluß, wobei das digitale Telefon im Arbeitsplatz integriert ist. Da ISDN zwei Basiskanäle für Sprache und Daten zur Verfügung stellt, reicht dieser Anschluß für die meisten Anwendungen. Neben den Vorteilen von Ansatz a) und b) ergeben sich hier weitere komfortable Möglichkeiten.

Es kann z.B. parallel zur Sprachverbindung eine Datenverbindung aufgebaut werden, über die im Arbeitsplatz gespeicherte Daten, Texte und Graphiken als Gesprächsgrundlage sofort ausgetauscht und auf dem Bildschirm visualisiert werden. Außerdem kann über den ISDN-Anschluß aufgrund der Identifikation des Gesprächspartners nicht nur auf lokale Datenbestände zugegriffen werden, sondern auch auf entfernte.

5. Der integrierte Anschluß von offenen multifunktionalen Arbeitsplätzen an ISDN

Um die in ISDN integrierten Funktionen wirklich für den multifunktionalen Arbeitsplatz nutzen zu können, muß der Anschluß in den Arbeitsplatz integriert werden, für offene Arbeitsplätze ist das möglich (siehe 3.). Durch einen ISDN-Anschluß in Form eines Coprozessors mit integrierten Telefon kann

- die Sprachkommunikation durch den Arbeitsplatz wirkungsvoll unterstützt werden bei voller Ausnutzung der ISDN-Dienstmerkmale

- die Datenkommunikation über ISDN effektiv betrieben werden bei ebenfalls voller Ausnutzung der Dienstmerkmale als auch der angebotenen Übertragungsrate.

Dem offenen multifunktionalen Arbeitsplatz wird erst damit die ISDN-Kommunikationswelt geöffnet, nämlich:

- Computerunterstütztes Komforttelefon mit der Integrationsmöglichkeit in die Anwendungssoftware

- Postdienste wie Teletex, Telefax, Btx

- Hostkommunikation über SNA/3270, X.31/PAD, Rate adaption mit üblichen Anwendungen über asynchronen Protokollen

- Im Zusammenspiel mit einer AP-AP-Kommunikation mit LAN-Funktionen (z.B: Netbios), wobei durch ISDN das LAN auch ein WAN sein kann

- Das integrierte digitale Telefon ermöglicht Sprachspeicherung und Sprachbehandlung durch den Arbeitsplatz.

6. Implementation

Der im vorigen Abschnitt skizzierte Anschluß von multifunktionalen Arbeitsplätzen an ISDN ist zweifellos eine elegante Lösung. Es gilt jedoch dazu eine ganze Reihe von Problemen zu lösen, die durch Zulassungsbestimmungen und Anwenderanforderungen gegeben sind; beispielsweise:

- Der Sprachteil muß auch bei ausgeschaltetem PC funktionieren; die Telefonfunktion des Coprozessors muß also mit der geringen Stromversorgung durch den ISDN-Anschluß arbeiten können; eine bestehende Verbindung soll natürlich nicht beeinträchtigt werden, wenn der Arbeitsplatz eingeschaltet wird.

- Bei eingeschaltetem Arbeitsplatz soll natürlich eine Wahl über die Datentastatur möglich sein; leider hat diese ein anderes Layout als die Telefontastatur.

- Die Abhandlung von Datenprotokollen mit 64kbaud erfordert eine kräftige Prozessorleistung; dies wirkt sich natürlich auch auf die Leistungsaufnahme aus und steht der ersten Anforderung entgegen.

- Für die Postdienste Teletex und Telefax wird ein großer gepufferter Speicherbereich zur Aufnahme von Empfangsdaten gefordert.

- Um vorhandene Kommunikationssoftware auf dem Arbeitsplatz nutzen zu können, ist es sinnvoll, die internen Schnittstellen kompatibel zu bestehenden (z.B. COM) zu halten.

- Die zur Implementation verfügbare Baugruppe (PC-Board) ist in ihrer Größe ziemlich beschränkt.

- Die Normierung der D-Kanal-Protokolle ist noch nicht abgeschlossen.

- Für Datenübertragung auf dem B-Kanal sind bislang keine
Standards vorhanden; durch die Telematikprotokolle sind Hinweise
gegeben, für multifunktionale Endgeräte sind diese Protokolle
(Point-to-point) nicht ausreichend. Eine Lösung könnte X.25 über
ISDN sein.

7. Fazit

ISDN bietet vor allem multifunktionalen Arbeitsplätzen eine noch
ungeahnte Vielfalt von Möglichkeiten, wenn der Anschluß wirklich
integriert erfolgt. Terminaladapter und andere nicht integrierten
Varianten des Anschlusses beschneiden einen großen Teil dieser
Möglichkeiten. Sicher bereitet der integrierte Anschluß eine
Reihe von nichttrivialen Problemen, diese können aber gelöst
werden (siehe tina*).

Innovative Entwicklungen mit Videotex (Vtx)

Ein Kommunikationsmedium überbrückt Europas Grenzen

D. Pfeiffer, Siemens AG, München

Unternehmensbereich Kommunikations- und Datentechnik

Kurzfassung

Die Bedeutung von VIDEOTEX (Vtx) ist in den europäischen Ländern unterschiedlich ausgeprägt. Entscheidenden Einfluß haben dabei die unterschiedlichen Marketingstrategien der Betreiber der Vtx-Netze, wie das Beispiel Frankreich zeigt.

Obwohl die technischen Ausprägungen der Vtx-Netze in den europäischen Ländern unterschiedlich sind, bilden diese nationalen Netze eine Basis für einen europäischen Verbund. Die Vtx-Netze sind die besten offenen Dialogsysteme, die in den Ländern verfügbar sind. Für einen europaweiten Zugriff zu diesen Netzen gibt es verschiedene Möglichkeiten.

- Mit Multistandardendgeräten können über Fernwahl alle europäischen Netze angesteuert werden.

- Anschluß von Endgeräten über PAD (Paketierungs-/Depaketierungseinrichtung)

- Ein Externer Computer, der an das Vtx-Netz der Bundesrepublik angeschlossen ist, kann ebenfalls z. B. in Frankreich als Server arbeiten.

Über Multistandardsysteme können Teilnehmer unterschiedlicher nationaler Netze gleichzeitig Zugriff auf einen Externen Computer in einem beliebigen Land haben. Bei der Struktur der Software für Multistandardsysteme gibt es zwei unterschiedliche Architekturen:

- Common Kernel
- Multigateway, Multistandard

Vtx bietet nicht nur den Zugang zu einer Vielfalt von Dienstleistungen, sondern gestattet auch den Netzübergang zu Teletex, Telex, Telefax, Telebox und Cityruf.

Innovative Techniken erweitern die Einsatzbreite von Vtx-Systemlösungen. Erwähnt seien ISDN und Bilddatenbanken.

1.   **Die Bedeutung von Videotex (Vtx) im europäischen Bereich**

Zu den drei klassischen Produktionsfaktoren Boden, Kapital und Arbeit kann man heute einen vierten Produktionsfaktor hinzunehmen: die Information (1). Es ist beeindruckend, welchen Stellenwert die Information bzw. Kommunikation in den modernen Industriestaaten schon erreicht hat. In den USA sind heute bereits ca. 50% der Beschäftigten im Informationsbereich tätig. In Europa liegt der Anteil um ca. 10% darunter. Die Geschwindigkeit, mit der sich der Anteil der Beschäftigten im Informationsbereich erhöht, ist gewaltig. In der Zeitspanne von 1951 bis 1971, also innerhalb von 20 Jahren, hat sich dieser Anteil in den Industrieländern um teilweise 10 oder gar mehr Prozent erhöht. Maßgeblich beeinflußt wird diese Entwicklung durch innovative Kommunikationsmedien.

Betrachtet man einzelne Gebiete des Kommunikationssektors, so kann man sehr hohe Zuwachsraten bei den Anschlüssen für Telefax (+ 92%) und Btx (+ 64%) feststellen, wohingegen traditionelle Sektoren wie Telefon (+ 3%) und Telex (+ 0,4%) sehr geringe Zuwachsraten aufweisen bei allerdings sehr hoher Ausgangsbasis (Stand Ende 1987). Die Zahlen zeigen eindeutig in Richtung neuer, komfortabler Kommunikationsmedien, zu denen auch Videotex zählt.

Vtx ist in Europa bereits zu einem wirtschaftlichen Faktor geworden. Z. Zt. sind etwa 3,73 Mio Teilnehmer an nationale Vtx-Systeme angeschlossen, wobei allerdings Frankreich den weitaus größten Anteil von 3,45 Mio Teilnehmern verzeichnen kann. In Europa (ohne Frankreich) sind ca. 560 Externe Computer an die nationalen Vtx-Netze angeschlossen. Allein in Frankreich sind 2850 Server angeschlossen, wobei ein großer Anteil der Server auf Personal Computer (PC) aufbaut.

Es ist allgemein bekannt, daß eine derartige Verbreitung des französischen Vtx-Systems und seines Terminals MINITEL auf zielgerichtete strategische Überlegungen der französischen Regierung zurückzuführen ist. Während in Deutschland und in den meisten übrigen europäischen Ländern ca. 80% der Teilnehmer Vtx geschäftlich oder halbgeschäftlich nutzen, sind es in Frankreich nur 40%. Durch gezielte Maßnahmen versucht nun Frankreich, den Anteil der geschäftlichen Nutzer zu erhöhen; so z.B. durch eine Luxussteuer auf bestimmte private Messagerie-Dienste.

2. Nationale Ausprägungen

In der Bundesrepublik Deutschland, in der die Deutsche Bundespost seit einigen Jahren das Medium Bildschirmtext (Btx) anbietet, und in fast allen anderen europäischen Ländern, sind inzwischen nationale öffentliche Videotex-(Vtx-)Netze aufgebaut worden. Sie haben jedoch unterschiedliche Architekturen und technische Ausprägungen, die zu erheblichen Schwierigkeiten bei der Netzkopplung führen.

Die Unterschiede dokumentieren sich nicht nur in den verschiedenen Namen für dengleichen Dienst, sondern

- Netzarchitektur
- Darstellungsstandard (Presentation Standard)
- Kommunikationsprotokoll (Gateway Protocol)

sind unterschiedlich ausgeprägt bzw. unterscheiden sich grundsätzlich.

Bezüglich der Netzarchitektur bilden heute die Vtx-Netze der Bundesrepublik Deutschland und Frankreichs die beiden extremen Gegensätze. In Deutschland wurde ein mächtiges, hierarchisches Rechnernetz mit Vtx-Vermittlungsanlagen und regionalen Informationsrechnern sowie einer überregionalen Zentrale aufgebaut. Dem Benutzer werden vielfältige Funktionen wie Mailbox, Aufbau geschlossener Benutzergruppen, Abspeicherung von Seiten im System, Inkasso von Seitengebühren etc. angeboten.

In Frankreich dagegen wird mit dem Vtx-Netz nur das Vermittlungsmedium zwischen Endbenutzer und Informationsanbieter bereitgestellt. Die meisten anderen europäischen Länder wählten ein Konzept, das zwischen den genannten Lösungen liegt.

Hinsichtlich des Darstellungsstandards am Endgerät gibt es unterschiedliche Ausprägungen der CEPT-Normen in den europäischen Ländern. Es zeigt sich jedoch ein Trend zum CEPT Profil 1 Standard. Schwerpunktmäßig wird CEPT Profil 3 (Prestel) nur noch in Belgien und Großbritannien eingesetzt. Die Niederlande bieten bereits einen CEPT Profil 1 - Anschluß an. In Frankreich wird CEPT Profil 2 (Antiope) verwendet. In einigen Ländern werden mehrere Profile parallel angeboten.

Die Technik des Rechnerverbundes, also das Protokoll für den Anschluß Externer Computer an ein nationales öffentliches Vtx-Netz (Gateway Protocol), ist die dritte Komponente, die die Inkompatibilität der länderspezifischen Lösungen kennzeichnet. Hier kann wenigstens von einer großen Ländergruppe gesprochen werden, die, abgesehen von einigen nationalen Besonderheiten, als Basisprotokoll Prestel wählte.

3. Vtx als Grundlage für ein europäisches Verbundnetz

Die fortschreitende Integration des europäischen Marktes erfordert auch eine Integration unterschiedlicher Datennetze.
Es sind Bestrebungen im Gange, europaweit ein einheitliches
Videotex Interworking Protocol (VI) zu verabschieden. Bis zu
seiner Realisierung in allen Ländern werden Übergangslösun-
gen für eine grenzüberschreitende Kommunikation von den Be-
treibern der nationalen Vtx-Netze und den Herstellern von
Externen Computern angeboten.

3.1 Verbindung nationaler Vtx-Netze

Durch die imkompatiblen, länderspezifischen Lösungen ist die
Forderung, nationale Vtx-Netze untereinander zu koppeln,
nicht ohne weiteres realisierbar. 1987 wurde zwischen Frankreich und Deutschland eine Zwischenlösung auf der Basis von
Gatewayrechnern eröffnet. Ein französisches Endgerät wird
über den in Paris installierten Gateway-Rechner Groom mit
dem deutschen Btx-System verbunden. Deutsche Btx-Terminals
werden über den Düsseldorfer Rechner mit Teletel in
Frankreich verbunden.

Nachteilig wirken sich bei dieser Verbindung die Tatsachen
aus, daß
    1. nicht alle Dienste in Teletel von Btx aus erreichbar
       sind und
    2. die Umsetzung der französischen Dialogfunktion
       über numerische Eingaben erfolgt.

Die belgische Post hat Mitte 1988 einen Vtx-Gateway zwischen
Belgien und Frankreich installiert. Die Verbindung von
Belgien aus wird mit einem Teletel-kompatiblen Terminal über
einen Gateway-Service (MinitelNet) zum Teletel-Kiosk
aufgebaut. Französische Benutzer haben mit Minitels über
einen Gateway in Brüssel Zugriff zum belgischen System.
Dieser Gateway nimmt eine Umsetzung zwischen Prestel und
Teletel vor.

Der erste "echte" Vtx-Verbund soll Ende 1988 zwischen Holland
und Deutschland eröffnet werden. Echt bedeutet

    - nationale Endgeräte können verwendet werden;

    - sämtliche Kommunikations- und Dialogfunktionen sind
      zugänglich (Mitteilungsdienst, Bestell-Service);

    - entgeltpflichtige Seiten können abgerufen werden;
      die Post übernimmt die Inkassogarantie.

Der gleiche Verbund mit der Schweiz ist für 1989 vorgesehen, die Einbindung Luxemburgs ist ebenfalls geplant.

3.2 Anschluß von Vtx-Endgeräten über Ländergrenzen hinweg

Über Fernwahl kann heute mit einem passenden Endgerät jedes Vtx-Netz angewählt werden, was jedoch nur in wenigen Fällen wirtschaftlich sein dürfte. Die Deutsche Bundespost bietet seit Mitte dieses Jahres auch den länderüberschreitenden Vtx-Endgeräteanschluß über Paketvermittlung an. Im Gegensatz zur Fernwahl zahlt hier der Benutzer im wesentlichen nur Gebühren für die übertragene Informationsmenge und nicht für die Zeit des gesamten Anschlusses.

Die technische Realisierung erfolgt durch die Installation eines PAD-Anschlusses (Packet Assembly/Disassembly facility) in demjenigen Land, von dem aus man das Btx-Netz in Deutschland anwählen möchte. Der Benutzer wählt über das Telefonnetz den PAD an und wird über die Schnittstelle X.25 mit dem Btx-Netz verbunden.

Der Anschluß an das französische Teletel-Netz über sog. VAP (Videotex Access Points) ähnlich den PAD ist sehr weit verbreitet. Entsprechende VAP sind in allen Ländern installiert, die Frankreich benachbart oder der französischen Sprache verbunden sind.

In China hat die Deutsche Bundespost einen entsprechenden PAD installiert, so daß europäische Firmen Zugang zum Btx-System haben. Abspeicherung und Abruf von chinesischen Zeichen im System sind möglich. Zur Zeit sind 40 Teilnehmer in China angemeldet.

Zur Olympiade in Seoul wird die Deutsche Bundespost einen Btx-Gateway zwischen Südkorea und der Bundesrepublik einrichten. Diese Btx-Brücke soll Sportlern und Funktionären zur Informationsbeschaffung und auch zur Nachrichtenübermittlung nach Deutschland dienen.

Der Anschluß an unterschiedliche nationale Vtx-Netze über Fernwahl oder PAD setzt ein Multistandardendgerät voraus. Neuere Entwicklungen auf dem Endgerätesektor verfügen über diese Möglichkeit der Auswahl zwischen CEPT 1 bis 3.

3.3   VTX mit fremden Schriftsystemen

Multistandardendgeräte   müssen   auch   verschiedene   Sprachen
"sprechen", um einem internationalen Einsatz gerecht zu werden. Multilingual heißt im einfachsten Fall, daß über ein Me-
nü die Auswahl einer europäischen Sprache möglich ist. Einerseits ist die Bedieneroberfläche davon betroffen, andererseits müssen gewisse Sonderzeichen eingebbar und auch abruf-
bar sein.
Im CEPT 1-Standard sind alle europäischen Sonderzeichen
festgelegt. Die Tastaturoberfläche ist in der Regel auf den
nationalen Zeichensatz eingestellt.

Weit komplexer stellt sich die Architektur eines Vtx-Termi-
nals für Sprachen wie chinesisch oder japanisch dar. Ein Zei-
chengenerator muß ca. 6500 chinesische Zeichen bedienen. Während die Generierung von Zeichen ein technisches Problem ist,
ist das Editieren von chinesischen Zeichen eine Frage der
Schnittstelle zum Benutzer. Es stehen mehrere Eingabemethoden
zur Verfügung, die in China unterschiedliche Verbreitung gefunden haben. Die bekanntesten Verfahren sind GB-Code und Fi-
ve-Stroke.

Beim GB-Code-Verfahren wird in einer 2 x 2-Byte-Tabelle den
ca. 6500 Zeichen je ein numerischer Code zugewiesen. Dieser
Code wird vom Benutzer über eine alphanumerische Tastatur
eingegeben.

Beim Five-Stroke-Verfahren werden über Tasten Striche und
Strichkombinationen eingegeben. Auswahl und Kombination werden durch eine intelligente Benutzeroberfläche unterstützt.

Die Darstellung der chinesischen Zeichen auf dem Bildschirm
erfolgt mit 24 x 24 Punkten. Dies bedeutet, daß nur 20 chinesische Zeichen pro Zeile und insgesamt 10 Zeilen dargestellt
werden können. In Btx wurden bereits von der Deutschen Bundespost chinesische Seiten abgelegt, die aber nur von Vtx-
Endgeräten mit speziellen Decodern abgerufen werden können.

Über eine Kooperation zwischen Blaupunkt, Detecon und Siemens
werden z. Zt. ein Vtx-Terminal für einen chinesischen Feld-
versuch und eine entsprechende Editiersoftware entwickelt.
Mitte 1987 wurde bereits ein erster Prototyp eines chinesischen Terminals in Peking auf der deutsch-chinesischen Elek-
tronikwoche vorgeführt.

4. Externe Computer als Multistandardsysteme

Eine wirtschaftliche Lösung, Daten und Anwendungen in einem Externen Computer allen Teilnehmern in allen nationalen Vtx-Netzen einheitlich zur Verfügung zu stellen, bietet sich durch den Einsatz von Multistandardsystemen. Durch die In-stallation der Multistandardsoftware in einem Rechner, der in einem beliebigen Land installiert sein kann, kann dieser Rechner als Externer Computer über X.25 an alle europäischen Vtx-Netze angeschlossen werden.

Die Multistandardsoftware baut auf dem Konzept der Externen Rechnersoftware für die unterschiedlichen nationalen Protokollvereinbarungen (Gateway-Protokolle) auf.

4.1 Softwarekonzept für nationale Gateways

Die Hauptschwierigkeit bei dem Einsatz von Externen Computern sind die unterschiedlichen Kommunikationsprotokolle der verschiedenen Länder. Deshalb hat sich Siemens für ein Konzept nach dem Prinzip der verteilten Verarbeitung entschieden. Zum Einsatz kommen dabei Rechner der Serie Siemens 7500 (Betriebssystem BS2000) mit vorgeschalteten Kommunikationsrechnern (KR) der TRANSDATA Ⓡ -Familie. Im Host (und teilweise im Kommunikationsrechner) befindet sich ein international einsetzbares Grundsystem (VTX-GA); die länderspezifischen Vtx-Komponenten (VTX-EC) sind in die Kommunikationsrechner ausgelagert. Das Grundsystem besorgt die eigentliche Verarbeitung der Benutzerdaten und den logischen Dialog zum Anwender. Basis hierfür ist der Universelle Transaktionsmonitor UTM, so daß die Kompatibilität zwischen herkömmlichen DV-Anwendungen und Vtx-Anwendungen gegeben ist. Dadurch können schon bestehende Dialoganwendungen, die bisher nur von DV-Terminals aus erreichbar waren, mit geringem Anpassungsaufwand auch am Vtx-Endgerät angeboten werden.

Anfang 1984 hat Siemens mit der Erstellung nationaler Vtx-Systeme begonnen. Basis für die Entwicklung war die damals für die Bundesrepublik Deutschland entwickelte Vtx-Software. Heute werden Vtx-Systeme von Siemens für nahezu alle westeuropäischen Länder, in denen ein nationales Vtx-Netz installiert ist, angeboten.

4.2 Multistandardsysteme

Die Inkompatibilitäten und die fehlenden Gateways zwischen den nationalen Netzen verhindern, daß der Teilnehmer eines nationalen Netzes direkten Zugriff zu einem Externen Computer hat, der an ein anderes nationales Netz angeschlossen ist. Unser Haus hat als eines der ersten Hersteller eine Software entwickelt, die den Anschluß eines Externen Computers gleichzeitig an mehrere nationale Vtx-Netze erlaubt.

So kann ein Multistandardsystem gleichzeitig als Externer Rechner des italienischen und deutschen Vtx-Netzes betrieben werden. Teilnehmer des deutschen Vtx-Netzes haben somit Zugriff auf dasselbe System wie italienische Vtx-Teilnehmer. Dies wird dadurch erreicht, daß im Host das Grundsystem (VTX-GA) und in den Kommunikationsrechnern die Software für beide Externe Computer-Anschlüsse (VTX-EC-I und VTX-EC-D) zum Ablauf kommen. Obwohl der Teilnehmer in Italien im Prestel-Standard und der Teilnehmer in der Bundesrepublik Deutschland im CEPT-Standard arbeiten, führen beide Dialoge mit derselben Anwendung im Host; die entsprechenden länderspezifischen Umsetzungen erfolgen in den Kommunikationsrechnern.

Bei der Realisierung von Multistandard-Externen Computern sind zwei Strategieansätze möglich:

- Konzept des Common Kernel

- und Konzept des Multigateway mit Multistandard.

4.2.1 Common Kernel

Unabhängig vom Darstellungsstandard am Endgerät (CEPT Profil 1 bis 3) werden systemintern immer CEPT 1-Masken geführt und verwaltet. Das entsprechende Umsetzen der Masken bei der Ein- und Ausgabe ist eine Aufgabe der ausgelagerten Gateway-Komponenten im Kommunikationsrechner. Außerdem werden in dieser Komponente das nationale Anschlußprotokoll zum öffentlichen Vtx-Netz abgehandelt und notwendige Dialoganpassungen durchgeführt.

Der wirtschaftliche Vorteil dieses Konzepts liegt auf der Hand: Die Bereitstellung eines nationalen Externen Rechners beschränkt sich auf die Erstellung einer entsprechenden Gateway-Komponente, während das Grundsystem für alle Länder gleich bleibt.

Es sei noch darauf hingewiesen, daß die Allgemeingültigkeit des Grundsystems VTX-GA darüber hinaus wirtschaftliches Vorgehen bei der Pflege, Wartung und Weiterentwicklung dieses

Produktes ermöglicht. Die nationalen Unterschiede schlagen
sich nur in einer Produktvielfalt in den Komponenten im Kommunikationsrechner nieder. Neben den wirtschaftlichen Vorteilen ergeben sich auch interessante anwenderorientierte Aspekte zum Aufbau eines Multistandardsystems.

4.2.2 Multigateway mit Multistandard

Im Gegensatz zum Common Kernel werden beim Multistandardsystem mit Multigateway die Vtx-Seiten jeweils in CEPT 1, 2
oder 3-Format abgelegt. Damit entfällt auch jegliche Umsetzung von einem Darstellungsstandard in den anderen. Nachteilig bei diesem Konzept ist die Tatsache, daß für einen europaweiten Einsatz jede Vtx-Seite in drei unterschiedlichen
Standards zu editieren und abzuspeichern ist. Sind dann noch
die Seiten in unterschiedlichen Sprachen bereit zu halten,
vervielfältigen sich die zu editierenden Seiten.

Einsatzfälle für Multistandardsysteme findet man bevorzugt im
Tourismus, Transportsektor und bei den Fluggesellschaften.
Typisches Beispiel im Tourismus sind Buchungssysteme. Hotels
in Österreich und Italien geben als Anbieter Informationen
über verfügbare Bettenkapazität in das Buchungssystem ein.
Reisebüros oder auch private Vtx-Teilnehmer in Deutschland
tätigen entsprechende Hotelbuchungen.

5. Vtx als integrierender Faktor für internationale Postdienste

Die Bedeutung von Vtx als integrierender Faktor für internationale Postdienste nimmt stetig zu. So gibt es über Btx
(oder wird es kurzfristig geben) Zugänge zu folgenden Diensten:

Telex, Teletex, Fax, Telebox und Cityruf.

Telex, Teletex

Die Möglichkeit des Dienstüberganges über spezielle Gateways
der Vtx-Betreiber von Vtx zu Telex und umgekehrt eröffnet
den Btx-Benutzern das komplette Telexnetz mit ca. 1.9 Millionen Teilnehmern im In- und Ausland. Bei Teletex sind es
international ca. 40.000 Teilnehmer. Dieser Dienst kann auch
über einen Externen Rechner eines privaten Anbieters realisiert werden. Der Übergang erfolgt über den Kommunikationsrechner des Externen Computers zum Telex-Netz.

Fax

Der Fax-Übergang wurde von der DBP noch nicht realisiert, jedoch bieten private Gateway-Rechner diesen Übergang schon an. Damit kann man über Btx ca. 90.000 Faxteilnehmer in Deutschland erreichen.

Telebox

Der Telebox-Dienst ist ein klassisches Mailbox-Netz, das für jeden Teilnehmer einen elektronischen Briefkasten bereitstellt. Der internationale Verbund über Telebox ist bereits realisiert. Der Austausch von Mitteilungen mit Teilnehmern aus dem Ausland ist bereits mit Großbritannien, Dänemark, Israel, Hongkong, Singapur, Australien, Kanada und den USA möglich. Bis Ende 1988 wird die Verbindung zwischen Btx und dem Telebox-Dienst hergestellt. Durch die Verbindung von Telebox mit dem Mitteilungsdienst können über Systemgrenzen hinweg Mitteilungen ausgetauscht werden. Es wird erwartet, daß zukünftig weitere Anbieter von Mailboxsystemen mit Verbundlösungen auf dem Markt erscheinen.

Cityruf

Cityruf heißt ein neuer Funkrufdienst der Deutschen Bundespost, der Ende 1988 eingeführt werden soll. Es handelt sich um einen scheckkartengroßen Empfänger, mit dem vier Fernsignale, 15 Ziffern oder kurze Texte wie bei einem Taschenrechner auf einem Display dargestellt werden können. Als Eingabemedium wird neben Telefon, Telex, Teletex auch Btx verwendet. Durch den vorhandenen und geplanten Verbund von Vtx ist dieser Cityruf auch international ansteuerbar.

6. Innovative Techniken als Ergänzung von Vtx-Systemlösungen

Vtx ist nicht nur ein Dienst, sondern ermöglicht den Aufbau von Systemlösungen. Dabei wird Vtx als Übermittlungsmedium betrachtet. Die Anforderungen an das System werden im Endgerät und/oder im Externen Computer implementiert.

Vtx und Bildplatten

Große Bestellsysteme weisen meistens den Mangel auf, daß zur Aufgabe einer Bestellung bestimmte Daten einem Katalog zu entnehmen sind. So muß der Disponent bei einem Ersatzteilbestellsystem einer Stückliste die Teilenummer entnehmen. Der Interessent, der eine Reise oder ein Hotel buchen möchte, kann sich meistens nur über Abbildungen in einem Katalog einen optischen Eindruck seines geplanten Reiseziels machen.

In beiden genannten Fällen kann auf einen Katalog verzichtet werden, wenn das Bestellsystem mit einer Bildplatte verknüpft wird. Dabei werden Stücklisten oder Hotelansichten auf der Bildplatte hinterlegt und wahlweise durch Aufruf bestimmter Vtx-Seiten am Bildschirm angezeigt. Die Anzeige kann in Form von Standbildern oder Bildsequenzen (Filme) erfolgen.

Der entsprechende Vtx-Arbeitsplatz besteht aus einem Vtx-fähigen PC, an den über eine V24-Schnittstelle der Bildplattenspieler angeschlossen wird. Der Bildschirm am PC hat einen Eingang für RGB(Vtx) und einen Eingang für VIDEO (Bildplatte).

Der Nachteil, dezentral an jeden PC eine Bildplatte anzuschließen, kann durch den zentralen Aufbau einer Bilddatenbank umgangen werden. Voraussetzung dafür ist jedoch eine Anbindung des jeweiligen Bildschirms zur zentralen Bilddatenbank über ein gesondertes Breitbandkabel. Über eine Kaskadierung der zentralen Bildplatten zu einer Bilddatenbank kann, abhängig von der Häufigkeit der aufgerufenen Bilder oder Bildsequenzen, eine Optimierung erreicht werden.

Vtx mit ISDN

Eine wichtige Erweiterung im Vtx-Dienst wird der Zugang über das neue diensteintegrierende digitale Fernmeldenetz ISDN sein. Bei Aufbau von privaten Vtx-Netzen kann heute schon der Vorteil der hohen Geschwindigkeit zwischen Endgerät und privater Zentrale genutzt werden.

Die Übermittlungsdauer einer Btx-Seite zum Endgerät wird durch die hohe Übertragungsgeschwindigkeit des ISDN gegenüber dem analogen Fernsprechnetz um den Faktor 50 verkürzt. Das bedeutet für eine umfangreiche Seite eine Reduzierung von 20 auf nur 0,5 sec Übertragungszeit. Die Reaktionszeiten des Btx-Systems bleiben beim ISDN-Zugang unverändert.

Der Verbindungsaufbau wird beim ISDN von derzeit etwa 30 sec auf etwa 2 sec verkürzt werden.

Vtx-Endgeräte mit einer Anschlußtechnik für 64 Kbit/s (S0-Schnittstelle) stehen für Pilotnetze zur Verfügung. Über private oder fallweise bereits öffentliche zur Verfügung

stehende 64 Kbit/s-Leitungen kann eine Verbindung zur privaten Zentrale mit einer SO-Schnittstelle aufgebaut werden.
Die Vermittlung erfolgt über eine digitale Nebenstellenanla-
ge. Bei öffentlichen Vtx-Systemen muß der Systemzugang um
eine ISDN-Anschlußtechnik erweitert werden. Auf Basis dieser
neuen Technik kann das Zeitverhalten verbessert werden.

In der Bundesrepublik werden für erste Tests Btx-ISDN-An-
schlüsse ab Herbst über das Ortsnetz München anwählbar sein.
Ab Frühjahr 1989 ist in einer Prototypphase über bestimmte
Vermittlungsstellen der ISDN-Zugang zum gesamten Btx-Angebot
möglich.

7. Ausblick

Durch technologische Weiterentwicklungen in den Vtx-Fernmel-
denetzen, bei den Rechnern und Endgeräten, zeichnen sich zusätzliche Anwendungsmöglichkeiten für Vtx ab. Einerseits
werden die nationalen Protokollunterschiede weitgehend über-
brückt werden, und das Potential der Teilnehmer und Anbieter
wird national und auch im europäischen Verbund stark anstei-
gen. Andererseits werden weitere innovative Entwicklungen
die Einsatzbreite von Systemlösungen erweitern.

Wichtig für den Anbieter und auch den Nutzer ist die Voraussetzung, daß Vtx entwicklungsfähig ist, daß aber trotzdem
bei Weiterentwicklung die Nutzbarkeit bestehender Anwendungen sichergestellt wird. Diese Voraussetzung ist gegeben.

<u>Literatur</u>

(1) Knecht, W.: Videotex das neue Medium; IBO-Verlag AG,
    Zürich,1984

(2) Daten nach OECD, Information Activities, Electronics and
    Telecommunications Technologies, Volume 1, Paris 1981

- DACNOS -
Ein Betriebssystem für heterogene Netze

Ulf Hollberg

IBM Europäisches Netzwerkforschungszentrum
Tiergartenstraße 15
D-6900 Heidelberg

Kurzfassung

Die heutige Situation an Universitäten und größeren Unternehmen ist durch ein *Nebeneinander* verschiedenartiger Rechensysteme gekennzeichnet. Diese *Heterogenität* ist in der Regel durch die Beschaffung von Rechnern für spezifische Zwecken, wie z.B. Prozeßsteuerung, Datenbanken, umfangreichen Berechnungen oder individuelle Programmierausbildung entstanden. Benutzer müssen sich mit den Gegebenheiten der jeweiligen Rechner vertraut machen, wenn sie deren Dienste nutzen wollen. Verbindungen der Rechner untereinander und Dienste wie „Remote Login" oder Dateitransfer erleichtern den physischen Zugang bzw. den Informationsaustausch, lösen aber nicht das Problem der Heterogenität. Verschiedene Ansätze sind bekannt, um diese Situation zu verbessern. Im *HECTOR*-Projekt zwischen der Universität Karlsruhe und der IBM wurde ein systematischer Ansatz entwickelt, das Nebeneinander der verschiedenen Rechner in einen „Informationsverarbeitungsverbund" zu verwandeln, in dem die Benutzer jedes Rechners transparent Dienste der anderen Rechner benutzen können, ohne ihre gewohnte Umgebung zu verlassen.

In diesem Artikel wird über diesen Ansatz, das „Distributed Academic Computing Network Operating System" (DACNOS), berichtet. DACNOS erweitert die verschiedenen *lokalen* Betriebssysteme um die Fähigkeit, Dienste anderer Rechner anzufordern bzw. zu erbringen. Im Artikel werden die Lösungen des DACNOS für entfernte Dienstaufrufe, Zugriffsschutz, Knotenautonomie, Heterogenität und Portabilität vorgestellt.

1. Einführung

Das *HECTOR*-Projekt (*HEterogeneous Computers TOgetheR*) ist ein gemeinsames Forschungsprojekt der Universität Karlsruhe und der IBM mit dem Ziel, Methoden und Verfahren zur *bequemen Benutzung von heterogenen Rechnern in einem Netzwerk* zu entwickeln. Das Projekt begann 1984 und läuft 1988 aus. Im Rahmen dieser Kooperation wurde das Projekt *Distributed Academic Computing (DAC)* von den Instituten für Telematik und für Dialog- und Betriebssysteme der Universität Karlsruhe und vom Europäischen Zentrum für Netzwerkforschung der IBM Deutschland durchgeführt [16]. Im DAC-Projekt wurde ein systematischer Ansatz zur *Unterstützung verteilter Anwendungen* und *gemeinsamer Nutzung von Betriebsmitteln in Netzen autonomer heterogener Rechner* entwickelt und als Prototyp implementiert.

Ein *verteiltes Betriebssystem* („*Distributed Operating System*") könnte die Forderungen nach gemeinsamer Nutzung von Betriebsmitteln und Unterstützung verteilter Anwendungen elegant erfüllen. Mit diesem Ansatz laufen alle Rechner im heterogenen Netz unter demselben Betriebsprogramm. Dieses bietet die üblichen Dienste eines Betriebssystems und nutzt dabei potentiell *alle verfügbaren Betriebsmittel im gesamten Netz* aus. Die Verteiltheit und Heterogenität wird vor dem Benutzer verborgen. Das gesamte Netz erscheint wie ein einziges System („*single system image*"). Meist läßt sich aus den Namen von Betriebsmitteln der Knoten ableiten, auf dem sie existieren. Dies dient jedoch nur als Hinweis für die Benutzer, für die Funktion des Systems ist es unerheblich. Verteilte Betriebssysteme erscheinen dem Benutzer *homogen*; sie lassen keinen Platz für gewachsene *heterogene* Benutzergemeinschaften, die ihre gewohnten Arbeitsumgebungen behalten wollen.

Daher haben wir im DAC-Projekt einen anderen Ansatz, den eines *Netzwerkbetriebssysteme* („*Network Operating System*") verfolgt. Die Knoten bleiben *autonom* und laufen unter ihrem lokalen Betriebssystem. Jedes dieser Betriebssysteme wird um eine Komponente erweitert, die entfernte Dienstaufrufe und -erbringung vermittelt. Neben dem *Netzwerkbetriebssystemkern* bieten weitere Komponenten Dienste, die für verteilte Anwendungen i.A. erforderlich sind: Katalog, Schutz und Abrechnung. Der Dateifernzugriff und die Programmfernausführung sind Beispiele für *transparente* Dienste, d.h. sie werden durch die Schnittstellen der lokalen Betriebssysteme benutzt. Alle genannten Komponenten bilden das „*Distributed Academic Computing Network Operating System*" („*DACNOS*"). (Abbildung 1)

Im folgenden Abschnitt werden die Entwurfsziele des DACNOS erläutert. Danach wird die Funktionalität des *Kerns* des DACNOS mit Benutzungsbeispielen beschrieben. Komponenten unterhalb der Kernschnittstelle werden in diesem Artikel nicht behandelt. Nach den *Systemdiensten* des DACNOS („management") werden zwei transparente Dienste vorgestellt („shared resources"). Der Artikel schließt mit einer Zusammenfassung und dem aktuellen Stand des Projekts.

2. Entwurfsziele

Anwendungen sind die Programme auf Rechnern, die den Benutzer direkt zugute kommen. Mit der Qualität und der Breite des Spektrums verfügbarer Anwendungen steht und fällt der Erfolg von Rechnerfamilien und Betriebssystemen. Das Erstellen von guten Anwendungen ist zeitaufwendig und teuer. Dies gilt insbesondere für verteilte Anwendungen. In vielen Bereichen stellen Anwendungen eine größere Investition dar, als die Rechner und die Betriebssysteme. Eine wesentliche Forderung an ein Netzwerkbetriebssystem ist daher die der *Koexistenz* mit den lokalen Betriebssystemen, d.h. existierende Anwendungen sollen *unverändert* benutzt werden können. Wir sprechen von *Zugriffstransparenz*, wenn neue Dienste durch die Schnittstellen der lokalen Betriebssystem benutzbar sind. Existierende, unveränderte Anwendungen können durch zugriffstransparente Dienste auch entfernte Betriebsmittel benutzen.

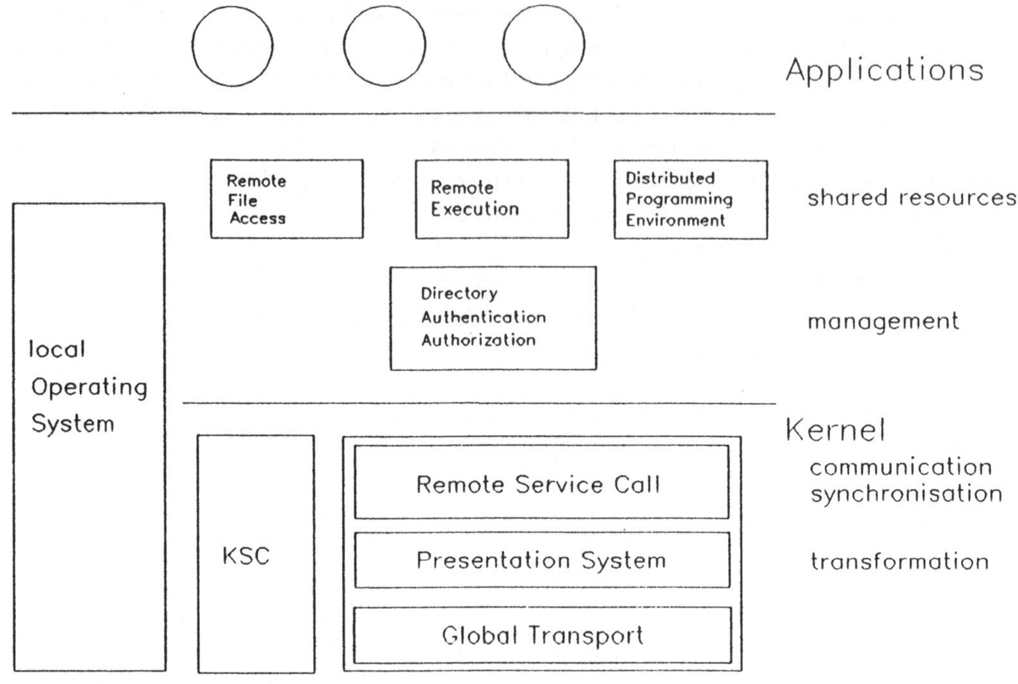

Abbildung 1. Die Struktur des DACNOS

Beim Entwickeln neuer verteilter Anwendungen sind zusätzlich aus der Verteiltheit resultierende Probleme zu beachten. Als wesentliche Problemfelder seien hier nur die *Heterogenität*
der beteiligten Rechner, die *Unzuverläßigkeit von Rechnern* und *Rechnerverbindungen* das
Fehlen eines gemeinsamen Arbeitsspeichers und die Notwendigkeit *entfernter Kommunikation*
genannt. Andere Problemfelder, wie *Zugriffsschutz, Abrechnung,* oder *Konsistenz von Daten*
erhalten durch die Verteiltheit eine neue Dimension. Die Funktionen des DACNOS sollen
die Entwicklung von verteilten Anwendungen von diesem zusätzlichen Ballast befreien; es soll
so „leicht" werden, wie die Entwicklung nichtverteilter Anwendungen.

Ein weiterer wesentlicher Aspekt ist die *Portabilität* von Anwendungen und von Komponenten des DACNOS selbst. Voraussetzung für portable Anwendungen sind einheitliche
Schnittstellen zu den Funktionen des Betriebssystems. Die Schnittstellen des DACNOS sind
systemunabhängig. Verteilte DACNOS Anwendungen sind portabel, wenn sie ausschließlich
Funktionen des DACNOS und aus standardisierten Bibliotheken der von DACNOS unter-
stützten Programmiersprachen verwenden. (Dies sind z.Z. C und Pascal.)

In gewachsenen heterogenen Benutzergemeinschaften tritt die Frage nach den Besitzverhält-
nissen der Betriebsmittel im Netz auf. Jeder Eigentümer eines Rechners soll sich an das
DACNOS-Netz anschließen können, ohne die Verfügungsberechtigung über seinen Rechner
zu verlieren. Er soll darüber entscheiden können, für welche Benutzern anderer Rechner

Dienste ausgeführt werden sollen. Wir nennen dies *Autonomie*. DACNOS enthält ein dezentrales Schutzsystem, um die Forderung der Autonomie zu unterstützen.

3. Zur Funktionalität des Kerns

In diesem Abschnitt wird die Funktionalität der Kernschnittstelle (*Anwendungsprogramm-schnittstelle*) des DACNOS vorgestellt. Diese Schnittstelle wird „*Remote Service Call*" (RSC) genannt. In diesem Artikel sollen nur die Konzepte und die Benutzung des RSC beschrieben werden. Zur Definition der Kernschnittstelle sei auf [4] verwiesen. In [7; 5] finden sich Diskussionen der Eigenschaften dieser Schnittstelle sowie Vergleiche mit verwandten Ansätzen aus der Literatur. Insbesondere findet sich dort auch eine Abgrenzung zum bekannten *Remote Procedure Call (RPC)* [14; 1].

Jedes heterogene DACNOS-Netz besteht aus einem *globalen Objektraum* und einer Menge von *logischen Knoten* mit eindeutigen Adressen. Die Rechner im Netz enthalten einen oder mehrere logische Knoten, je nach Art des Rechners und des Betriebssystems. (PCs sind logische Knoten; virtuelle Maschinen im VM/CMS und Prozesse im VMS sind logische Knoten.) In jedem logischen Knoten sind mehrere RSC-Prozesse aktiv. Diese Prozesse kommunizieren innerhalb ihres logischen Knotens und zwischen verschiedenen logischen Knoten mittels globalen RSC-Objekten. Potentiell kann jeder RSC-Prozeß auf ein globales RSC-Objekten zugreifen; Einschränkungen ergeben sich aus den vom Eigentümer gewährten Zugriffsrechten und Zugriffsarten.

Die Objektarten des RSC

Ports sind benannte Nachrichten- bzw. Auftragspuffer und Prozeßwarteräume in einem. Sie repräsentieren Dienste im DACNOS (*Service Access Points*). Prozesse kommunzieren über Ports miteinander. *Carrier* entsprechen *Aufträgen mit Rückmeldung*. *Notices* entsprechen *einfachen Nachrichten*. *Locks* dienen der *Synchronisation*. *Windows* bieten *gemeinsam benutzbaren Speichersegmente* ! RSC-Objekte werden erzeugt, ausgewählten Benutzern für bestimmte Zugriffsarten veröffentlicht, gegebenenfalls zur Benutzung an einen RSC-Prozeß gebunden, freigegeben und gelöscht.

3.1 Klienten - Bedienerbeziehungen

Betrachten wir das *Klienten-Bediener*-Szenario in Abbildung 2. Ein RSC-Prozeß will einen Dienst anbieten. Er erzeugt einen *Port*, um Dienstanforderungen zu empfangen (1). Er registriert diesen Port unter einem *sprechenden* Namen im Katalog (2). Er veröffentlicht den Port unter einem Objektnamen (3). Das Paar, Adresse der logischen Knotens diese Prozesses und der Objektname identifizieren den Port eindeutig im globalen Objektraum. Damit ist ein Dienst im Netz eingerichtet und potentiell allen RSC-Prozessen verfügbar. Der Bedienerprozeß wartet auf Aufträge, die am erzeugten Port eintreffen (4).

```
Bediener:
(1)    Port := CreatePort
(2)    DS-register( ServiceName, NodeId, ObjId, Attributes )
(3)    offer( Port, ObjId, SEND, AuthGroup )
(4)    Carrier := wait( Port )
(5)     'process service request using parameters from carrier'
(6)    return( Carrier )


Klient:
(7)    ( NodeId, ObjId ) := DS-inquiry( ServiceName )
(8)    Port := share( Node, OBJId, SEND )
(9)    Carrier := CreateCarrier( .. )
(10)   send( Carrier, Port )
(11)   wait( Carrier )
```

Abbildung 2. Klienten-Bediener-Szenario

Will ein RSC-Prozeß einen Dienst benutzen, so sucht er sich aus dem Katalog mit dem *sprechenden* Namen oder charakteristischen Eigenschaften des Dienstes die Identifikation des Ports, d.h. die Adresse des logischen Knotens und den Objektname (7). Der Klientenprozeß versucht mit der *share*-Operation (8), den Port zur Benutzung zu binden und gibt dabei die gewünschten Zugriffsarten an. Sind die Zugriffsarten zulässig und ist der Klient autorisiert, den Dienst zu benutzen, so wird das Binden durchgeführt. Nun hat der Klienten ein Zugriffsrecht auf den Port. Als Auftragsbeschreibung erzeugt der Klient einen *Carrier* (9) und füllt ihn mit *Parametern*, dies sind *Werte* und *Zugriffsrechten* auf eigene RSC-Objekte. Mit der *send*-Operation (10) wird der Auftrag an den Port geschickt. Diese Operation arbeitet asynchron, d.h. sie ist mit dem Einfügen des Auftrags in die Warteschlange des Ports beendet. Die Fertigstellung des Auftrags kann mit *wait* (11) abgewartet werden.

Der Carrier trifft am Port des Bedieners ein; dieses Ereignis läßt den Bediener wieder aktiv werden (4). Der Carrier enthält eine Nachricht und Zugriffsrechte auf weitere RSC-Objekte (Windows, Locks, ..). Nach Empfang des Carriers besitzt der Bediener die enthaltenen Zugriffsrechte auf RSC-Objekte des Klienten. Dies ist die *auftragsspezifische* Bindung von Objekten an Prozesse; es sind *Parameter* des Auftrags. Nun kann der Bediener den Auftrag bearbeiten und dabei die gebundenen Objekte des Auftragsgebers benutzen (5). Hat der Bediener den Auftrag ausgeführt, so fügt er eine Quittungsnachricht in den Carrier ein und gibt ihn zurück (6). Damit werden ihm auch alle im Carrier enthaltenen Zugriffsrechte wieder entzogen. Der Bediener kann sich weiteren Aufträgen zuwenden.

Der Klient empfängt seinen Carrier **(11)** und entnimmt der Quittungsmeldung, ob und wie der Auftrag bearbeitet wurde. Sollte die Auftragsbearbeitung dem Klienten zu lange dauern, so kann er jederzeit mit der *retract*-Operation seinen Auftrag zurückziehen. Der Bediener verliert daraufhin sämtliche Zugriffsrechte des Carriers und muß die Bearbeitung des Auftrags abbrechen.

3.2 Gemeinsam benutzbare Speichersegmente

Lokale Anwendungen mit mehreren Prozessen benutzen Nachrichten und gemeinsam bekannte Objekte im Arbeitsspeicher (*Kommunikationsobjekte*) zum Informationsaustausch und zur Synchronisation. Monitore [2] sind ein Beispiel für Kommunikationsobjekte. Bei verteilten Anwendungen fehlt der gemeinsame Speicher. Daher findet man häufig reine Nachrichtenkommunikation vor. Dies mag in einigen Fällen ein effizienter Mechanismus sein, in anderen Fällen erfordert dies aber die Implementierung eines Protokolls mittels Nachrichten, das ein Art gemeinsamen Speicher simuliert. In heterogenen Netzen kommt noch die Problematik der unterschiedlichen Datendarstellung hinzu. In dem Bestreben, die Erstellung von Anwendungen auf der Basis von RSC so einfach zu machen, wie im lokalen Fall, wurde ein Mechanismus in das RSC integriert, der gemeinsame Speichersegmente als globale Objekte anbietet.

Die *Window*-Objekte des RSC sind Deskriptoren für Speichersegmente im Adreßraum von RSC-Prozessen. Beim Erzeugen eines Windows wird die Lage und Größe dieses Segmentes im Adreßraum des erzeugenden RSC-Prozesses festgelegt (Abbildung 3 **(1)**). Der logische Knoten des erzeugenden RSC-Prozesses wird zur *Basis* des Objektes. Nun kann das Window durch einen Auftrag, wie oben beschrieben, oder explizit (Abbildung 3 **(2)**, **(3)**) an einen Bediener gebunden werden. Beim expliziten Binden kontrolliert RSC die Autorisierung und die Zugriffsarten. Bei gebundenen Windows lassen sich die Daten des Speichersegmentes von anderen RSC-Prozessen so schreiben **(4)** oder lesen **(5)**, wie Daten in deren lokalen Speichern.

```
Objektbasis:
(1)   Window := CreateWindow( Addr, Length, .. )
(2)   Offer( Window, ObjId, .. )


andere logische Knoten:
(3)   Window := Share( Node, ObjId, .. )
(4)   Write-to( Window, from-area, Length, W-Offset )
(5)   Read-from( Window, to-area, Length, W-Offset )
```

Abbildung 3. Benutzung eines RSC-Windows

3.3 Heterogene Datendarstellung

In heterogenen Netzen werden Informationen zwischen Prozessen auf Knoten mit unterschiedlicher Datendarstellung ausgetauscht. Damit die ausgetauschten Daten auf allen Netzknoten gleich interpretiert werden können, müssen sie entsprechend ihrem Datentyp zwischen den verschiedenen Darstellungen konvertiert werden. Bei Erzeugen von RSC-Objekten wird die *Typbeschreibung* der enthaltenen Daten festgelegt. Immer wenn Zugriffe auf Objekte durchgeführt werden, sorgt der Datentransformator des RSC für die entsprechende Konversion.

3.4 Verteilte Semaphore

In verteilten Prozeßsystemen werden Mechanismen zur Synchronisation der Prozesse benötigt. Bei den RSC-*Locks* handelt es sich um *binäre Semaphore*. Der Umgang mit ihnen entspricht dem der RSC-*Windows* (siehe Abbildung 4). Ein Prozeß erzeugt ein *Lock*; er wird dadurch zur Basis dieses Objekts. Er gibt das Lock als Parameter eines Auftrags weiter oder veröffentlicht es (2). Weitere RSC-Prozesse können Zugriffsrechte darauf erwerben (3), wie bei Windows oder Ports, und das Lock so benutzen wie im lokalen Fall (4), (5) und (6).

```
Objektbasis:
(1)      Lock := CreateLock
(2)      Offer( Lock, ObjId, .. )


andere logische Knoten:
(3)      Lock := Share( Node, ObjId, .. )
(4)      Wait( Lock )
(5)          Kritischer Bereich
(6)      Release( Lock )
```

Abbildung 4.   Benutzung eines RSC-Locks

3.5 Weitere RSC-Objekte

Auf die bereits genannten RSC-*Notices* wird nicht näher eingegangen, da die Verwendung von einfachen Nachrichten bekannt sein dürfte. Notices enthalten keine Zugriffsrechte.

Ein weiteres interessantes Objekt ist die *Event-Liste*. Sie wird benötigt, wenn ein Prozeß auf eines von mehreren Ereignissen warten will. Solche Ereignisse können sein: die Rückkehr eines *Carriers*, das Eintreffen eines *Carrier* oder einer *Notice* an einem *Port*, das Freiwerden eines *Locks* und ein Ereignis einer *Event-Liste*. Objekte, auf deren Ereignisse gewartet werden soll, werden in einer Event-Liste zusammengefaßt. Die *wait*-Operation wird auf diese Liste ausgeführt. Das Warten ist beendet, sobald das erste der Ereignisse der Liste eintritt.

4. DACNOS Systemdienste

In diesem Abschnitt werden die Systemdienste des DACNOS vorgestellt: der *Authentifizierer/Autorisierer*, der *Katalog* und der *Abrechnungsdienst*.

4.1 Der Authentifizierer/Autorisierer

Der Schutz von Betriebsmitteln ist in Netzwerken mit Knoten verschiedener Eigentümer von noch größerer Bedeutung als in lokalen Systemen. Bei jeder Benutzung eines Diensten durch einen entfernten Rechner muß sichergestellt werden, daß die Benutzung gestattet ist (*Autorisierung*). Dies kann nur geschehen, wenn jeder Benutzer im Netz eindeutig und *nicht-fälschbar* identifiziert ist (*Authentifizierung*).

Im DACNOS wurde daher ein netzweites Schutzsystem integriert. Der *Authentifizierer/Autorisierer (AAS)* überprüft die Identität jedes Benutzers beim *Login* durch geeignete Maßnahmen (Password, o.ä.). Ist die Identität eines Benutzers festgestellt, so wird vermerkt, daß Benutzer „X" *zur Zeit* auf dem logischer Knoten mit der Adresse „Y" arbeitet. Dieser Vermerk wird gelöscht, wenn der Benutzer das System verläßt (*Logout*). Der *Autorisierer* führt Listen von Benutzergruppen. Unter dem Namen einer Benutzergruppe sind die Benutzernamen eingetragen, die dieser Gruppe angehören. Fordert nun ein Benutzer einen Dienst an, so wird seine Netzwerkadresse als versteckter, *unverfälschbarer* Parameter im Carrier mitgegeben. Der Bediener führt Zugriffslisten, in denen die für einen Dienst autorisierten Benutzergruppen eingetragen sind. Mit dieser Liste von Benutzergruppen und der Netzwerkadresse des Klienten wendet sich der Bediener an den AAS Dienst. Dessen Antwort ist positiv, wenn der aktuelle Benutzer an der Netzwerkadresse des Klienten Mitglied in einer der Benutzergruppen ist. Zur weiteren Diskussion sei auf [13] verwiesen.

4.2 Der Katalog

Das Wissen über Dienste und Systemzustände ist von größter Bedeutung für den Betrieb und die Benutzung von verteilten Systemen. Ein allgemeiner Katalog sorgt im DACNOS für diese Dienste [12].

Eine Menge von Katalogbedienern sind im Netz aktiv. Jedem logischen Knoten ist ein solcher Bediener zugeordnet. Damit ist das Netz in *Domänen* zerlegt. Katalogeinträge haben netzweit eindeutige Namen, die aus dem Namen der Domäne ihres Bedieners und einem eindeutigen Namen innerhalb der Domäne bestehen. Ein Namensverwaltern pro Domäne sorgt für deren Eindeutigkeit. Katalogeinträge sind Tupel beliebiger Zusammensetzung. Beliebige Prädikate über diesen Tupeln können zum Auffinden von Tupeln netzweit verwendet werden. Tupeltyp, Tupel und Tupelattribute können geschützt werden.

In der Regel tragen Bediener ihre Adresse und ihre Dienste mit Namen und spezifischen Eigenschaften im Katalog ein. Der oben eingeführte AAS-Dienst benutzt den Katalog, um seine Informationen sicher zu speichern.

4.3 Abrechnung

Neben der Adresse des Absenders ist auch das *Abrechnungsobjekt* ein versteckter Parameter jedes Carriers. Dieses Objekt enthält Felder für den Betriebsmittelverbrauch in verschiedenen Maßeinheiten: *CPU-Zeit, Ein-/Ausgabevolumen* und hat Platz für weitere eventuell dienstspezische Einheiten. Während ein Bediener einen Auftrag ausführt, werden die verbrauchten Betriebsmittel vom RSC in diesem Abrechnungsobjekt akkumuliert. Dienstspezische Einheiten muß der Bediener explizit abrechnen. Beendet der Bediener den Auftrag, so wird vom RSC das Abrechnungsobjekt ebenfalls an den Klienten zurückgegeben. Eine Kopie geht auch an den zuständigen Abrechnungsdienst, der die Daten pro Benutzername oder -konto sammelt und Abrechnungen zusammenstellt. Eine detailierte Beschreibung des Abrechnungssystems findet sich in [8].

5. Transparente Dienste

In diesem Abschnitt werden zwei transparente Dienste des DACNOS vorgestellt: der *Dateifernzugriff* und die *Programmfernausführung*. Beim Design dieser Dienste wurde größtmögliche Transparenz angestrebt. Ein Kommando genügt, um ein entferntes Betriebsmittel unter einem lokalen Namen in das lokalen System einzubinden. Danach kann das Betriebsmittel wie gleichartige lokale benutzt werden.

5.1 Dateifernzugriff

Der Zugriff auf Dateien gehört zu den häufigen Tätigkeiten der Benutzer. In Netzen entsteht schnell der Wunsch, von einem Rechner auf die Dateien eines anderen Rechners zuzugreifen, sei es um allgemeine Informationen zu lesen, oder um mit einem anderen Benutzer gemeinsam einen Artikel zu schreiben. Bibliotheken ausführbarer Programme sind ein weiteres Beispiel.

In existierenden Netzen kann solch ein Informationsaustausch durch *Remote Login* und *Mailing* oder mit einem *Dateitransferdienst* [10] durchgeführt werden. Dabei ruft ein Benutzer den Dateitransferdienst auf seinem Rechner auf, und gibt die Netzwerkadresse seines Zieles an. Der Dateitransferdienst nimmt Verbindung mit dem entsprechenden Dienst auf dem Zielknoten auf. Nun kann der Benutzer mit einigen Kommandos die gewünschten Dateien herausfinden und zu seinen lokalen Rechner übertragen lassen, bzw. vom lokalen auf den entfernten übertragen. Beide Vorgehensweisen erfüllen zwar meist ihren Zweck, haben jedoch einige unerfreuliche Eigenschaften. Die Benutzer müssen die Gegebenheiten, die

Kommandos und die Dateinamensstruktur der entfernten Rechnern zumindest ansatzweise kennen. Dateien müssen vor ihrer Benutzung auf dem lokalen Rechner gespeichert werden, was oft nicht wünschenswert und manchmal nicht möglich ist. Effizienter und komfortabler ist ein *Dateifernzugriffsdienst*, der in das lokale System *transparent* integriert ist, d.h. der durch die Schnittstellen des lokalen Dateisystems benutzbar ist. Die *Remote File Access (RFA)*-Komponente des DACNOS bietet diesen Dienst an [9]. Hier soll nur beschrieben werden, wie der transparente Dateifernzugriff in heterogener Umgebung benutzt werden kann.

RFA bietet ein *globales Dateisystem* über das gesamte Netz hinweg an (Abbildung 5).

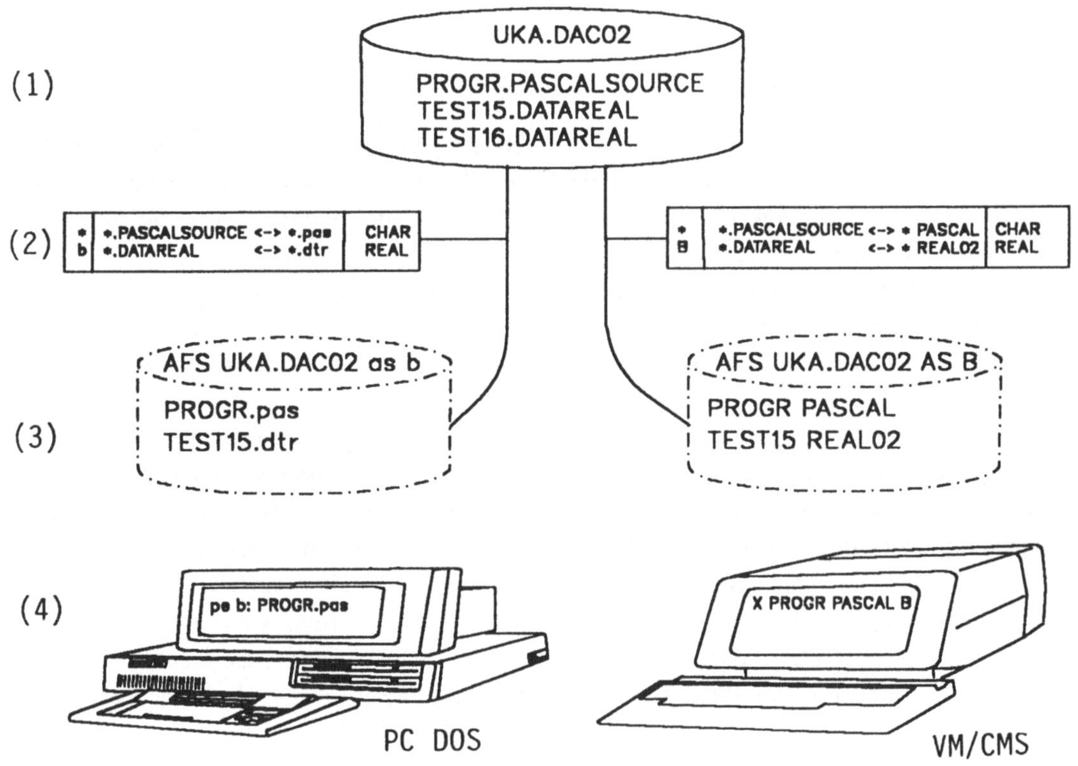

Abbildung 5. Dateifernzugriff

Globale Dateien haben *hierarchische Namen*. Präfixe dieser Namen werden zur *Bildung von Dateimengen* verwendet (1). RFA-Klienten *binden globale Dateimengen explizit* in ihre lokale Umgebung ein und vergeben dabei einen lokalen Dateimengennamen (in Abbildung 5 (3): **AFS UKA.DAC02..**). Beim Binden werden die Suffixe der globalen Dateinamen in lokale Dateinamen *übersetzt*, damit sichergestellt ist, daß die Namen der jeweiligen lokalen Syntax für Dateinamen entsprechen. Die Übersetzung der Dateinamen wird mit einer Reihe von Regeln gesteuert, die der Benutzer für sich selbst definieren kann (2). In [9] sind Beispiele für die Ausdruckskraft und Flexibilität der Regelsprache angegeben. Nach dem Binden sind die globalen Dateien der gebundenen Menge unter ihren lokalen Namen genauso benutzbar, wie andere lokale Dateien **(4)**. Diese voll-transparente Benutzung erfordert Eingriffe in solche lokalen Betriebssystem, die keine Möglichkeit bieten, Systemaufrufe umzudefinieren.

Eine Menge von RFA-Bedienern bieten die Basis für das globale Dateisystem. Diese Bediener bieten Speicherplatz für neue Dateien (*„file store"*) und vermitteln Zugriffe auf *„veröffentlichte"* Dateien ihres lokalen Dateisystems. Veröffentlichte Dateien befinden sich im „Besitz" des RFA-Bedieners bis ihre Veröffentlichung rückgängig gemacht wird. Die Bediener sind logische Knoten im DACNOS Netz und lassen sich von ihrem Administrator konfigurieren.

5.2 Programmfernausführung

In heterogenen Netzen entsteht leicht der Wunsch, Programme auf anderen Knoten ausführen zu lassen, sei es wegen spezieller Fähigkeiten der dortigen Hardware (Vektorrechner, gesicherter Rechengenauigkeit, ..), besonderer Software oder einfach wegen der größeren Rechengeschwindigkeit. Es genügt meist nicht, die Ausführung eines entfernten Programms zu veranlassen; man will über sein Terminal mit dem Programm kommunizieren und mit dem Programm Dateien aus der eigenen lokalen Umgebung bearbeiten. Im folgenden soll skizziert werden, wie der *„Remote Execution (RX)"*-Dienst des DACNOS arbeitet [15].

Einfache Terminalein- oder ausgabe („line mode") läßt sich in manchen lokalen Betriebssytemen umlenken, bei anderen sind Modifikationen des Betriebssystems erforderlich. Auch wenn sich komplexe Terminalein- oder ausgabe (*full screen mode*) umlenken läßt, kann ein Anpassungsproblem entstehen, wenn das entfernte Programm ein spezielles Terminal erwartet, also hardwareabhängig ist, und das lokale Terminal nicht die erwarteten Eigenschaften hat. Vollständige Lösungen dieses Problems sind erst zu erwarten, wenn alle Terminaleigenschaften im Netz gleich oder aufeinander abbildbar wären (*„virtual terminal"*). Aus naheliegenden Gründen wurde für den DACNOS-Prototypen auf arbeitsaufwendige Teillösungen verzichtet.

Die Dateiumgebung des entfernten Programms läßt sich mit Hilfe des RFA-Dienstes an die lokale Umgebung des Klienten angleichen. In der lokalen Benutzermaschine wird ein RFA-Bediener gestartet, und alle lokalen Dateien „veröffentlicht". Damit sind sie über RFA global benutzbar, also auch von entfernt ausgeführten Programmen. Am Ende der Fernausführung wird der RFA-Bediener wieder beendet. Eventuell geänderte Dateien sind dann in der lokalen Umgebung des Klienten.

Zum transparenten Aufruf entfernter Programme mußten die Kommandointerpretierer der lokalen Systeme geändert werden, um lokale und entfernte Ausführungen zu unterscheiden.

6. Schlußbemerkungen und Ausblick

In diesem Artikel wurde in kompakter Form ein Überblick über das *Distributed Academic Computing Network Operating System (DACNOS)* gegeben, ein Betriebssystem für heterogene Netze. Damit sollte das DACNOS-Projekt vorgestellt und Interesse für die angegebene Literatur geweckt werden. Die Entwurfsziele und die Struktur des DACNOS wurden erklärt. Die Funktionalität und der Umgang mit der Anwendungsprogrammschnittstelle RSC des DACNOS wurde beschrieben. Die Systemdienste *Katalog, Authentifizierer / Autorisierer* und *Abrechnung* wurden vorgestellt. Die Problematik zweier transparenter Dienste, des *Dateifernzugriffs* und des *Programmfernausführungs* wurde besprochen.

Es konnten nicht alle Dienste des DACNOS vorgestellt werden. Weiter sollen hier erwähnt werden. Der „*Task Setup Service (TSS)*" erlaubt netzweite *verteilten Stapelprogrammausführung* [6]. Der *Datenbankfernzugriff* im Dialog auf SQL-Datenbanken [11] und auf eine experimentelle AIM-Datenbank [3] wird angeboten. Es ist möglich, Fortran-Unterprogrammen auf entfernten Rechnern ausführen zu lassen (*Unterprogrammfernausführung*).

Ein Prototyp des DACNOS und der beschriebenen Dienste ist zur Zeit auf drei Rechnertypen verfügbar: IBM /370 unter VM/CMS, DEC VAX unter VMS und IBM PC unter PC DOS. Portierungen auf AIX und OS/2 werden folgen.

DACNOS erfüllt die Forderungen nach *Koexistenz* mit existierenden Betriebssystemen und Anwendungen und nach *Autonomie der Knoten*. Es *erweitert* lokale Betriebssysteme. Dabei bleiben die gewohnten lokalen Arbeitsumgebungen der Benutzer erhalten. Existierende Anwendungen können weiterhin unverändert ausgeführt werden und zusätzlich über transparente Dienste des DACNOS entfernte Betriebsmittel benutzen. DACNOS erfüllt damit die Forderungen nach *Transparenz*, die Heterogenität der Benutzerschnittstellen und der Datendarstellung wird verborgen.

DACNOS vereinfacht die *Entwicklung verteilter Anwendungen*. Besonders die drei letztgenannten Dienste sind Beispiele für die „Leichtigkeit", mit der verteilte Anwendungen im Rahmen des DACNOS geschrieben werden können. Alle diese Dienste wurden in wenigen Monaten von Studenten - zum Teil als Diplomarbeiten - geschrieben. Die Portierung der jeweiligen Klientenprogramme von CMS auf PC DOS und auf VMS hat nur wenige Wochen gedauert.

Mit DACNOS wurde ein Modell und ein Prototyp für die *gemeinsame Benutzung von Betriebsmitteln in Netzen autonomer, heterogener Rechner enwickelt..* DACNOS bietet eine komfortable Grundlage für die Entwicklung neuer verteilter Anwendungen in heterogener Umgebung.

Literatur

[1]   A.D.Birell, B.J.Nelson: *Implementing Remote Procedure Calls.* ACM TOCS, Vol. 2, No. 1, pp.39-59 (1984)

[2]   C.A.R.Hoare: *Monitors: an operating system structuring concept.* Comm. ACM, Vol. 14, No. 10, pp.549-557, Oktober 1974

[3]   P.Dadam, K.Küspert, F.Andersen, H.Blanken, R.Erbe, J.Günauer, V.Lumm, P.Pistor, G.Walch: *A DBMS Prototype to Support Extended NF2 Relations: An integratetd View on Flat Tables and Hierarchies.* Proc. ACM SIGMOD Conf., Washington, D.C., May 1986, pp.356-367

[4]   H.Eberle, K.Geihs, M.Seifert: *Remote Service Call: Object and Operation Reference.* DAC Technical Memorandum, No.16 (1985), *vom Autor zu beziehen)*

[5]   H.Eberle, K.Geihs, A.Schill, B.Schoener, H.Schmutz: *Generic Support for Distributed Processing in Heterogeneous Networks. in: G.Krüger, G.Müller (Eds.), HECTOR - Heterogeneous Computers Together, A Joint Project of IBM and the University of Karlsruhe, Volume II, 1988, ISBN 3-540-19137-2 and 0-387-19137-2*

[6]   C.Förster: *Processing Distributed User Tasks in Heterogeneous Networks. in: G.Krüger, G.Müller (Eds.), HECTOR - Heterogeneous Computers Together A Joint Project of IBM and the University of Karlsruhe, Volume II, 1988, ISBN 3-540-19137-2 and 0-387-19137-2*

[7]   K.Geihs, B.Schoener, U.Hollberg, H.Schmutz, H.Eberle: *An Architecture for the Cooperation of Heterogeneous Operating Systems. in: Proceedings of the IEEE Computer Network Symposium, Washington, April 1988*

[8]   G.Harter: *Funktionen zur Systemverwaltung in einem Netzbetriebssystem für heterogene Umgebungen. Diplomarbeit, Universität Karlsruhe, Institut für Telematik, April 1988*

[9]   U.Hollberg: *Transparent Access to Remote Files in Heterogeneous Networks. in: G.Krüger, G.Müller (Eds.), HECTOR - Heterogeneous Computers Together A Joint Project of IBM and the University of Karlsruhe, Volume II, 1988, ISBN 3-540-19137-2 and 0-387-19137-2*

[10]   IBM Corporation: *IBM Transmission Control Protocol/Internet Protocol vor VM; Command Reference Manual. IBM Bestellnummer GC09-1204*

[11]   B.Kieser: *Entwurf und Implementierung des Zugriffs auf das Datenbanksystem SQL/DS in einem heterogenen, verteilten Netz. Diplomarbeit, Fachhochschule Mannheim, Dezember 1987*

[12]   B.Mattes, H.v.Drachenfels: *Ein Verteiltes Katalogsystem für einen heterogenen Rechnerverbund. Infomatik Forschung und Enwicklung, Vol.2, No.4 (1987), pp.171-181, Springer Verlag*

[13]   B.Mattes: *Authentication and Authorization in Resource Sharing Networks. in: G.Krüger, G.Müller (Eds.), HECTOR - Heterogeneous Computers Together A Joint Project of IBM and the University of Karlsruhe, Volume II, 1988, ISBN 3-540-19137-2 and 0-387-19137-2*

[14]   B.J.Nelson: *Remote Procedure Call. Technical Report CSL-81-9, Xerox Palo Alto Research Center, 1981*

[15]   R.Oechsle: *Remote Program Execution. in: G.Krüger, G.Müller (Eds.), HECTOR - Heterogeneous Computers Together A Joint Project of IBM and the University of Karslruhe, Volume II, 1988, ISBN 3-540-19137-2 and 0-387-19137-2*

[16]   H.Wettstein, H.Schmutz, O.Drobnik: *Cooperative Processing in Heterogeneous Networks. in: G.Krüger, G.Müller (Eds.), HECTOR - Heterogeneous Computers Together A Joint Project of IBM and the University of Karslruhe, Volume II, 1988, ISBN 3-540-19137-2 and 0-387-19137-2*

Verteiltes Rechnen in heterogenen Umgebungen

T. Mundt, R. Süß[*] - Apollo Domain Computer GmbH

Kurzfassung :

In den kommenden Jahren wird sich der Trend, die EDV Systeme innerhalb der Unternehmen miteinander zu verbinden, verstärken. Die große Herausforderung an die Datenverarbeitung der 90'er Jahre besteht darin, Systeme verschiedener Hersteller und Betriebssysteme (Unix und andere) miteinander zu verbinden. Für die Funktionen Terminalemulation, Filetransfer und Fileaccess existieren bereits Standards bzw. Quasi-Standards. Es fehlt eine Architektur, die ein verteiltes Rechnen in heterogenen Umgebungen ermöglicht. Mit dem Network Computing System (NCS) von Apollo wurde eine solche Architektur geschaffen. Sie enthält folgende Elemente: Network Interface Definition Compiler (NIDC), Remote Procedure Call Library (RPC Lib), Broker und den Kommunikationsprotokollen. NCS ist ein Werkzeug um aus einer Applikation mit Procedure Calls eine verteilte Applikation mit Remote Procedure Calls (RPC) zu machen.

Jedoch sind nicht alle Applikationen für eine Verteilung geeignet. Eins der beiden folgenden Kriterien muß erfüllt sein:
- Die Applikation ist parallelisierbar
- Es steht ein dedizierter Rechner
  (Compute Server) zur Verfügung.

Ist diese Vorraussetzung erfüllt, können Teile der Applikation auf einen oder mehrere Server ausgelagert werden. NCS basiert auf einem Client-Server-Modell. Der Client ruft mittels eines RPC's den zugehörigen Serverteil auf. Der RPC sowie dessen Parameter (Variablen, Felder etc.) müssen zu einem Datenpaket zusammengefaßt und zum Server übertragen werden. Dieser führt die geforderte Funktion (RPC) aus und sendet die Ergebnisdaten an den Client zurück.

Die Schnittstellen der RPC's werden mit Hilfe der NIDL (Network Interface Definition Language) beschrieben. Der zugehörige Compiler (NIDC) erzeugt die Stubs, die benötigt werden, um Client und Server der Applikation zu verbinden. Die Stubs sorgen für die Aufbereitung der Übergabedaten, schnüren daraus die Datenpakete und rufen die RPC Library auf. Die RPC Library kann auf verschiedenen Netzwerkprotokollen aufsetzen. So auch auf dem auf Ethernet basierenden Datagram Socket Mechanismus des Berkeley-Unix.

Für eine flexible und elegante Benutzung wurde eine Binding-Struktur geschaffen. Das Binding, die dynamische Verbindung zwischen Server und Client, erfolgt durch den Broker (Vermittler). Jeder Server, der einen Service anbietet, meldet sich beim Broker. Ein Client Programm fragt den Broker, welche Rechner den benötigten Service anbieten und erhält eine Liste der Server Rechner für diesen Service. Diese Liste wird zum Verteilen der Aufrufe verwendet. Der Binding-Mechanismus ist ein wesentliches Element der NCS-Architektur und ermöglicht erst den wirklich flexiblen Einsatz für das verteilte Rechnen in heterogenen Rechnernetzen.

NCS wurde in C entwickelt und ist leicht auf andere Unix-Systeme portierbar. Es existieren bereits eine Reihe von Portierungen für Unix- und andere Betriebssysteme. Mit NCS wurde eine Basisarchitektur geschaffen, die weitergehende Lösungen ermöglicht. Einige Beispiele hierfür sind das Remote Debugging , Licensing Server, oder der Attribut Broker. Mit NCS wurde eine zukunftsweisende Architektur geschaffen für die Integration heterogener Rechnernetze. Das System ist offen, auf Unix-Rechnern sehr leicht portierbar und unabhängig vom Netzwerk. Mit der Entwicklung der NCS-Architektur wurde ein Forum gegründet, das Network Computing Forum (NCF), an dem sich eine Reihe namhafter Hardware-Hersteller und Softwarehäuser beteiligen. Ziel des Forums ist die Entwicklung eines Standards, sowie die Weiterentwicklung von NCS.

[*] Ralf Süß , Apollo Domain Computer GmbH,
Rosenkavalierplatz 10, 8000 München 81
Telefon 089/928003 - 27

Verteiltes Rechnen in heterogenen Umgebungen

Vom Batchprocessing zum Network Computing

Die relativ hohen Hardwarepreise in der Vergangenheit führten zu DV-Konzepten mit Rechnern, die für fast alle Aufgaben geeignet waren, die General Purpose Computer. In den Anfängen der kommerziellen Datenverarbeitung waren dies die Batch-Computer. Ihnen folgten die Timesharing-Systeme. Die anfänglichen Erwartungen an diese Systeme – kurze Antwortzeiten bei vielen Teilnehmern zu erreichen – erfüllten sich nicht. Das Zentralrechnerkonzept zeigte trotz immer schneller werdender Systeme Engpässe bei stärkerer Belastung.

Es werden heute zunehmend unterschiedliche Systeme zur Lösungen verschiedener Aufgaben eingesetzt. Kaum ein Hersteller ist heute in der Lage, eine Produktpalette anzubieten, die PC's, Workstations und spezialisierte Rechner umfaßt. Deshalb wird man zunehmend Heterogenität antreffen. Viele dieser Rechner nutzen Unix als Betriebssystem, doch werden andere Betriebssysteme ebenso vorhanden sein. Eine Herausforderung an die Datenverarbeitung der 90'er Jahre wird die Integration solcher heterogener Rechnernetze sein.

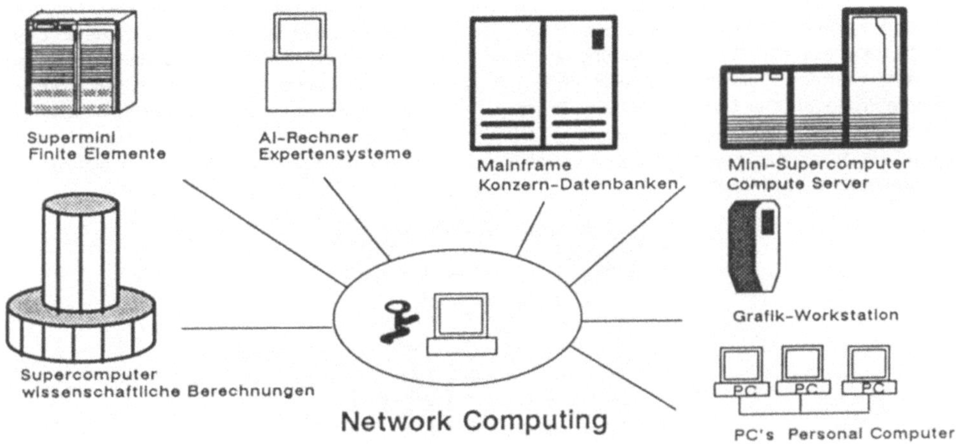

Die in den letzten Jahren stark gefallenen Hardwarepreise ließen neue Rechnerkonzepte entstehen. Das neue Stichwort hieß Dezentralisierung: Nach Möglichkeit für jeden Benutzer einen leistungsfähigen Rechner auf den Arbeitsplatz. PC's und Workstations eroberten die Märkte. Der andere Aspekt dieses Trends: Es entwickelten sich spezialisierte Rechner, die ein bestimmtes Problem besonders gut lösen können: Einen Lisp-Computer für ein komplexes Expertensystem; einen Vektorrechner zur Lösung von komplexen mathematischen Modellen wie die der Finiten Elemente; einen Datenbankrechner für die Unternehmensdatenbank.

Workstations und PC's dienen dabei als grafische Front-Ends, mit denen ein Benutzer transparent eine heterogene Rechnerlandschaft bedienen kann.

Produkte in heterogenen Rechnernetzen

Für die Verbindung von heterogenen Rechnernetzen haben sich bereits einige Lösungen als Standards bzw. Quasi-Standards durchgesetzt: Mit Hilfe serieller Schnittstellen und den Unixprotokollen wie uucp, cu und tip lassen sich Verbindungen zwischen verschiedenen Systemen verwirklichen. Benötigt man schnellere Ankopplungen, muß man Local Area Networks (LAN) benutzen. Ethernet mit TCP/IP ermöglicht den Datenaustausch mit sehr vielen verschiedenen Systemen. Die ARPA-Dienste Telnet und FTP ermöglichen in heterogenen Rechnerumgebungen Terminalemulation und Filetransfer. Mit RFS und NFS kann ein transparenter Dateizugriff in heterogen Netzen verwirklicht werden. Für die Ausnutzung der verteilten Ressource wie zum Beispiel Peripherie oder Rechenleistung in heterogenen Rechnernetzen gibt es bisher nur wenige Ansätze. Um ein verteiltes Rechnen zu ermöglichen oder die verteilten Unternehmensressourcen zu nutzen, wurde eine neue Architektur geschaffen, das Network Computing System (NCS) von Apollo.

Die NCS Architektur

Zur Nutzung der verteilten Unternehmensressourcen wurde die NCS-Architektur geschaffen. Sie besteht aus den folgenden Komponenten: Network Interface Definition Compiler (NIDC), Remote Procedure Call Library (RPC Lib), Broker und den Kommunikationsprotokollen. Mit NCS wurde ein Werkzeug geschaffen, um verteilte Applikationen zu entwickeln.

Ein schwieriges Problem entsteht durch die Parameterübertragung. Alle Parameter des Calls (Variablen, Felder, Records) müssen an den Server Rechner gesendet werden. Was passiert wenn Server und Client Rechner nicht dieselbe Characterdarstellung verwenden oder sich die Floating Point Formate unterscheiden?

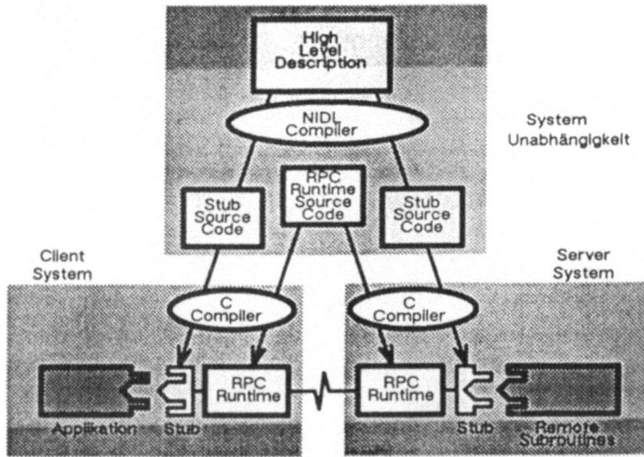

Sinnvoll ist der Einsatz einer verteilten Struktur, wenn eine der folgenden Bedingungen erfüllt wird: Entweder kann die Applikationen parallelisiert werden oder für einen bestimmten Programmteil steht ein dedizierter Rechner (Compute Server) zur Verfügung. Die Unterprogrammaufrufe (Procedure Calls) einer Applikation müssen in Remote Procedure Calls verwandelt werden. Dies soll möglichst einfach und transparent erfolgen, das heißt die Applikation soll möglichst wenig modifiziert werden.

Eine mögliche Lösung ist die prinzipielle Konvertierung der Daten in eine kanonische Form. Dieses Verfahren ist jedoch unnötig aufwendig, wenn Rechner mit gleichen Datenformaten RPC's verwenden. Daher wurde bei NCS der Ansatz gewählt: 'Receiver makes it right'. Der jeweilige Empfänger eines Datenpaketes muß dafür sorgen, daß er die empfangenen Daten interpretieren kann.

Der Network Interface Definition Compiler (NIDC)

In der NCS-Architektur werden diese Probleme durch den Compiler (NIDC) gelöst. Mit Hilfe der NIDL (Network Interface Definition Language) wird der RPC und seine Parameter in einer C ähnlichen Syntax beschrieben. Aus der NIDL erzeugt der Compiler die Stubs für den Server und den Client. Die Stubs sind die Versatzstücke, die ein verteiltes Programm benötigt, damit die Remote Procedure Calls so funktionieren wie Local Procedure Calls. Sie sorgen für die Aufbereitung der Übergabedaten, erzeugen daraus die Übertragungspakete und rufen die RPC Library auf.

Zudem erzeugt der Compiler einen Unique Identifier (UID). Diese UID ist eine weltweit eindeutige Kennung, die aus der Maschinenkennung und einem Zeitstempel mit 4 Mikrosekunden Auflösungen erzeugt wird. Die UID definiert einen Verbindungsschlüssel, der für Client und Server eindeutig ist. Dies ist wichtig, da in einer heterogenen Umgebung mit sehr vielen Benutzern Procedure Calls verschiedener Applikationen den selben Namen haben können.

Die Remote Procedure Call Library

Die RPC Lib sorgt für die Datenübertragung der Pakete von einem Rechner zu einem anderen über das Netzwerk. Die RPC Libraries können veschiedene Netzwerkprotokollen nutzen. Die NCS Architektur benötigt für die Verbindung einen schnellen Kommunikationskanal und ist daher im allgemeinen nur in Verbindung mit Local Area Networks (LAN) sinnvoll. Aus Geschwindigkeitsgründen wird der Layer 3 des OSI Modells verwendet, das sind 'Unreliable Datagram Services'. Ein solcher Service ermöglicht es, ein Datenpaket von einem Rechner zu einem anderen Rechner zu senden. Die beiden Rechner müssen nicht direkt miteinander verbunden sein. Der Nachrichtentransport und damit die Pfadsuche geschieht durch das sogenannte Routing.

Bei einem Layer 3 Protokoll können folgende Zustände eintreten :
- Ein Paket erreicht nicht den Empfänger
- Ein Paket wird mehrfach übertragen
- Die Empfangssequenz der Pakete ist anders als die Sendesequenz

Diese Aufgaben werden durch den Layer 4 gelöst. Da der Layer 4 im allgemeinen nicht schnell genug ist, setzt NCS auf dem Layer 3 auf und übernimmt die notwendigen Prüfungen und Wiederholsequenzen selbst.

Das zur Zeit am meisten gebräuchliche Verbindungsmedium bei LAN's ist Ethernet mit TCP/IP. NCS kann unter anderem den Datagramm-Socket-Mechanismus (UDP/IP) von Berkeley, der auf Ethernet basiert, verwenden.

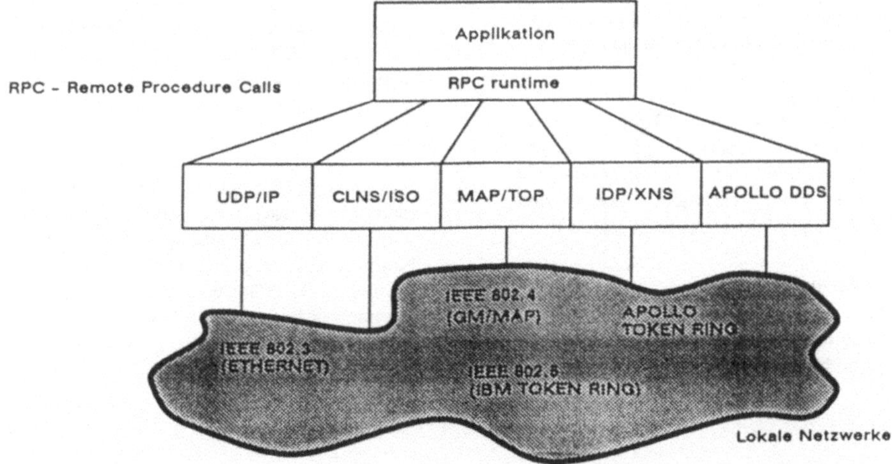

Das NCS Modell

Als Modell für die RPC's dient ein Server Client Modell. Ein Client Prozeß schickt seinen Compute Request an einen Server, den Compute Server. Der Server befindet sich zum Beispiel im Listening Mode und wartet auf ankommende Compute Requests. Erfolgt ein solcher Aufruf durch einen RPC, wird die geforderte Procedure vom Server aufgerufen. Die Ergebnisdaten werden mit dem gleichen Mechanismus zum Client zurückgesendet, mit dem der Server die Eingabedaten erhalten hatte.

Um die NCS Architektur flexibel und elegant zu nutzen, wurde eine Binding Struktur geschaffen.

vern, die den gewünschten Service anbieten. Anschließend führt die Applikaton ein Binding durch, bei dem ein oder mehrere Rechner als Server ausgewählt werden. Alle folgenden RPC's des Programms werden danach auf den oder die selektierten Server geschickt.

3) Automatic Binding

Beim Automatic Binding wird bei jedem RPC neu selektiert, zu welchem Server der RPC gehen soll. Diese Strategie läßt sich bei gleichartigen Rechnern noch recht gut praktizieren.

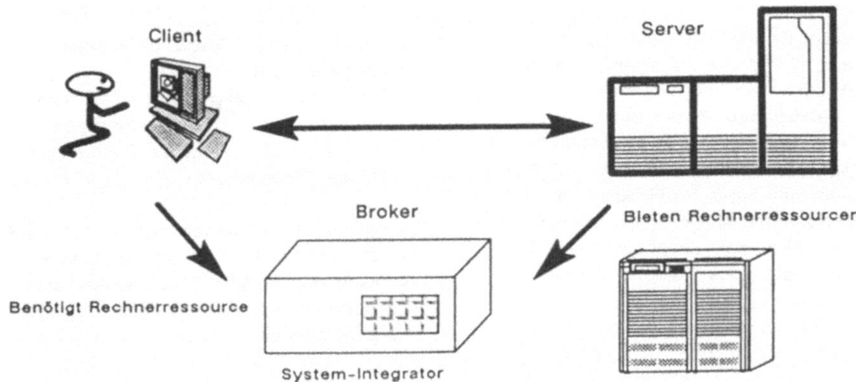

Das Binding, die logische Verbindung zwischen Server und Client, erfolgt durch den Broker (Vermittler). Jedes Programm auf den beteiligten Rechnern, das einen Compute Service anbietet, meldet sich beim Broker. Mit NCS lassen sich verschiedene Binding Methoden realisieren:

1) Explicit Binding
Beim Explicit Binding wird vom Client Programm ein ganz bestimmter Server angefordert, wie zum Beispiel ein bestimmter Vektorrechner. Ist der Rechner nicht verfügbar, kann das Programm zur Zeit nicht ausgeführt werden.

2) Implicit Binding
Ein Client Programm fragt zu Beginn den Broker, welche Rechner den benötigten Service anbieten. Es enthält daraufhin eine Liste von Ser-

So kann man die Steuerung anhand der jeweiligen Auslastung vornehmen. Stellt man sich jedoch eine komplexere heterogene Rechnerwelt vor, so ist es mit den heutigen Mitteln äußert schwierig zu bewerten, wie Auslastungen auf unterschiedlichen Systemen vergleichbar sind. Der Aufwand, der bei einer solchen Verteilungsstrategie entsteht, ist außerdem sehr hoch.

Aus diesen Gründen ist derzeitig das Implicit Binding die bevorzugte Methode. Das Binding und der Einsatz der Broker ist ein wesentliches Element der NCS-Architektur und ermöglicht erst den wirklich flexiblen Einsatz für das verteilte Rechnen in heterogenen Rechnernetzen.

Portierbarkeit

Die gesamte NCS-Architektur wurde in C entwickelt und ist leicht auf andere Unix-Systeme portierbar. Ein C-Compiler, Ethernet mit TCP/IP und den Unix Berkeley Sockets sind die Vorraussetzungen für eine sofortige Portierung von NCS auf der Basis von Ethernet. Eine Reihe von Portierungen wurden bereits durchgeführt, wobei sich diese nicht nur auf Unix-Systeme beschränken. Es existieren neben den Unix Portierungen auch solche für PC's mit MS-DOS, oder für VMS.

Eine Reihe von Portierungen wurden von Apollo durchgeführt. Darüberhinaus gibt es bereits eine Reihe von Hardwareherstellern wie Alliant, Convex, Prime, Stratus, Pyramid und Multiflow, die bereits selbst NCS anbieten und vermarkten.

NCS hat eine objektorientierte Struktur. Die Applikationen definieren "Was gemacht werden soll", die Systemarchitektur sorgt für das "Wo und Wie etwas geschieht".

Weiterentwicklung

Interessant ist die NCS-Architektur besonders als Basis für weitergehende Lösungen. Einige Beispiele hierfür sind das Remote Debugging, Licensing Server, oder der Attribut Broker.

Ein wichtiges Ergänzungsprodukt zum NCS ist das Remote Debugging. Haben die heutigen Debugger schon Probleme nach einem einfachen fork(), so werden die Probleme bei mehrfacher Parallelisierung und bei RPC's auf anderen Rechnersystemen erheblich zunehmen. Sind zudem Systeme anderer Hersteller involviert, wird es noch komplizierter. Daher gibt es als Ergänzungsprodukt von Apollo einen Debugger, der die NCS-Architektur nutzt und auch RPC's zu Fremdsystemen verfolgen kann.

Ein weiteres NCS Produkt ist der Network License Server (NLS). Kommerzielle Softwarepakte für Workstations sind im allgemeinen an eine Kennung der Workstation gebunden. Kauft ein Anwender zum Beispiel drei Lizenzen, so kann er das betreffende Paket nur auf drei vorher zu bestimmenden System laufen lassen. Sind die entsprechenden Workstations durch andere Aufgaben belegt, kann die Software nicht genutzt werden, obwohl es zur Zeit eine Reihe verfügbarer Systeme gibt. Der Wunsch der Anwender geht dahin, eine bestimmte Anzahl von Lizenzen zu kaufen und die

Software entsprechend oft auf verschiedenen Systemen zu nutzen.

Dies ist mit bisherigen Softwaremitteln kaum möglich. Mit NLS auf der Basis von NCS wird eine solche Möglichkeit geschaffen. Eine Anwendung nutzt die Locks (Schlösser) von NLS. Ein Anwender kauft nun eine bestimmte Anzahl von Keys (Schlüsseln). Jeder Benutzer des Softwarepaketes erhält einen der verfügbaren Schlüssel. Dies entspricht der Anzahl der gekauften Lizenzen. Sind alle Schlüssel vergeben, wird ein nächster Request abgewiesen. Derjenige Benutzer, der abgewiesen wurde, kann sich in eine Warteschlange einreihen lassen. Die Zuteilung erfolgt, wenn ein Schlüssel wieder frei wird. Der Kauf weiterer Lizenzen wird sehr einfach gemacht, da lediglich der Schlüssel (eine Kennziffer von Typ UID) dem Anwender mitgeteilt werden muß.

Ein weiteres in der Zukunft geplantes NCS Produkt wird ein Attribut Broker sein. Der Attribut Broker erlaubt es, in komplexen heterogenen Netzwerken Ressourcen aufgrund von Attributbeschreibungen zu finden. Zum Beispiel kann an ihn die Frage gestellt werden: Wo ist zur Zeit ein DIN A0 Plotter frei? Oder auch: Auf welchem Rechnersystem sind 500 MB Plattenspeicher verfügbar? Diese Beispiele zeigen die Verwendbarkeit von NCS außerhalb der reinen CPU Leistungsverteilung.

Network Computing Forum (NCF)

Mit NCS wurde eine zukunftsweisende Architektur geschaffen für die Integration heterogener Rechnernetze. Das System ist offen, auf Unix-Rechnern sehr leicht portierbar und netzwerkunabhängig. Mit der Entwicklung der NCS-Architektur wurde ein Forum begründet, das Network Computing Forum (NCF), an dem sich eine Reihe namhafter Hersteller beteiligen.

Das Forum umfaßt bereits mehr als 100 Mitglieder. Im NCF sind Softwareanbieter, Rechnerhersteller und wissenschaftliche Institutionen vertreten. Ziel des Forums ist die Entwicklung eines Standards sowie die Weiterentwicklung von NCS.

A Distributed Abstract Object Machine for the Office

J.-P. Behr, B. Fink, R. Kraemer, R. Stecher
Philips GmbH Forschungslaboratorium Hamburg

Abstract

The ESPRIT Project 237 *Communication Systems. Architecture* (CSA) is concerned with the development and demonstration of an architecture for distributed office systems. The architecture is based on an object oriented approach. The system view which it supplies to the application programmer hides the distribution of the system components.

The system view is provided by a three layered hierarchy of abstract machines. In the first abstraction step a local but unique object interface is provided which is independent from the heterogeneity of the underlying system software and hardware. In the second abstraction step the individual systems are interconnected to a distributed object machine with a single system image. Finally the third abstraction step provides facilities for the interaction with non–CSA architectures.

This paper outlines the concepts of the distributed abstract object machine which itself is constructed from objects.

1. Introduction

The ESPRIT Project 237 *Communication Systems Architecture* (CSA) aims at a software architecture for intensively interacting office systems integrating computations and communications. The requirements for this architecture are the following:

1. It should support a suitable method for the description
   and implementation of office applications.

2. It should abstract from heterogeneity of different
   hardware and operating systems and thus support portability.

3. It should abstract from distribution, thus applications
   become location transparent.

4. It should support communication with non–CSA systems.

The CSA starting-point for an architecture which fulfills these requirements is an object oriented approach supported by a hierarchy of abstract machines. The first machine level abstracts from heterogeneity, the second abstracts from distribution, while the third abstraction level supports communication to non–CSA architectures. Object orientation provides a computational model and a paradigm which seems appropriate to many applications, particularly to office applications and to operating systems design. For the latter reason the CSA project uses the object oriented approach as a method for both structuring and implementation of the aspired architecture.

We call a system which conforms to the CSA architecture a *domain*, having in mind an office of a plant or of an enterprise. From a hardware point of view a domain consists of a number of local systems such as work stations, personal computers, and mini-computers which are connected via possibly different kinds of networks like LANs and WANs. From the software and the users point of view a domain provides a surface which hides the fact that the system is distributed over the hardware elements. This "single machine image" surface will be provided by a distributed object machine kernel which we also call the *domain machine kernel*.

This paper concentrates on the description of the machine architecture while the object model was already described in more detail in another paper [1]. The second section enumerates a few basic facts of the CSA object model. Section 3 describes the hierarchy of the abstract machines. Section 4 describes the object management and the invocation management. An outlook on future work completes this paper in section 5.

2. Object Model

The qualities and merits of the object model for software structuring are dealt with widely in the literature e.g. [2]. Therefore we concentrate on the primary features and the terminology of the CSA object model.

An object consists of a collection of information and a set of operations on that information. The collection of information is called the state of the object. Operations are functions or procedures that are applied to the state and are the only way to access it.

Interaction between objects is by invocation. An invocation initiates the execution of an operation in another object. The CSA approach to invocation is similar to that of the Actor [3] model. Many approaches restrict invocation to a synchronous mechanism e.g. [4]. In CSA, objects may invoke other objects synchronously or asynchronously at the discretion of the invoking object. Either type of invocation may be applied to any operation.

Objects are instances of object types. Each instance is created and encapsulated according to a template which describes the type specification. The CSA object model uses an explicit inheritance scheme that allows individual attributes, rather than all the attributes, of existing object types to be inherited. Moreover objects may alternatively be specified as private sub–objects of other object types by importation as public shared objects.

Each object consists of an object executor and an object controller. The object executor comprises the operations of the object. The object controller provides mechanisms for controlling access to the object's operations, maintaining the state of the object, enforcing concurrency constraints, and validating parameter types for operations.

Execution of operations is performed in threads. A thread is the execution of a single operation for one invocation and does not cross the boundary of an object. More than one thread may be active in an object at the same time.

Objects are identified and managed as distinct entities by an object management system. The object management system, in the form of an abstract machine kernel, maintains a machine internal representation for each existing object.

3. Abstract Machine Hierarchy

The architecture described in this paper is based on a set of abstract object machines (AOM). Each machine provides an environment for the implementation of objects confirming to the object model described in section 2 of this paper. There are three AOMs in the hierarchy which correspond to the three levels of abstraction as identified within the architectural design requirements 2 to 4 in section 1.

The first abstract object machine is the local object machine (LOM) which encompasses a set of resources normally managed by a single instance of an underlying operating system. The main purpose of this machine is to deal with heterogeneity of computing and communication systems and to provide an object view.

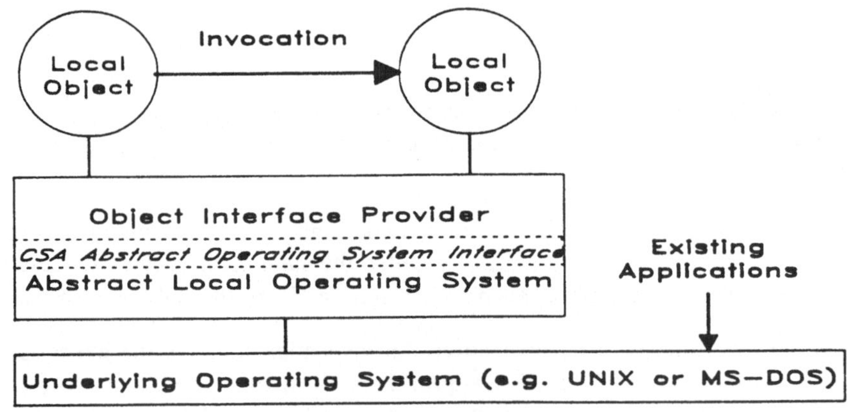

Figure 1: Local Abstract Object Machine Kernel

On each individual system a LOM is implemented which can coexist beside existing local applications (fig. 1). To support portability the LOM kernel is separated into two parts. The first part – the abstract local operating system – deals with the problem of heterogeneity and provides an operating system interface which is identical for all systems forming a domain and is independent from the various underlying operating systems. The second part – the object interface provider – presents the object view to the next higher level. Fig. 1 shows the relationships of the LOM kernel to the underlying system and the local objects (LO) it supports. It also indicates the logical invocation path between local objects. The actual invocation path is via the LOM kernel.

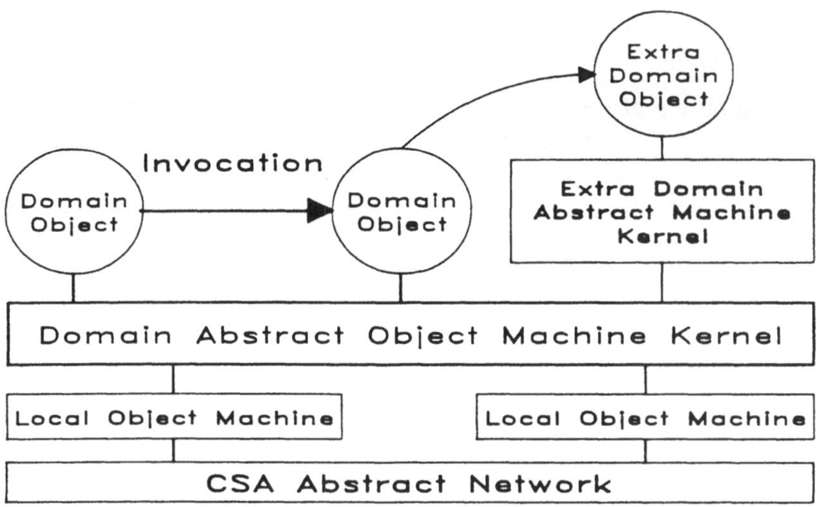

Figure 2: Domain Abstract Object Machine

The second of the abstract object machines is the domain object machine (DOM) shown in fig. 2. A set of LOMs is interconnected via an abstract network. This network abstracts from all the details of the underlying data transfer facilities. A DOM kernel is built on top of the collection of LOMs that constitute a domain. This distributed machine kernel is constructed from kernel components each consisting of local objects. It provides the application systems above this level with the view of a single resource sharing system. While local objects residing on different LOMs are not able to communicate by invocation it is the quite normal way for the domain objects supported by the DOM. However, a domain object is represented by one or more local objects. A domain object is location transparent in the sense that to perform an invocation no knowledge is required about the location of its representation.

To cope with the requirement for openness to other architectures an additional extra-domain object machine (EXDOM) as illustrated in fig. 2 is required. Extra-domain communication between CSA domains is relatively simple because they are constructed according to the same principles. For an invocation of an object residing in another domain only a domain identifier has to be added because all domains have separate name spaces.

For extra-domain communication to other architectures specific two-sided objects are installed as gateways. From the CSA domain side they look and behave like objects while from outside they look like elements of the architecture for which they are provided.

4. The Distributed Abstract Object Machine

4.1. Overview

The distributed abstract object machine kernel is built on top of the collection of systems that constitutes a CSA domain. This distributed kernel is itself constructed from kernel components each consisting of local objects. The DOM can be seen as a distributed application running on top of a set of local object machines.

Objects residing on top of the DOM are called *domain objects* (DO). Domain objects are constructed according to the same object model as local objects. However, domain objects are location transparent. I.e. the application programmer does not need to know where the representation of a domain object actually resides. Like local objects domain objects interact by invocation.

The domain object machine kernel consists of a number of managers which can be roughly separated into two categories:

- Object management
- Communication management

Some of the managers themselves are distributed i.e. they consist of a number of components residing on different systems. The communication between components within a distributed manager is called *intra manager communication* (fig. 3). Since the manager components consist of local objects residing on different systems the intra manager communication cannot be implemented by normal invocations between local objects. An additional mechanism is required for the communication between remote local objects. We call this mechanism *remote activation*. The fundamental difference between remote activation and invocation is that the former requires explicit addressing of the system on which the destination object resides. Remote activation is also applied to implement the invocation mechanism between domain objects and is therefore described in more detail in section 4.3.

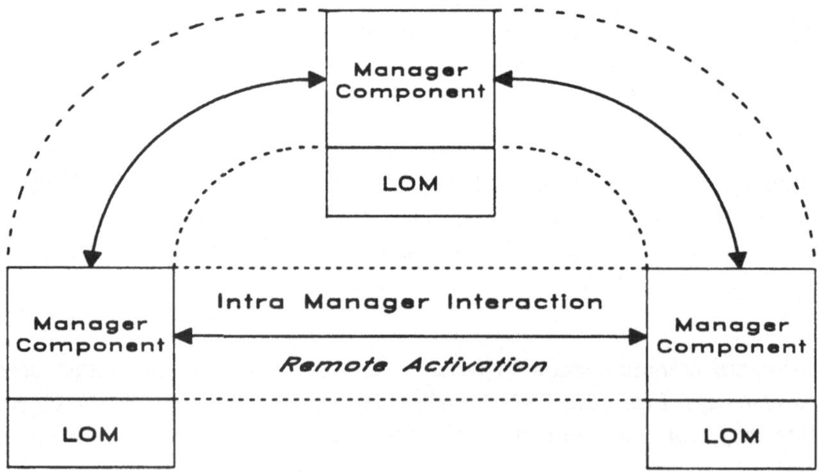

Figure 3: A Distributed Manager

4.2. Object Management

The object management consists of the type manager, the instance managers, the identification manager, and the location manager.

Type Manager

On each system there resides a local object instance which acts as a type manager for domain object types. Its main task is the generation of new object types by collecting type definitions and creating their respective representations called instance managers.

Instance Managers

The instance managers are not actually part of the domain object machine kernel but domain object instances of type instance manager. The main task of an instance manager is the representation of an object type and the creation of object instances of the type it represents. For each specific type there exists at least one associated instance manager.

Location Manager

The location manager is a distributed manager. As such it consists of object instances of type location manager component. It has two fundamental tasks:

– The determination of object location and administration of
  object movement,

– The creation of object representations.

The determination of an object location is the strategic task to decide where to locate an object according to a set of rules. These rules may be very complicated taking into account the current state of the system and may e.g. result from strategies for load balancing.

The second task of the location manager is to provide a set of operations for the creation and deletion of object representations. These are run time structures of domain object instances represented by local objects.

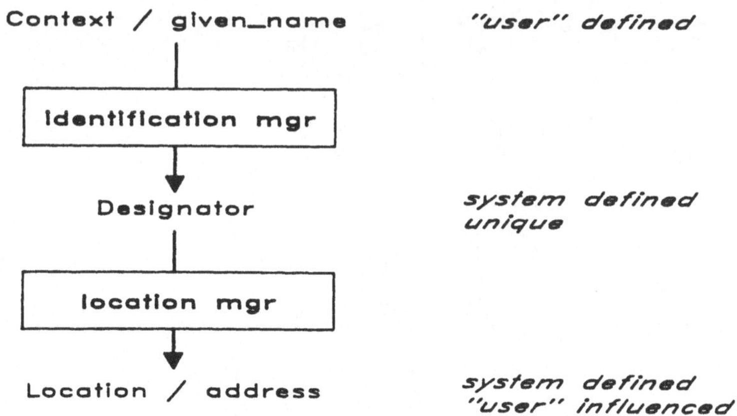

Figure 4: Identification Scheme

Identification Manager

The identification scheme within CSA consists of three identification levels according to fig. 4. *Given-names* are the highest level of object identifiers within an abstract object machine. They have to be unique within one context. Contexts are powerful facilities providing means of structuring identification spaces in a recursive way. Identical given-names in different contexts do not conflict. Given-names may be arbitrarily assigned to designators. A *designator* is a unique identifier within an abstract object machine associated with precisely one object instance. Multiple given-names may be assigned to a single designator thus allowing aliasing.

Designators are generated and linked to given-names by the identification manager. As the identification manager is a distributed manager it consists of object instances of type *identification manager component*. It is used to create designators, to register contexts and to find the designator associated with a given-name in a certain context.

Fig. 5 demonstrates the interaction of the object management parts upon the creation of an object type and an object instance. The creation of a new type resulting in the creation of the associated instance manager as a domain object X in the domain system service (DSS) level as well as the creation of an ordinary domain object A both require the creation of the respective representations as local objects on an arbitrary local machine. This is performed for local objects of type *domain object representation* by the instance manager which resides as a local object in the system service level of the local machine (LSS). The dotted arrows indicate the steps which have to be executed to create a new type, while the full arrows indicate the creation of a domain object instance.

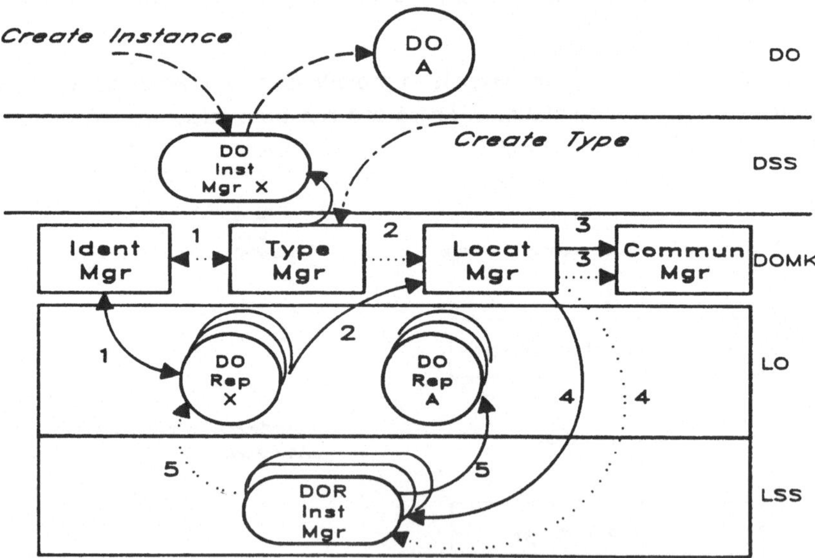

Figure 5: Interaction of Machine Components

4.3. Invocation Management

The invocation management consists of a reliable data transfer handler (RDTH) and the communication manager. It was already mentioned, that the implementation of location transparent invocations between domain objects requires a *remote activation* mechanism for the interaction between local objects residing on different systems. This is illustrated in fig. 6.

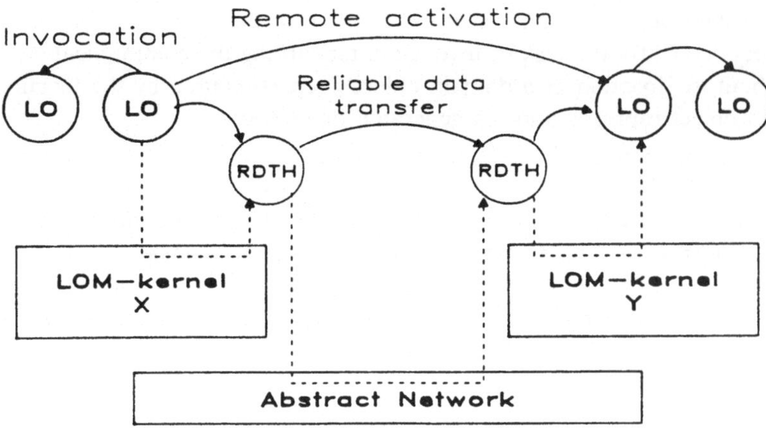

Figure 6: Remote Activation of Local Objects

Reliable Data Transfer Handler

The remote activation is performed by the RDTH. It provides for transparent transfer of data between an originating object and a destination object. The data transfer is reliable in the sense that the object originating a remote activation is informed about any failure to deliver the transferred data to the destination RDTH.

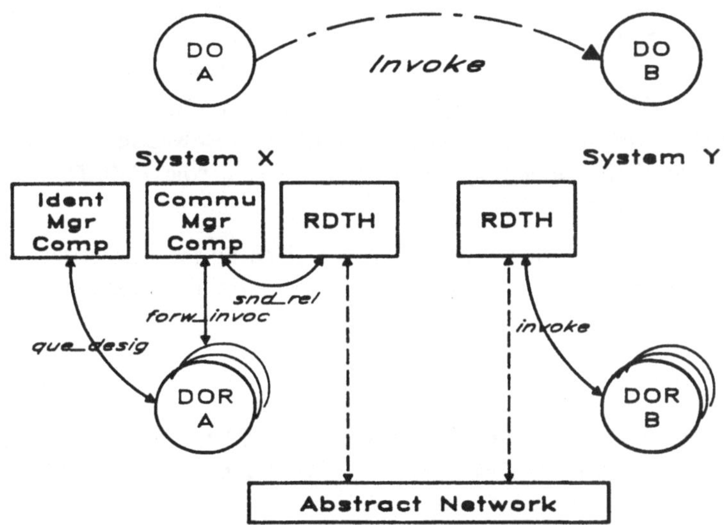

Figure 7: Invocation Between Domain Objects

Communication Manager

The communication manager is a distributed manager consisting of object instances of type *communication manager component*. Its main task is to forward invocations to the destination system depending on the actual location of the representation of the invoked domain object. To fulfill the task of invocation forwarding the communication manager is informed about the location of a domain object's representation by the location manager whenever an object representation is generated or moved.

Fig. 7 demonstrates how the kernel components of the domain machine interact upon an invocation between domain objects, where the respective representations by local objects reside on different systems X and Y. The invocation of an operation of domain object B by domain object A is implemented by a sequence of invocations according to the numbering in fig. 7. The physical transfer of data representing the invocation is initiated by the communication manager component of system X making use of the *send_reliable* operation of its local RDTH.

5. Future Work

In the remaining two years of the project duration the CSA architecture will be implemented as a prototype for demonstration purposes. This prototype will mainly be based on a number of SUN-3 work stations running UNIX. To demonstrate that heterogeneous hardware and software systems can be managed by the architecture also some PCs running MS-DOS and a VAX running VMS will be incorporated in the prototype. The workstations are linked to a distributed system by means of existing protocols like Ethernet, TCP/IP or X.25.

Acknowledgements

CSA is being developed by a consortium of four organizations, namely MARI Advanced Microelectronics Ltd. (UK), Plessey Research and Technology (UK), Synergie Informatique et Developpement (F), and Philips GmbH Forschungslaboratorium Hamburg (D). Additionally two subcontractors namely Informationstechnologie Kiel GmbH (D) and Universite Pierre et Marie Curie (F) are involved in this development. The work is being partially funded by the CEC as part of the ESPRIT work area 4.3.1 Communication Systems.

The authors wish to acknowledge the assistance given by the project team in producing this paper and the management of their respective organizations for permission to publish it.

References

1. J.-P. Behr, U. Killat, R. Kraemer, and R. Stecher, *CSA, a Hierarchical Object Oriented Architecture for Distributed Office Systems*, NTG Communication in Distributed Systems, RWTH Aachen, Informatik Fachberichte Nr. 160, Springer Verlag, 1987.

2. A. K. Jones, *The Object Model: A Conceptual Tool for Structuring Software*, Operating Systems – An Advanced Course, Lecture Notes in Computer Science 60, pp. 8–16, Springer-Verlag, 1978.

3. C. Hewitt, *Viewing Control Structures as Patterns of Passing Messages*, Artificial Intelligence 8, 1977.

4. G. T. Almes, A. P. Black, E. D. Lazowska and J. D. Noe, *The Eden System: A Technical Review*, IEEE Trans. Soft. Eng., vol. 11, no. 1, pp. 43–58, January 1985.

Konzeption eines aktiven, portablen Software-Dictionary mit integriertem Datenbank-Design-Tool

Jörg-Uwe Beyer, Falk Janotta

ADV/ORGA F.A.Meyer AG

Kurt-Schumacher-Straße 241

2940 Wilhelmshaven

0. Abstract

Nach einer kurzen Vorstellung des UNIBASE-Projektes wird in diesem Beitrag zunächst definiert, was unter einem aktiven, portablen Software-Dictionary zu verstehen ist. Danach werden die Zielsetzung sowie die Anforderungen ausführlich erklärt und beschrieben, mit welchen Konzepten diese realisiert werden sollen.

Das voll Software-Dictionary-integrierte Datenbank-Entwurfswerkzeug wird im Anschluß daran erläutert, wobei die zugrundeliegende Methode vorgestellt und die Funktionalität des Werkzeugs herausgestellt werden.

Zum Abschluß werden die Ausführungen zusammengefaßt und interessante Ausblicke auf weitere Betätigungsfelder auf diesem Gebiet gegeben.

1. Einleitung

Die hier beschriebene Konzeption eines Software-Dictionary ist Thema einer gemeinsamen Diplomarbeit, die von den Autoren im Rahmen eines Praktikums bei der ADV/ORGA F.A.Meyer AG erstellt wird.

Betreuer dieser Diplomarbeit ist Herr Prof. Dr. G. Schlageter von der Fernuniversität Hagen.

1.1 Das UNIBASE-Projekt

Das UNIBASE-Projekt ist ein Verbundprojekt, das vom Bundesminister für Forschung und Technologie gefördert wird [TIMM86]. In diesem Projekt arbeiten vier industrielle und vier wissenschaftliche Partner zusammen an der Realisierung einer Software-Produktionsumgebung.

Die ADV/ORGA F.A.Meyer AG ist innerhalb dieses Projektes für das Teilprojekt ANIMOS verantwortlich.

Das Teilprojekt ANIMOS umfaßt im wesentlichen drei Ziele:

- Entwicklung von Datenbankentwurfs- und Datenbankzugangswerkzeugen

- Entwicklung von System- und Programmentwurfswerkzeugen

- Bau der Benutzeroberfläche für Anwendungssoftware

Die Entwicklung eines komfortablen Software-Dictionary gehört von der Thematik her in den ersten Zielbereich. Gleichzeitig dient es aber auch als Grundlage für die Entwicklung der Werkzeuge aus den anderen Zielbereichen.

2.1 Definition Software-Dictionary

Ausgangspunkt der Betrachtung ist die Situation eines unabhängigen Software-Entwicklers. Aus diesem Blickwinkel werden die folgenden wesentlichen Anforderungen an ein zentrales und aktives Software-Dictionary erläutert.

Die zunehmende Vernetzung von Datenverarbeitungssystemen in Unternehmen, Organisationen und Institutionen verlangt eine weitgehende Verträglichkeit zwischen unterschiedlichen Hard- und Software-Systemen. Bei den heute verfügbaren Betriebssystemen und der Vielzahl an Netzen ist die Erstellung von echt verteilten Anwendungen kaum möglich.

Die Vielfalt der am Markt vorhandenen Datenhaltungssysteme führt zu ebenso vielfältigen Datenzugriffssprachen. Applikationen, die unabhängig von einer speziellen Datenmanipulationssprache sein sollen, benötigen daher eine einheitliche Datenzugriffsschnittstelle. Die Programme müssen so konzipiert sein, daß sie in verschiedenen Rechnerumgebungen und Betriebssystemen lauffähig sind.

Für das Software-Dictionary-System ergeben sich daraus im wesentlichen die nachfolgend dargestellten Anforderungen.

2.1.1 Portabilität

Die Portabilität des Software-Dictionary ist Voraussetzung für eine breite Anwendbarkeit dieses Produktes und aller darauf aufbauenden Anwendungssoftware-Systeme. Das Software-Dictionary-System ist in der Grundkonzeption völlig neutral definiert, um seine universelle Einsetzbarkeit sicherzustellen.

2.1.1.1 Datenbanksysteme

Grundsätzlich müssen alle drei Datenbankkonzepte (relational, hierarchisch, Netzwerk) sowie die weitverbreiteten index-sequentiellen Datenverwaltungssysteme (ISAM, VSAM) unterstützt werden.

Um dies zu ermöglichen, wird eine universelle SQL-Schnittstelle zur Verfügung gestellt. Diese SQL-Schnittstelle dient dazu, die weitgehend dem ANSI-Standard folgenden SQL-Befehle der einzelnen Werkzeuge und Anwendungsprogramme in die Datenmanipulationssprachen des jeweils verfügbaren Datenbanksystems umzusetzen.

Die SQL-Schnittstelle bedient sich dabei selbst aus der Meta-Datenbank des Software-Dictionary, um die für die Umsetzung notwendigen Informationen zu erhalten.

Die Meta-Datenbank des Software-Dictionary wird wiederum nur über die SQL-Schnittstelle angesprochen.

SQL als Datenbankabfragesprache wurde gewählt, da sie sich zu einer Standard-Sprache entwickelt hat. Viele Anbieter relationaler Datenbanksysteme passen ihre Produkte an den SQL-Standard an, bzw. bieten FULL-ANSI-SQL-Schnittstellen an.

2.1.1.2 Rechnerumgebung

Das Software-Dictionary soll in jeder relevanten Rechnerumgebung lauffähig sein. Als für den Einsatz relevant sind dabei anzusehen:

- Host-Rechner

- PC

- PC-Netze

- UNIX-Workstations.

Als mögliche Betriebssysteme sind interessant:

- MVS

- VM

- MS-/PC-DOS

- OS/2

- UNIX.

Unabhängig davon ist eine Implementierungssprache auszuwählen. Die Wahl fiel auf die Sprache "C", die mehrere Vorteile bietet:

"C" ist

- prädestiniert für systemtechnische Anwendungen

- weitverbreitet in PC-Umgebungen

- verfügbar für verschiedene Mainframe-Umgebungen mit Trend zu Standard

- die einzige Alternative für UNIX-Unterstützung.

2.1.2 Laufzeitunterstützung

Das Software-Dictionary ist ein aktives System und bildet als solches die Grundlage für alle Anwendungssysteme.

Ein Anwendungsprogramm hat die Möglichkeit zur Laufzeit auf Inhalte der Software-Dictionary-Meta-Datenbank zuzugreifen. Das Software-Dictionary steht dem Anwendungsprogramm als Informationslieferant für die Überprüfung der Zugriffsberechtigung auf Datenbanken, für Datenbank-, Entitäten-, Attribut- und Maskenbeschreibungen zur Verfügung.

Identifikation und Zugriffskontrolle

Applikationsdatenbanken, aber auch die Software-Dictionary-Meta-Datenbank werden von vielen Benutzern zu verschiedenen Zwecken genutzt. Aus Gründen der Datensicherheit und des Datenschutzes muß sichergestellt sein, daß nicht jeder Benutzer unkontrolliert und möglicherweise unberechtigt auf eine Datenbank zugreift oder Werkzeuge benutzt, für die er nicht autorisiert ist. Der Zugriff auf Datenbanken oder Werkzeuge wird vom Software-Dictionary überwacht.

Die Überwachung erfolgt in der Art und Weise, daß der Benutzer an einer graphischen Oberfläche die ihm zur Verfügung stehenden Werkzeuge zur Auswahl angezeigt bekommt. Bei einem interaktiven Datenbankzugriff werden dem Benutzer in einer geeigneten Folge die Datenbanken, Entitäten und Attribute angezeigt. Der Benutzer wählt hieraus diejenigen aus, die ihn interessieren. Die Zugriffsüberwachung stellt sicher, daß die angezeigten Objekte auch von dem Benutzer ausgewählt werden dürfen. Dadurch wird verhindert, daß ein Benutzer etwas auswählt und danach erst erfährt, daß der Zugriff verweigert wurde.

Dem Benutzer wird nicht verboten, was er nicht darf, sondern ihm wird das angeboten, was er für seine Arbeit braucht!

Im Vergleich zum Datenbankbetrieb entspricht diese Vorgehensweise der Einrichtung von Benutzersichten auf die Datenbestände.

Innerhalb der angebotenen Informationsauswahl lassen sich natürlich vom Benutzer eigene Sichten einrichten.

2.1.3 Entwicklungsunterstützung

UNIBASE ist eine Software-Produktionsumgebung, die mit Hilfe integrierter Methoden und Werkzeuge den gesamten Lebenszyklus komplexer Software-Produkte von der Spezifikation bis zur Versionsverwaltung unterstützt. Im ANIMOS-Teil des Projektes sind konstruktive Entwicklungswerkzeuge für die Benutzeroberflächenimplementierung, für den Programm- und Systementwurf und für den Datenbankentwurf zu entwickeln.

Zum Umfang der Entwicklungsunterstützung gehört zunächst einmal, daß jedem Entwickler die vom ihm benötigten Werkzeuge zur Verfügung gestellt werden. Zu diesen Werkzeugen gehören neben den im ANIMOS-Projekt enstandenen Datenbank- und Programmentwicklungswerkzeugen auch konventionelle Programmierhilfsmittel wie Editoren, Libraries, Compiler usw... .

Eine weitere Komponente betrifft die Daten, die von dem zu entwickelnden Programm bearbeitet werden sollen.

Es wird sichergestellt, daß alle mehrfach verwendeten Daten konsistent gehalten werden.

Die Software-Dictionary-Meta-Datenbank enthält Beschreibungen aller im Gesamtsystem vorhandenen Daten. Diese Informationen dienen als Basis für die Generierung von Programmen, Masken, Reports und Dokumentation, daß heißt, daß Namen, Typen und Wertebereiche automatisch berücksichtigt werden.

Für jedes Datum wird festgehalten, von welchem Programm es gebraucht wird, bzw. in welchen Masken und Reports es auftritt.

Die Auswirkungen von Änderungen an den Datenstrukturen lassen sich so leichter überwachen

2.1.4 Der Gesamtsystem-Entwurf

Das in Abbildung 1 dargestellte Konzept ist die Grundlage für die Entwicklung von echt verteilten Applikationen. Es folgt den Vorstellungen des PPD-Modells (Presentation / Processing / Data), welches die strikte Trennung von Präsentations-, Verarbeitungs- und Datenzugriffskomponenten vorschreibt. Jede dieser Komponenten kann prinzipiell auf einem eigenen Rechner bzw. Prozessor ablaufen.

Dieses Konzept ist beliebig ausbaufähig. Es können beliebig neue Präsentations- und Verarbeitungskomponenten, aber auch Datenbanksysteme hinzugefügt werden. Auf den SQL-Generator und den Programmgenerator kann hier nicht näher eingegangen werden.

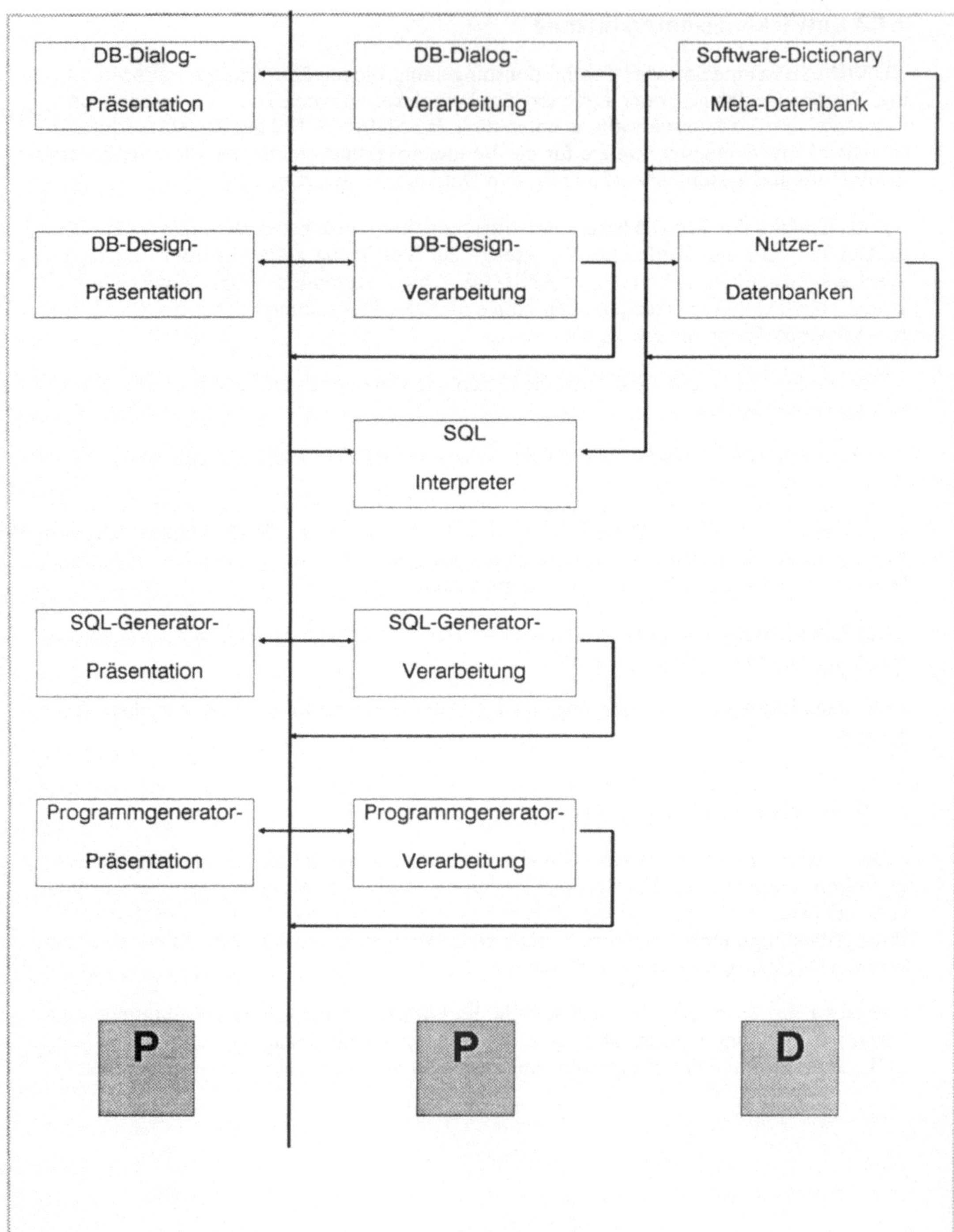

Abbildung 1: PPD-Gesamtentwurf des Software-Dictionary

2.1.5 Entwicklungsstand

Im Rahmen der Diplomarbeit war es nicht möglich, alle funktionalen Anforderungen an das Software-Dictionary in einem Programmsystem zu realisieren. Aus diesem Grund galt es, zunächst einen möglichst umfassenden Entwurf zu erstellen. Für eine Realisierung des ersten Prototyps wurde dann die Funktionalität auf das unbedingt notwendige Minimum (im folgenden: Kernsystem) eingeschränkt.

2.1.5.1 Kernsystem

Das Software-Dictionary-Kernsystem bildet die Grundlage für das gesamte Software-Dictionary-System. Alle für den weiteren Aufbau des Dictionary notwendigen Informationen werden vom Kernsystem zur Verfügung gestellt.

Bei dem Kernsystem handelt es sich im wesentlichen um Einträge in die Software-Dictionary-Meta-Datenbank. Dabei handelt es sich um:

- Tabellen für den Betrieb des SQL-Interpreters

- Tabellen für die Zugriffskontrolle

- Tabellen für den Betrieb des Datenbank-Design-Tools

2.1.5.2 Datenbank-Dialog-System

Ein wesentlicher Bestandteil des Software-Dictionary ist eine Komponente für den interaktiven Zugriff auf Datenbanken. Diese Komponente ist notwendig, da auch die Meta-Datenbank des Software-Dictionary damit von einem ausgezeichneten Benutzer, dem Master-User, manipuliert wird.

Über eine graphische Oberfläche werden dem Benutzer alle für ihn zugänglichen Datenbanken angezeigt. Anschließend werden die Entitäten der vom Benutzer ausgewählten Datenbanken in Abhängigkeit von der geplanten Aktivität auf diesen Daten angezeigt. Wiederum kann sich der Benutzer durch Auswahl mittels Maus die zu den Entitäten gehörenden Attribute anzeigen lassen und hat dann die Möglichkeit, werteabhängig Attribute auszuwählen.

Während dieser graphischen Dialogführung wird intern ein SQL-Befehl generiert, der über die einheitliche SQL-Schnittstelle auf die Meta-Datenbank des Software-Dictionary wirkt.

Für die erste Realisierung bis Anfang September 1988 ist die Rechnerkonfiguration der Abbildung 2 geplant.

Bis Mitte November 1988 soll dann eine Konfiguration mit Host-Anbindung realisiert sein. Diese Konfiguration ist in Abbildung 3 dargestellt.

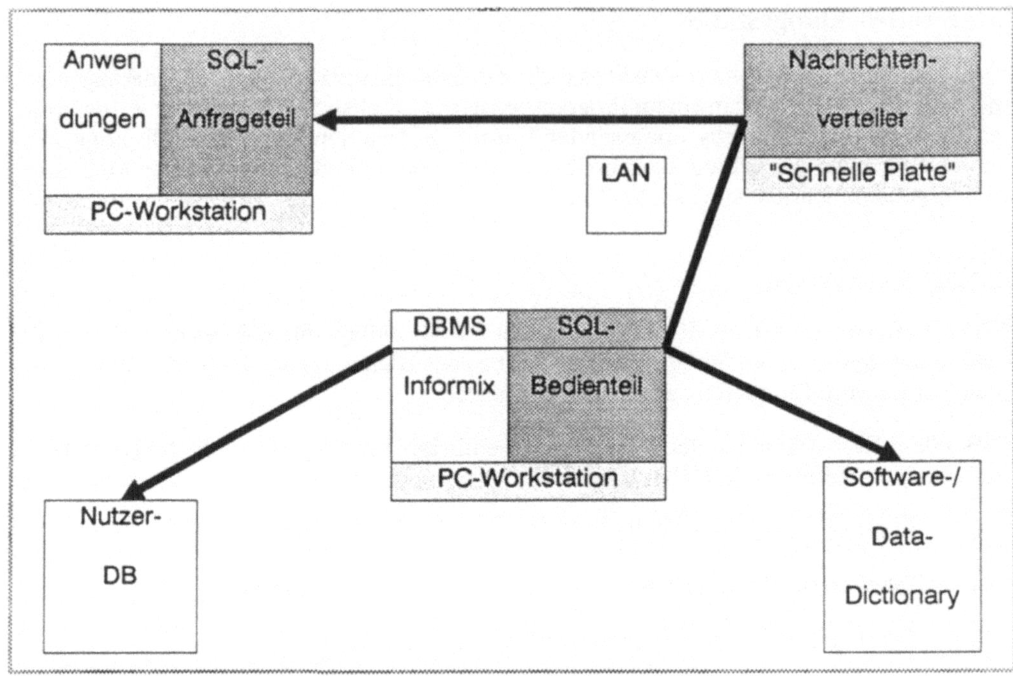

Abbildung 2: Prototyp 1 (September 1988)

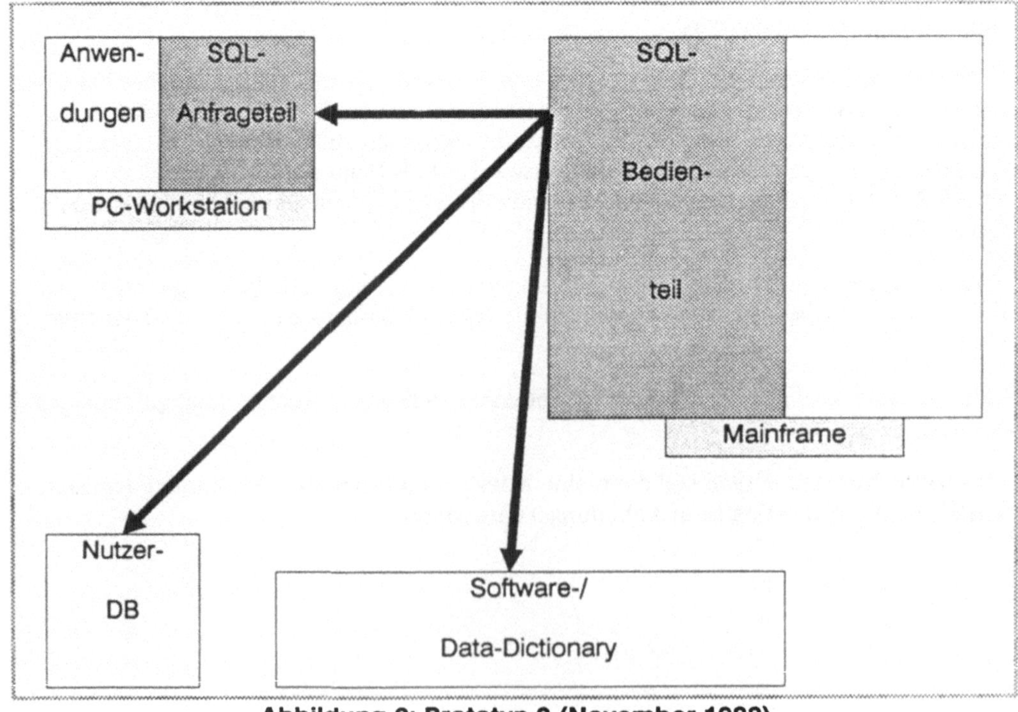

Abbildung 3: Prototyp 2 (November 1988)

2.2 Ein Datenbank-Entwurfswerkzeug

2.2.1 Der Datenbank-Entwurfsprozeß

Man kann den Datenbank-Entwurfsprozeß in Anlehnung an die verschiedensten Autoren, die über den Entwurf von Datenbanken publiziert haben ([YAO78], [SMITH78], [KAHN78], [WITT87], [CONV84]), in die folgenden sechs Phasen unterteilen.

- Analyse der Anforderungen aus der Realwelt

- Modellierung einzelner Benutzersichten (Views)

- Integration der Benutzersichten in eine globale Sicht der Datenbank (View-Integration)

- Restrukturieung der globalen Sicht in ein geeignetes konzeptuelles Schema

- Transformation des konzeptuellen Schemas in ein externes Schema (Sichten), das den Benutzern zur Verfügung steht

- Generierung des internen Schemas durch Analyse des konzeptuellen bzw. externen Schemas

Das im folgenden beschriebene Datenbank-Entwurfswerkzeug setzt genau im Punkt d) an. Es wird also vorausgesetzt, daß die verschiedenen aus der Analyse der Anforderungen entstandenen Sichten zu einer globalen Sicht der Datenbank integriert wurden und die Attribute, die in der Datenbank nachher enthalten sein sollen, zur Eingabe bereit stehen.

Das voll in das Software-Dictionary integrierbare Datenbank-Entwurfswerkzeug verfährt nach dem Entity-Relationship-Modell in einem von Bonczek [BONC84] beschriebenen 7-Schritte-Verfahren, das noch etwas erweitert wurde.

Bei der Benutzung dieses Werkzeugs wird der Datenbankadministrator mit Hilfe einer graphisch orientierten Fensteroberfläche (THESEUS unter MS-WINDOWS bzw. unter Presentation-Manager) geführt.

2.2.1.1 Der 7-Schritte-Algorithmus

Dieser von Robert H. Bonczek, Clyde W. Holsapple und Andrew B. Whinston 1984 [BONC84] vorgestellte Algorithmus basiert auf sieben nacheinander auszuführenden Schritten. Er ist einfach im Verfahren, erzeugt logisch korrekte Strukturen und der Datenbankadministrator erhält eine klare und genaud Darstellung der konzeptuellen Struktur der Applikation. Da die ursprüngliche Zielsetzuung des Algorithmus' ein gültiges CODASYL-Netzwerkschema war, mußte er an einigen Stellen so modifiziert werden, daß er ein allgemein verwendbares konzeptuelles Schema liefert. Die einzelnen Schritte werden im folgenden dargestellt.

Schritt 1

Es wird eine Liste aller Attribute erstellt. Diese Liste steht wie oben beschrieben zur Eingabe bereit. Für jedes Attribut werden entgegen des ursprünglichen Algorithmus' am Ende des Programms die entsprechenden DetailInformationen wie Typen, Größen, Wertebereiche, Zweckbeschreibungen usw. eingegeben. In diesem ersten Schritt werden lediglich die Namen der Attribute eingegeben.

Schritt 2

Alle 1:1Beziehungen zwischen Attributen werden zu einer Entität zusammengefaßt. Jede Entität bekommt einen Namen, der ihre Attribute beschreibt. Einzubeziehen sind hier auch sogenannte Fast1:1Beziehungen wie z.B. die zwischen Produktcode und Quantität.

Schritt 3

Es wird eine Entität für jedes Attribut gebildet, das bis jetzt noch nicht in einer Entität erscheint.

Schritt 4

Die 1:N-Beziehungen zwischen Entitäten werden in diesem Schritt festgelegt. Ihnen wird ein eindeutiger Name gegeben.

Schritt 5

Unnötig definierte 1:N-Beziehungen werden wieder entfernt. Es dürfen allerdings nur solche 1:Neziehungen entfernt werden, die nach der Entfernung keinen Informationsverlust bewirken.

Folgendes Beispiel soll das deutlich machen:

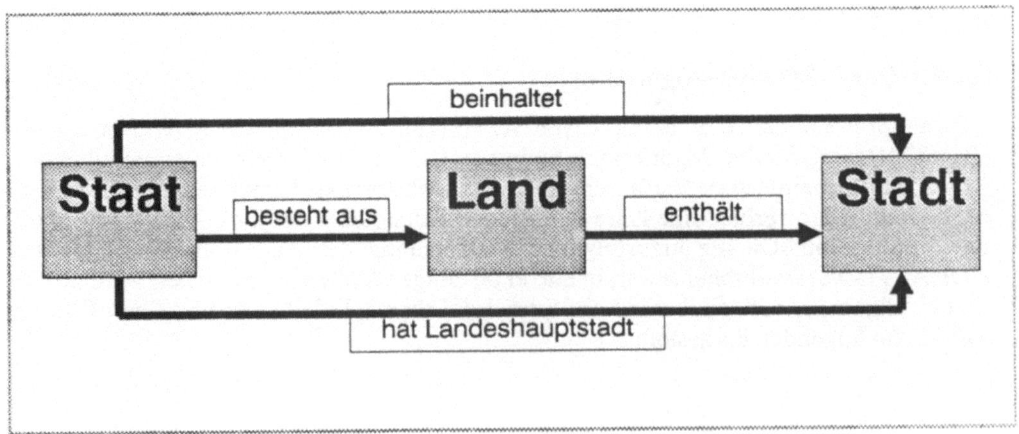

Die Beziehung "beinhaltet" ist überflüssig, da diese Beziehung transitiv durch die beiden Beziehungen "besteht aus" und "enthält" ausgedrückt wird, während die Beziehung "hat Landeshauptstadt" eine Information enthält, die bei Weglassen dieser Beziehung verloren gehen würde.

Schritt 6

Für jede Entität, die noch zu keiner 1:N-Beziehung gehört, wird vom Datenbankadministrator eine Entität ausgewählt, zu dem sie eine M:N-Beziehung hat. Diese Beziehung wird dann definiert und es wird ein eindeutiger Name vergeben.

Schritt 7

Gibt es jetzt dennoch M:N-Beziehungen der Realwelt, die für die Reporterzeugung benötigt werden, aber noch nicht erzeugt sind, müssen sie durch 1:NBeziehungen zu künstliche Entitäten erzeugt werden.

2.2.1.2 Die Funktionsweise des Datenbank-Entwurfswerkzeugs

Zunächst einmal wird der Datenbankadministrator das Ziel-Datenbanksystem spezifizieren. Danach richtet sich das Angebot verschiedener Spezifikationsmöglichkeiten beim Entwurf, die für das eine DBMS gelten, für ein anderes jedoch nicht. Als Beispiel sei hier die Möglichkeit von verzweigten Beziehungen genannt, wie sie vom erweiterten Netzwerk-Datenbanksystem MDBS III angeboten wird, die jedoch in anderen Systemen nicht möglich ist.

In den Metadaten werden alle unternehmensweit bisher schon definierten und benutzten Attribute verwaltet. Damit besteht bei der Spezifikation der Attribute für eine Datenbank die Möglichkeit, schon bestehende Attribute mit in den Entwurfsprozeß einzubeziehen. Das gewährleistet die Verwendung von einheitlichen Attributen, deren Eigenschaften unternehmensweit in allen Datenbanken gleich sind. Außerdem vereinfacht diese Vorgehensweise den Entwurf der Attribute erheblich. Der Datenbankadministrator vergibt nun für die ausgewählten Attribute datenbankspezifische Namen.

Bei der Implementierung des Datenbank-Entwurfswerkzeugs wurde darauf geachtet, daß der Nutzer durch die Ablaufsteuerung dazu gezwungen wird, die Schritte des Entwurfsalgorithmus' weitestgehend einzuhalten. Dies entspricht zwar nicht der allgemein üblichen Benutzeroberflächen-Philosophie der freien Dialogführung durch den Nutzer, stellt aber den Datenbankentwurf nach einer bestimmten Methode sicher.

Bei dieser Methode werden nun nacheinander die 1:N- und die M:N-Beziehungen spezifiziert, was sich sofort in der graphischen Darstellung des Entity-Relationship-Modells auswirkt. Der Datenbankadministrator hat also ständig das aktuelle ER-Modell auf dem Bildschirm präsent und kann mit seinen Objekten operieren, d.h. er kann die Graphik und damit das Modell verändern.

Nachdem auf diese Art und Weise das gewünschte Entity-Realtionship-Modell entstanden ist, wird der Datenbankadministrator die Funktion "Ausführen" aktivieren, die das entstandene Schema durch eine generierte Standard-ANSI-SQL-Befehlsfolge in ein physisches Datenbankschema im jeweiligen Ziel-Datenbanksystem überführt.

An dieser Stelle sei schon ein kleiner Ausblick in die Zukunft erlaubt. Es ist neben der reinen Sicherungsfunktion, die den jeweiligen Stand des Entwurfs sichert, um am nächsten Tag daran weiter arbeiten zu können, auch an eine Art Prototyping für den Datenbankentwurf gedacht [EFFEL87]. Dabei kann zu jedem Zeitpunkt des Entwurfs - sofern schon Entitäten definiert wurden - eine Testversion der Datenbank, wie sie sich zu dem Zeitpunkt darstellt, mit Testdaten erstellt werden, so daß der Entwerfer schon frühzeitig schwerwiegende Fehler im Entwurf erkennen und beseitigen kann. Diese Datenbank hat aber nur temporären Charakter, d.h. sie wird beim Fortgang des Entwurfs wieder verworfen.

2.2.1.3 Weitere Aufgaben des Datenbank-Entwurfswerkzeugs

Neben der eigentlichen Hauptaufgabe des Datenbankentwurfs stellt das Werkzeug aber noch eine Reihe weiterer nützlicher Funktionen zur Verfügung:

Änderung

Die Änderung eines bestehenden Entity-Relationship-Modells (einer Datenbank) erfolgt im kleinen Rahmen mit einer eigenen Funktion, z.B. Änderung eines Attributtyps oder Hinzunahme eines neues Attributes.

Löschung

Alle Löschfunktionen für eine Datenbank sind unter einer gemeinsamen Funktion zusammengefaßt, d.h. die Löschung von Attributen, ganzen Entitäten, Beziehungen oder Sichten erfolgt über diese Option.

Redesign

Ein völliges Redesign - also eine Änderung eines bestehenden Entity-Relationship-Modells im großen Rahmen - ist das Ziel einer eigenständigen Funktion, die über die oben schon erwähnte Prototyp-Funktion erlaubt, die geplanten Strukturänderungen der Datenbank mit einer generierten Test-Datenbank zu überprüfen.

Normalisierung

Mit dieser Funktion kann man die verschiedensten aus der Literatur bekannten Normalisierungsalgorithmen aktivieren und somit das konzeptuelle Schema den jeweiligen konkreten Bedürfnissen anpassen

Metadaten

Diese Funktion bleibt einzig dem Master-User vorbehalten und dient der Möglichkeit, die Struktur der Meta-Datenbank (Software-Dictionary) in einem bestimmten Rahmen zu verändern.

2.2.2 Die Zusammenarbeit mit dem Software-Dictionary

Es gibt viele Datenbank-Entwurfswerkzeuge, die mittels einer mehr oder weniger komfortablen graphischen Oberfläche in der Lage sind, Entity-Relationship-Modelle eines konzeptuellen Datenbankschemas aufzubauen, darzustellen und zu edititeren. Es gibt allerdings nur sehr wenige, die die Informationen, die in einem solchen Modell enthalten sind, in das Dictionary zu übernehmen und zu verwerten. Dabei lassen sich die anfallenden Metainformationen vielfältig von Systemkomponenten verwenden, die das Software-Dictionary benutzen. Man denke zum Beispiel an Programm-und Systementwurfs-Werkzeuge, Masken- und Report-Generatoren sowie Datenbank-Anfragesysteme.

Das im Rahmen des ANIMOS-Projektes zu erstellende Datenbank-Entwurfwerkzeug nutzt alle Möglichkeiten aus, um die beim Entwurf anfallenden (Meta-) Daten dem Software-Dictionary zur Verfügung zu stellen, aber umgekehrt auch schon vorhandene Informationen wie z.B. bereits bestehende Attribute an den Entwerfer weiterzuleiten.

Konkret besteht nun die Zusammenarbeit des Datenbank-Entwurfswerkzeugs mit dem Software-Dictionary in folgenden Punkten:

- Erfassung aller Attribute, Entitäten, Beziehungen etc. im Software-Dictionary (Metadatenbank)

- Speicherung des kompletten ER-Modells zu jeder im System existierenden und mit dem Entwicklungswerkzeug erzeugten Datenbank

- Speicherung der Zwischenstände von ER-Modell-Entwürfen und Kennzeichnung als nicht nutzbare Datenbank

- Sofortige Mitführung aller Änderungen am ER-Modell im Software-Dictionary (Funtionen "Änderung", "Löschung", "Redesign", "Normalisierung", "Metadaten")

- Speicherung und Verwaltung erzeugter Test-Datenbanken zu Unterstützung des "Prototyping" für den Datenbank-Entwurf

2.2.3 Entwicklungsstand

Der zum Erscheinungsdatum realisierte Prototyp 1 des Datenbank-Entwurfswerkzeugs ist in der Lage, die elementare Funktion, nämlich den Entwurf einer Datenbank über ein ER-Modell, mit voller Integration des Software-Dictionary durchzuführen. Dazu gehören neben der vollen Funktionalität der Neuanlage auch das Ändern eines ER-Modells in kleinem Rahmen und das Löschen von Attributen, Entitäten oder Sichten.

Gerade in der Entwicklung befindet sich die Implementierung der Normalisierungsalgorithmen. Die nächsten Meilensteine werden der Komplex "Redesign" und Generierung einer Test-Datenbank sein.

3. Zusammenfassung

Das hier vorgestellte Software-Dictionary zeichnet sich durch ein zukunfts-orientiertes Konzept aus. Das liegt zum einen in der fast unbegrenzten Portabilität, die es ermöglicht, das Software-Dictionary in jeder gängigen Rechner- Betriebssystem- und Netzwerkarchitektur einzusetzen. Zum anderen garantiert die Benutzung einer Standard-SQL-Schnittstelle den Zugriff auf alle weit verbreiteten Datenbanksysteme gleich welchen Typs und unabhängig von einer konkreten DML/DDL. Durch die Realisierung der sehr wichtigen Eigenschaft aktiv zu sein, leistet das Software-Dictionary eine wirkliche Laufzeit- und Entwicklungsunterstützung aller integrierten Programmsysteme und Werkzeuge.

Die Einbindung eines komfortablen Datenbank-Entwurfswerkzeugs sowie eines Programm-Generator-Systems in die Entwicklungsumgebung macht zudem einen vollständigen Entwurf des unternehmerischen Realwelt-Modells möglich. Doch nicht nur hier läßt sich das Software-Dictionary sinnvoll einsetzen. Auch in wissenschaftlichen und technischen Umgebungen ist eine Ausnutzung der Vorteile wegen der großen Systemunabhängigkeit des Software-Dictionary denkbar.

Damit erfüllt das Software-Dictionary viele der an komfortable und leistungsfähige Software-Produktionsumgebungen gestellte Ansprüche.

4. Ausblick

Wie so oft, zeigt sich auch in diesem Projekt sehr schnell, daß längst noch nicht alle Grenzen des wünschenswerten und machbaren erreicht sind. Man kann beispielsweise darüber nachdenken, inwieweit Expertensysteme in Zukunft die Leistung des Software-Dictionary unterstützen bzw. ergänzen können. Da die Expertensysteme selbst aber noch weit davon entfernt sind, standardmäßig eingesetzt werden zu können, muß man die Entwicklung auf diesem Gebiet beobachten und versuchen, die eigenen Wünsche und Vorstellungen mit einfließen zu lassen.

Ein weiterer wesentlicher Punkt in naher Zukunft wird die Einbeziehung von echt verteilten Datenbanken in die Konzeption sein, wobei auch darüber zu entscheiden sein wird, ob man das Software-Dictionary selbst nicht auch verteilt!

Auf dem Gebiet der Künstlichen Intelligenz wird man früher oder später auch an objektorientierten Datenbanken und deduktiven Datenbanken nicht vorbeikommen, so daß für die Zukunft auf diesem Gebiet sicherlich noch genug Entwicklungsarbeit zu leisten sein wird.

Literatur

[BONC84]

Bonczek, Robert H.; Holsapple, Clyde W.; Whinston, Andrew B.

"Micro Database Management - Practical Techniques for Application Development"

Volume in Computer Science and applied mathematics, Academic Press, Inc., Orlando, 1984

[CONV84]

Bernhard Convent

"Ein formaler Ansatz zum rechnergestützten Entwurf von Datenbankschemata mittels View-Integration"

Diplomarbeit an der Universität Dortmund, Abteilung Informatik, Dortmund 1984

[EFFEL87]

Wolfgang Effelsberg

"Datenbankzugriff in Rechnernetzen" in:

Informationstechnik it, 29. Jahrgang, Heft 3/1987

[KAHN78]

"LDDM - A structured logical database design methodology" in:

Database Design Techniques I: Requirements and logical Structures NYU Symposium, New York, May 1978, in:

Lecture Notes in Computer Science 132, G. Goos and J. Hartmanns (ed.)

[SMITH78]

Smith, John Miles; Smith, Diane C.P.

"Principles of database conceptual design" in:

Database Design Techniques I: Requirements and logical Structures NYU Symposium, New York, May 1978, in:

Lecture Notes in Computer Science 132, G. Goos and J. Hartmanns (ed.)

[TIMM86]

"Die erweiterbare und portable Software-Produktionsumgebung Unibase" in:

SOFTWAREprofessional Nr.6, Nov./Dez.86 sowie

"UNIBASE Software-Produktionsumgebung auf UNIX-Basis" in:

Computer Magazin 10/86, Sonderteil

[WITT87]

Witt, Kurt-Ulrich; Preising, Claudia

"Anforderungen an und Konzeption für eine Design-Workstation für relationale Datenbanken" in:

Angewandte Informatik 12/87, S. 509 - 517, Vieweg & Sohn Verlagsgesellschaft mbH

[YAO78]

Yao, S.B.; Navathe, Shamkant B.; Weldon, Jay-Louise

"An integrated approach to database design" in:

Database Design Techniques I: Requirements and logical Structures NYU Symposium,
New York, May 1978, in:

Lecture Notes in Computer Science 132, G. Goos and J. Hartmanns (ed.)

Die Siemens Retrievalsysteme TAURUS und GOLEM

von
Thomas Mohrenweis
Siemens AG
Otto-Hahn-Ring 6
8000 München 83

Zusammenfassung

Nach einer Erläuterung des Begriffes "Information Retrieval" werden die Einsatzfälle für solche Systeme und der Zusammenhang zwischen Texterschliessung und Suchergebnis dargestellt. Es folgt eine Beschreibung der SIEMENS Information-Retrieval-Systeme GOLEM und TAURUS. GOLEM läuft im Betriebssystem BS2000 und bietet mit PASSAT auch ein System zur automatischen Textanalyse. TAURUS läuft im Betriebssystem SINIX und setzt auf Dokumenten des Textsystems HIT auf. Abschließend werden noch die vielfältigen Möglichkeiten der Kopplung von anderen Systemen mit den IR-Systemen beschrieben.

Inhalt

1. Einleitung

1.1 Information Retrieval Systeme

Information Retrieval Systeme (IRS) sind spezielle Informationssysteme, die überwiegend zur Speicherung und zur Suche von Textdokumenten, und damit von unformatierten Informationen , genutzt werden.
Somit unterscheiden sich IRS von der zweiten Gruppe der Informationssysteme, den Datenbanksystemen: diese dienen der Speicherung, Wiedergewinnung und Auswertung von formatierten Informationen.

Um das gezielte Wiederfinden von Textdokumenten in einem IRS zu ermöglichen, ohne alle im System gespeicherten Texte zu durchsuchen, muß der Speicherung dieser Texte ein inhaltlicher Erschließungsprozess vorausgehen. In diesem werden den Textdokumenten beschreibende Merkmale, die Deskriptoren, zugeordnet.
Deskriptoren können formale Kriterien sein, wie z.B. der Autor oder das Erscheinungsdatum eines Textes. Es können auch den Inhalt eines Textes charakterisierende Begriffe sein, die selbst nicht im Text vorkommen müssen.
Über die Deskriptoren erfolgt dann die Suche nach den im IRS gespeicherten Dokumenten.

"Information Retrieval" im engeren Sinne ist definiert als das Suchen und Auffinden bestimmter Informationen innerhalb eines gespeicherten Informationsbestandes.
Ein "Information Retrieval System " hat außer diesen Suchfunktionen auch noch Aufgaben, die das Aufbereiten, Speichern und Verwalten der Informationen beinhalten. Die im Information Retrieval System gespeicherten Informationen besitzen eine beliebige Struktur - ein wichtiger Unterschied zu den Datenbanksystemen, wo die immer in Tabellenform gespeicherten Informationen innerhalb der Datenbank die gleiche Struktur besitzen.
Die Informationen bestehen jedoch nicht nur aus Texten: sie besitzen auch formale Teile.
Zum Beispiel wird der Krankenbericht eines Arztes nicht nur seine Diagnose (= Textteil) enthalten, sondern auch Patientendaten (= formaler Teil), die sowohl alphanumerisches (persönliche Daten) wie auch numerisches (Bsp. Fiebertemperatur) Format haben können.

Bei solchen Daten besteht nicht nur ein Bedarf des Wiederfindens im Archiv; es ist auch notwendig, sie nachzubearbeiten und aufzubereiten.

1.2 Einsatzfälle für Information Retrieval Systeme

Für IRS gibt es eine Vielzahl von Einsatzfällen:
Das beginnt bei großen Informationssystemen, die eine Vielzahl von Dokumenten für eine große Anzahl von Benutzern zugänglich machen. Als Beispiel sei hier der Bereich Informationsanbieter (data star, GENIOS, JURIS etc.) genannt, dazu gehören auch die Fachinformationszentren , wo Volltext-Dokumente bzw. Literaturnachweise für wichtige Sachgebiete aus Forschung, Technik , Wirtscchaft und Wissenschaft zur Verfügung stehen. Auch große Unternehmen setzen für ihre interne Dokumentation zunehmend IRS ein.

Der Einsatz von IRS ist jedoch nicht auf große Anwendungen beschränkt. In Fachabteilungen von Firmen oder Behörden stellt sich zunehmend das Problem, Dokumente, Briefe, Vorgänge, Projekte, Testberichte etc., die sich zu immer größeren Papierbergen auftürmen, sinnvoll zu archivieren. Wichtig ist hier, daß die Unterlagen unter verschiedenen Gesichtspunkten wiedergefunden werden können. Die Menge der Daten und die Anforderungen an die Suchmöglichkeiten erfordern ein IRS.
Sogar im Bereich eines Arbeitsplatzes, auf PC-Ebene also, ergeben sich Einsatzfälle für IRS:
Jeder Anwender eines Textverarbeitungssystems hat früher oder später mit einem Problem zu kämpfen: Im Laufe der Zeit sammelt sich eine Menge von abgeschlossenen Texten an, die nicht mehr für die aktuelle, laufende Tätigkeit benötigt werden.
Sie können jedoch nicht verworfen werden, da immer die Möglichkeit besteht, daß sie doch noch einmal nachgewiesen oder benutzt werden müssen.

Vor allem in den letztgenannten Bereichen, als "Elektronisches Archiv" werden IRS in den nächsten Jahren zunehmend an Bedeutung gewinnen. Die Marktprognosen verschiedener Institute versprechen hohe Wachstumsraten.

2. Arbeitsweise von Information Retrieval Systemen

Es gibt im wesentlichen zwei verschiedene Techniken, mit denen Information Retrieval Systeme arbeiten. Das sind

- die Systeme mit Volltextinvertierung und

- die Deskriptorsysteme

Bei der Volltextinvertierung wird jedes Wort eines Textes in der Form, in der es im Text gefunden wird, zum Suchbegriff. Ausgenommen von dieser Regel sind lediglich die sog. Stopworte, das sind im allgemeinen Trivialwörter wie "und", "der", "von", "fast" usw. Abgesehen von der Erstellung der Stopwortliste entsteht dem Anwender dabei kein zusätzlicher Aufwand.

Bei den Deskriptorsystemen werden nur ausgewählte, den Text charakterisierende Wörter zum späteren Suchbegriff. Die Auswahl der Suchbegriffe erfolgt entweder intellektuell durch den Anwender oder programmgesteuert durch Textanalyseprogramme.

Beide Techniken haben ihre Vor- und Nachteile:

Aufgrund der weniger selektiven Zuteilung von Suchbegriffen bei der Volltextinvertierung und wegen linguistischer Probleme ist die Suche in Volltextinvertierungssystemen entweder ungenauer ("unschärfer") oder aufwendiger. Unschärfer deswegen, weil jedes Wort in jeder möglichen Form abgespeichert wird: der Suchbegriff "Wort" zum Beispiel als "Wort", "Worte", "Wörter", "Wörtern". Wird also nur nach "Wort" gesucht, werden die anderen Formen des Suchbegriffes nicht gefunden. Dies kann zum Teil kompensiert werden durch mehr Aufwand in der Recherche: durch Maskierungen.Mit dieser Technik werden möglicherweise alle zutreffenden, aber auch viele überflüssigen Informationen gefunden.Die Zahl der überflüssigen Treffer nimmt mit der Größe der Datenbank zu. Bei den Deskriptorsystemen wird dieser "Aufwand" bereits vor der Abspeicherung der Dokumente in das Information Retrieval System erbracht: es ist entweder eine intellektuelle oder eine automatische Analyse des Dokumentinhalts notwendig, um ihm Suchbegriffe zuzuteilen. Dafür liefert die Suche in Deskriptorsystemen genauere Ergebnisse und schnellere Antworten als in volltextinvertierenden Systemen.

Auf Arbeitsplatzsystemen mit ihren noch begrenzten Möglichkeiten zur Dokumentabspeicherung kommen die Vorteile der Volltextinvertierung zum Tragen: es entsteht kein Aufwand vor der Abspeicherung der Dokumente und diese werden immer nach zwar unselektiven aber einheitlichen Kriterien abgespeichert.

Auf großen Hostsystemen ist die Problematik anders: es ist sinnvoller, den Aufwand zur Erschließung des Dokumentinhalts einmal vor Abspeicherung des Dokuments zu erbringen, denn sonst muß jeder Nutzer des Retrievalsystems durch eine komplexere Recherche diesen Aufwand immer wieder erbringen, um sein Rechercheziel zu erreichen. Dieser Aufwand umfaßt neben dem Zeitaufwand des Benutzers häufig auch die Kosten für die Nutzung der Anlage. Auf diesen Systemen haben also die Deskriptorsysteme ihre Vorteile.
Dieser Logik folgend bietet Siemens auf den SINIX-Systemen das Volltextinvertierungssystem TAURUS, und im BS2000 das Deskriptorsystem GOLEM für die Zwecke des Information Retrieval an.

3. GOLEM - ein Retrievalsystem für BS2000-Rechner

GOLEM eignet sich für alle Information-Retrieval-Anwendungen, denn

- es läßt Datenbanken von nahezu beliebiger Größe zu (GOLEM-Datenbanken mit mehreren Millionen Dokumenten sind keine Seltenheit!). Umso effizienter werden selbstverständlich kleinere Datenmengen bedient.

- der gleichzeitige Zugriff durch viele Rechercheure wird unterstützt durch den Transaktionsmonitor UTM.

- wirksame und umfangreiche Möglichkeiten des Datenschutzes gewährleisten sowohl durch das Betriebssystem und UTM als auch durch GOLEM selbst, daß jeder Rechercheur in der Datenbank nur das findet, was er auch sehen darf. Dies bezieht sich sowohl auf Funktionen (getrennte Befugnisse zum Ändern, Suchen oder Administrieren), als auch auf die Daten selbst (auf Dokument-, Abschnitts- oder Deskriptorenebene). Eine Before-image-Sicherung schützt gegen Datenverlust während Änderungsvorgängen. Während der Suche verhindert UTM, daß der Benutzer in das Betriebssystem wechseln kann (Abschottung des Betriebssystems)

- es bietet als Benutzungsoberfläche die Common Command Language (CCL); hierbei handelt es sich um einen Kommandoset, der als Vorschlag für eine gemeinsame Oberfläche für Retrievalsysteme vorliegt; laut Euronet DIANE, dem europäischen Informationssystem, bieten über 10 europäische Hosts die CCL als Retrievaloberflächen an und 50% der bibliographischen Dateien in Europa sind mit dieser gemeinsamen Befehlssprache zugänglich. Endbenutzer, die bereits auf diesem Gebiet tätig sind, brauchen deshalb bei Einsatz von GOLEM keine neuen Kommandos zu lernen. Um auch Laien den Zugang zu den Systemen zu erleichtern, ist auch eine komfortable Bedienerführung verfügbar. Um andererseits Spezialisten jede Möglichkeit zu geben, ihr Datenmaterial möglichst genau zu selektieren und auszugeben, wurde die CCL um viele spezielle Such- und Ausgabefunktionen angereichert, die sonst nicht zur Standardausstattung von Retrievalsystemen gehören. Um nur einige davon zu nennen: Es gibt die komfortable Möglichkeit mit Wortlisten zu arbeiten. Wortlisten sind Behälter mit Suchbegriffen, die z.B. durch einfaches Markieren beim Blättern im Wörterbuch in die Wortliste geholt wurden. Die Wortliste kann dann auf einfache Weise in Suchfragen einbezogen werden. Dokumente, die im Laufe der Suche gefunden wurden, können in Dokumentbehältern datenbankübergreifend gesammelt werden und erst am Ende der Session ausgedruckt werden. Die Suche kann zweistufig durchgeführt werden: in einer Grobrecherche werden Suchfragen formuliert bis ein erstes Ergebnis erreicht wird. In einer zweiten Stufe, der sog. Feinrecherche kann dieses Ergebnis durch Stringsuche auf Dokumente oder Dokumentteile des Suchergebnisses beliebig präzisiert werden.

- Situationsbezogene Hilfe-Funktionen sind Bestandteil des GOLEM-Systems.
- GOLEM ist auch für kleinere BS2000-Maschinen, wie Personalcomputer PC-2000 und Abteilungsrechner 7500-C30 geeignet. GOLEM und PASSAT sind die im deutschen Sprachraum am meisten verbreiteten Systeme ihrer Größenklasse.
- Zum Produkt GOLEM gehören auch Dienstprogramme mit folgenden Funktionen
    - Definieren der GOLEM-Datenbank und Ändern von Datenbankkennwerten.
    - Laden und Ändern von Dokumenten
    - Strukturieren des GOLEM-Wörterbuches
    - Programme zum Überprüfen der Konsistenz der GOLEM-Datenbank
- GOLEM ist reorganisationsfrei.

Ergänzen kann man GOLEM durch die Textanalysekomponente PASSAT. Dieses Programm indexiert jeden Text an Hand eines Vergleichswortlexikons, das in einer Standardausführung mit dem Produkt PASSAT mitausgeliefert wird. Dieses Vergleichswortlexikon kann vom Anwender jederzeit fachspezifisch modifiziert werden. Durch PASSAT werden nicht nur im Text vorkommende Wörter als

Suchbegriffe identifiziert. Die Wörter werden auf ihre grammatikalische
Grundform reduziert. Sie können durch andere Suchbegriffe ersetzt ,oder es
können zusätzliche Suchbegriffe vergeben werden. Suchbegriffe, die aus mehr
als einem Wort bestehen (z.B. "Deutsches Rotes Kreuz") werden erkannt und an
GOLEM weitergegeben. Auch werden zusammengesetzte Wörter identifiziert,
in Einzelbestandteile zerlegt und diese dann je nach Festlegung in der Vergleichswortliste ebenfalls als Suchbegriff zugeteilt

Textwörter	werden zum	Suchbegriff durch linguistisch orientierte Methoden	
… den *Patienten* …		Patient	Eliminierung von Flexionen
… in vielen **Krankenhäusern** gibt es …		Krankenhaus	Eliminierung von Flexionen, Umlaut-erkennung
… **Lärmschutz** …		Lärm Schutz Lärmschutz	Zerlegung von Kompositabegriffen
von der **Bayerischen Ärztekammer** wurde ..		Bayerische Ärztekammer	Erkennung von Mehrwortbegriffen
… **Kalzium** kommt in …		Kalzium Calcium	Behandlung von Synonymen

PASSAT ist ein mächtiges Instrument um Texte vor der Abspeicherung in einem
Retrieval System zu indexieren. Die Vorteile gegenüber anderen Deskribierver-
fahren sind vor allem:

- eine einheitliche Deskribierung ist gewährleistet, da immer mit derselben
  Vergleichswortliste gearbeitet werden kann (bei intellektuellen Verfahren
  besteht die Gefahr unterschiedlicher Deskribierung derselben Begriffe)
- die Suchbegriffe werden auf das Wesentliche reduziert (da jedes Wort bzw.
  Teilwort nur in der Grundform vorkommt). Dies bringt erhebliche
  Speicherplatz- und Performancegewinne. Außerdem erspart dies das oft
  lästige Maskieren von Suchbegriffen während der Suche.

- durch die vielen Möglichkeiten von Wortsubstituierungen, Komposita und
  Mehrworterkennung ist eine qualitativ hochwertige Deskribierung
  gesichert. Der spätere Rechercheur im Retrievalsystem, der ein genaues
  Ergebnis für seine Suche erwartet, wird dies zu schätzen wissen.

4. TAURUS - ein Retrievalsystem für SINIX-Rechner

In jeder Büroumgebung ist die textorientierte Informationsverarbeitung eine
Schwerpunktanwendung. Diese textorientierte Informationsverarbeitung
besteht nicht nur aus dem Erstellen und Bearbeiten von Texten; aus bereits
vorhandenen und kontinuierlich wachsenden Informationsbeständen müssen
diese archivierten Textinformationen stets im Zugriff und eine relevante
Herausfilterung möglich sein. Eine schnelle, umfassende und aktuelle
Informationsbereitstellung direkt am Arbeitsplatz ist eine wichtige
Voraussetzung, damit entscheidungsunterstützende Arbeitsvorgänge durch den
Sachbearbeiter oder die Fachkraft durchgeführt werden können.
Für SINIX-Rechner bietet Siemens für das Information Retrieval Problem
folgende Lösung an:
Das Erfassen , Archivieren und Verwalten von Textdokumenten sind Tätigkeiten,
die mit dem Textbearbeitungssystem HIT durchgeführt werden. Ergänzt wird
dies durch das Wiederauffinden, Aufbereiten und Weiterleiten von Texten; dies
ist die Aufgabe des IR-Systems TAURUS, das die Volltext-Recherche auf mit HIT
erstellten Texten ermöglicht. Volltext-Retrieval bedeutet, daß jedes einzelne
Wort im Dokumenttext suchbar ist. Ausgenommen sind nur diejenigen Wörter,
die in einer Stopwortliste explizit ausgeschlossen werden: z. B. die Trivialwörter
"der", "die", "das".
TAURUS ist an das Textsystem HIT angepaßt und sucht auf den Original-HIT-
Dokumenten nach den gewünschten Informationen. Hierdurch ist eine doppelte
Datenhaltung, d. h. ein Duplizieren der Dokumente aus HIT in das Recherche-
programm, nicht erforderlich. Dies wirkt sich positiv auf die Performance der
Produkte aus. Darüberhinaus bedeutet es für den Anwender ein Höchstmaß an
Datensicherheit.
TAURUS kann auch mit Dokumenten arbeiten, die mit dem SINIX-Standardeditor
CED erstellt wurden.
TAURUS ist menügesteuert, besitzt Funktionstasten und bietet Hilfe-Funktionen.
Die Formulierung der Suchfrage erfolgt in Bildschirm-Masken.

TAURUS stellt HIT-Dokumente zu sogenannten "Kollektionen" zusammen und
erstellt zu jeder Kollektion ein Wörterbuch und Verweislisten auf die Dokumente. Es werden in einer Recherche also nicht alle Dokumente durchsucht,

sondern TAURUS findet die Dokumente über seine Verweislisten;deshalb ist die Suche auch extrem schnell .

In der Suchkomponente werden in eine Bildschirmmaske die Suchkriterien eingetragen und der Suchvorgang aktiviert. Als Suchergebnis gibt TAURUS eine Trefferliste aus, in der alle den Suchkriterien entsprechenden Dokumente aufgelistet sind.

Suchkriterien können sein:
- einzelne Wörter
- Wortanfänge
- Sätze bzw. Satzteile
- bestimmte Merkmale des Dokumentes, z. B. Autor, Erstellungsdatum usw

Eine beliebige Kombination der Suchkriterien ist möglich.
Bei manchen Anwendern ist es zweckmäßig, Schlüsselmerkmale zu einem Dokument zu definieren. Jedem Dokument kann ein Profil zugeordnet werden, das den Dokumentnamen, den Eigentümer, das Eingabedatum sowie weitere vom Anwender vergebene Deskriptorenfestlegt.
Dieses Dokumentprofil wird getrennt vom Dokument im Katalog abgelegt und dient dazu, Informationen, die nicht Inhalt des Dokumenttextes sind, zusätzlich aufzunehmen.

Für den Anwender bedeutet der Einsatz von TAURUS eine volle Integration mit dem Textsystem HIT auf den SINIX-Arbeitsplatzcomputern MX2, MX4, MX300 und MX500.
Recherche-Ergebnisse sind mit HIT weiterverarbeitbar, d.h. unter TAURUS können die in HIT zur Verfügung stehenden Textbearbeitungsfunktionen genützt werden.

5. Kopplungsmöglichkeiten und Integration in andere Systeme

5.1 Textsystem und Archivsystem

Zwischen beiden besteht eine enge Beziehung, da häufig die Texte sofort nach ihrer Erstellung im Archiv abgelegt - und damit auch für andere zugänglich gemacht - werden sollen. Die Archivdokumente wiederum sollen jederzeit zur Änderung oder Weiterverarbeitung ins Textsystem übertragen werden können.

Siemens bietet hier integrierte Systeme:

Auf den SINIX-Rechnern HIT und TAURUS, wie in Kap. 4 beschrieben.

Für die Anlagen des Betriebssystems BS2000 bietet Siemens das leistungsfähige Bürosystem OASE. Der Textbaustein OASE-TEXT kann durch einen Kopplungsbaustein mit GOLEM verbunmden werden. Die Dokumente können beliebig zwischen Archiv und Textsystem übertragen werden. Auch zwischen HIT und OASE existiert eine Kopplung, so daß die Dokumente zwischen den Textsystemen des PC und des Hosts ausgetauscht werden können.

Hit kann auch direkt mit GOLEM gekoppelt werden: Die MMC (Micro-Mainframe-Connection), ein Siemens-Produkt, das das Arbeiten vom PC aus in BS2000-Datenbanken und das Übertragen von Daten in PC-Anwendungen ermöglicht.

Den Leistungsumfang zeigt folgende Abbildung:

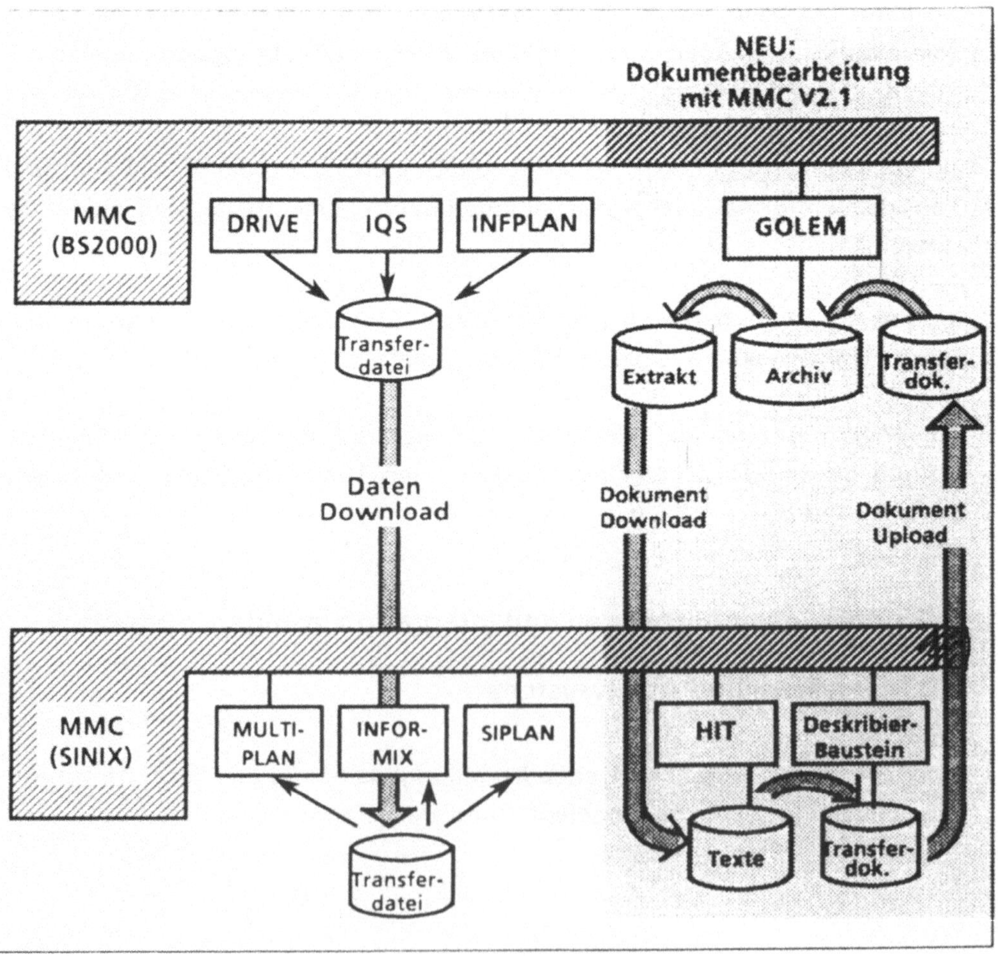

Bei der Archivierung von HIT-Dokumenten können auf mehrere Arten Suchbegriffe vergeben werden:

- Deskriptoren werden automatisch aus Schlüsselfeldern im Dokumenttext extrahiert

- Deskriptoren werden manuell eingegeben

- Deskriptoren werden durch Ankreuzen imDokumenttext selektiert

- Deskriptoren werden automatisch durch PASSAT erzeugt

Die in GOLEM archivierten Dokumente können jederzeit ins Textsystem zurückgeholt werden, das ursprünglichr Format bleibt dabei erhalten.

5.2 GOLEM und die Individuelle Datenverarbeitung (IDV)

Die individuelle Datenverarbeitung ist definiert als flexible Lösung von spontan auftretenden Problemen durch den Benutzer mit Hilfe von Softwarewerkzeugen, deren Funktionsumfang und Benutzeroberfläche einen unmittelbaren Nutzen am Arbeitsplatz gewährleistet. In diesem Sinne ist auch GOLEM ein typisches IDV-Werkzeug. Das zentrale IDV-Produkt von Siemens im BS2000 ist ES (Endbenutzer-Service). ES bietet unter zentraler Steuerung die vier wichtigsten Komponenten der IDV:

- eine Query, abhängig von der verwendeten Datenhaltung DRIVE oder IQS

- einen Listengenerator: ADILOS

- Software für Tabellenkalkulation und spread sheets: INFPLAN

- Software zur Erstellung von Geschäftsgrafiken: BUGRAF

Diese vier Standardbestandteile von ES sowie eine wachsende Anzahl von anderen Softwareprodukten, die auch dem Gebiet der IDV zuzurechnen sind, tauschen untereinander Daten aus. Dies geschieht über eine Datei, die ein Standardformat besitzt: die ES-Transferdatei. Auch GOLEM benutzt diese Schnittstelle, so daß die formatierten Teile eines Dokumentes entsprechend weiterverarbeitet werden können.

Ein Beispiel für eine Nachbearbeitung von GOLEM-Daten zeigt folgende Abbildung.

Aus Krankengeschichten wurde ein Tortendiagramm erstellt, das die Verteilung der Entlassungen aus dem Krankenhaus über die Wochentage zeigt.

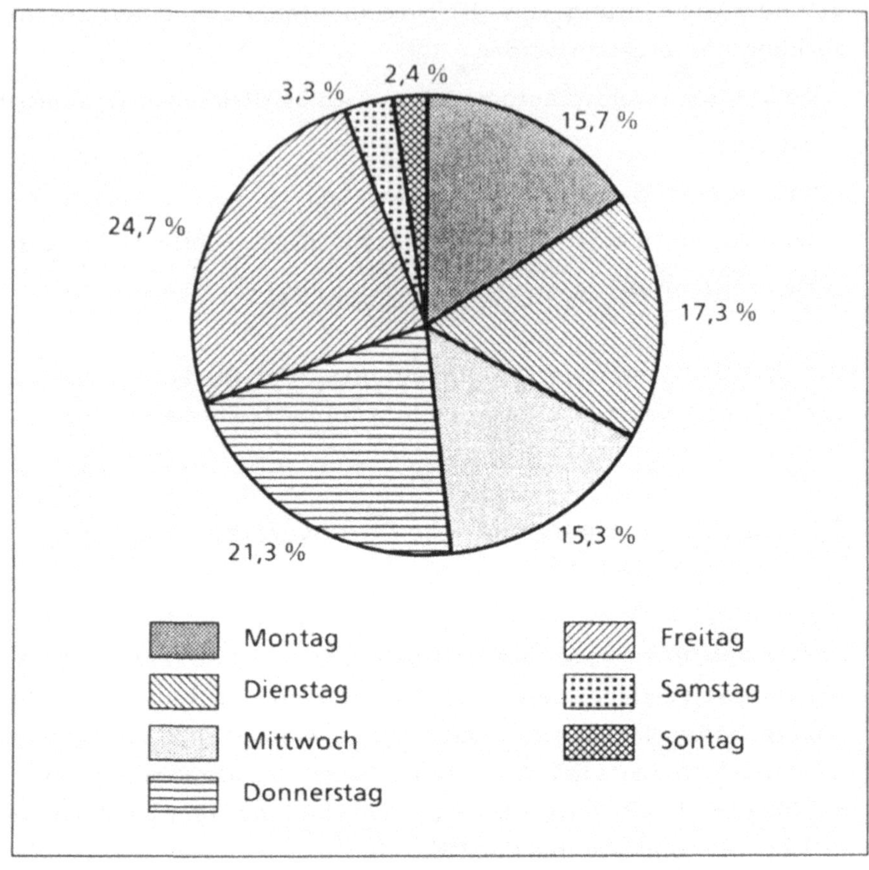

5.3 Einsatz von Scanner und optischen Speicher

Häufig stellt sich das Problem, daß Dokumente nur in Papierform vorliegen und eine manuelle Erfassung zu aufwendig ist. In diesem Fall können die Dokumente gescannt werden, wobei aber nicht die Buchstaben, sondern nur die Hell/Dunkel-Werte (Pixel) gespeichert werden; man spricht von Faksimile-Speicherung. Nachteil dieser Technik ist ein erhöhter Speicherbedarf und die Tatsache, daß die Texte nicht weiterverarbeitet werden können (Textsystem, automatische Indexierung). Für die Archivierung müssen deshalb zusätzlich Informationen erfaßt werden (Schlagwörter, Abstracts). Mit Schriftenlesern (OCR, ICR: optical bzw. intelligent character recognition) kann der Text interpretiert werden, d.h. die Buchstaben werden erkannt und in Code umgesetzt.

Bei Archiven kann großer Bedarf an Speicherplatz entstehen, so daß sich der Einsatz (billiger) optischer Speicher (WORM-Platte) anbietet. Bei der Siemens-Tochtergesellschaft SIETEC, Berlin, wurde bereits ein Anschluß einer optischen Platte an GOLEM realisiert.

Verteilte Datenbanken in kommerziellen Umgebungen

Helmuth Gümbel

Digital Equipment GmbH, München

ABSTRACT

Die Technik der verteilten Datenbanken breitet sich auch in
der kommerziellen Anwendungswelt aus. Es wird der Stand der Technik
diskutiert und das hieraus resultierende Potential.

Digital Equipment bietet als Hersteller hier interessante Systemlösungen, die als Beispiel dargestellt werden. Die Einbindung dieser
Lösungen im System und ihre Integration werden geschildert. Fragen
wie nach künftigen Trends (wie z. B. Standardisierung und heterogener Verbund) werden adressiert.

Da sich die Datenbanktechnik immer mehr zur Grundlagentechnologie
entwickelt, erhalten Standard-Anwendungen (4GL-Sprachen, Generatoren)
größeres Gewicht. Der Anwender nutzt hiermit die vermehrt verfügbare
Produktivität.

Anschließend wird die Frage der Datenbankverteilung aus praktischer
Sicht und der Zusammenhang zur unternehmensweiten Datenmodellierung
angesprochen.

<u>TECHNISCHE DATENBANKSYSTEME</u>
<u>FÜR DIE MONTAGEPLANUNG</u>

J. BOIDOL   (IKOSS)

ABSTRACT

Es wird über den Stand einer Anwendungsentwicklung
zur Planung der elektrischen und pneumatischen In-
stallation von Montageanlagen berichtet. Die Entwicklung erfolgt unter einer Softwareentwicklungs-
umgebung und auf Basis der Relationalen Datenbank
ORACLE im Rahmen des BMFT-Projektes PRIMOS
(Konzeption und Auslegung von Montageanlagen, Förder-
kennzeichen 02 FT 16038).

Partner in diesem Projekt sind die Firmen Robert
BOSCH, GMO, IKOSS, FIX-Maschinenbau, TEAM und die
Fraunhoferinstitute IAO und IPA.

Teil 1 und 2 beziehen sich auf gemeinsame Projekter-
gebnisse, Teil 3 auf das PRIMOS-Teilprojekt 7, in
welchem ROBERT BOSCH und IKOSS zusammenarbeiten. Die
Entwicklung im TP7 wird durch ein Expertenteam aus
Anwendern der Firmen Robert BOSCH, FIX-Maschinenbau
und TEAM begleitet.

1.   PROBLEMSTELLUNG

Im BMFT-Projekt PRIMOS wird in Ergänzung zu bestehenden modular gestalteten Montageanlagenkonzepten ein
modular gestaltetes System zur Planung solcher Montageanlagen entwickelt.

Es besteht aus

-   Anwendungsmodulen, welche Aufgabenbereiche der
    Montageanlagenplanung unterstützen

-   Von den spezifischen Anwendungen unabhängigen
    Basissystem-Modulen, welche die Systemressourcen
    für die Anwendungen liefern

Dabei stellen die Anwendungsmodule die Umsetzung von Planungshilfsmitteln dar und werden in Form von manuellen Planungshilfsmitteln bzw. daraus abgeleiteten DV-gestützten Planungshilfsmitteln dem Markt zur Verfügung gestellt.

Wichtigste Komponente des Basissystems ist eine Datenbank, welche zwar anwendungsunabhängig gestaltet ist, jedoch im integrierten System die Basis für die Implementierung der für den Verlauf der Planung notwendigen Fachinformationen (Katalogdaten, Modelldaten) ist.

Die Anwendungsmodule und die Fachdatenbank sollen Anlagenplanern stufenweise zur Verfügung gestellt werden. Sie verbessern und ersetzen auf die Anlagenkonzepte bezogene, konventionelle Planungs- und Informationsmedien.

Folgende Effekte sind dabei zu erwarten:

1. Systematisierung und Übertragbarkeit von Planungs-Know-how

2. Verbesserung der Planungsqualität

3. Reduzierung der Aufwände für Projektierung und Konstruktion von Montageanlagen

4. Aktualität, Sicherheit und Kontrollierbarkeit der Informationen über Angebot und Einsatzspektrum standardisierter Anlagenkomponenten

2. AUFGABENSTRUKTUR

Aus der in 1. dargestellten Problemstellung leitet sich die Aufgabenstruktur für das Projekt ab. Sie war eines der Ergebnisse der Definitionsphase des Projektes, welche im Juli 1986 abgeschlossen wurde.

Hauptaufgabe 1 Entwicklung eines fachlichen Gesamtmodells für die Montageplanung bestehend aus einem funktionalen Modell und einem Datenmodell

Hauptaufgabe 2 Entwicklung eines integrierenden Basissystems zur übergreifenden Aufnahme der im fachlichen Gesamtmodell definierten Anwendungsmodule und Daten

Hauptaufgabe 3   Entwicklung einer Projektstruktur
                   und eines Vorgehensmodells, angepaßt
                   an die fachlichen und organisato-
                   rischen Projekterfordernisse und
                   Auswahl und Anpassung einer Soft-
                   ware-Entwicklungsumgebung an dieses
                   Modell

Die Hauptaufgabe 3 wurde in einer Weise gelöst,
welche sowohl dem PRIMOS-Ziel eines integrierten
Gesamtsystems gerecht wird als auch schnelle Teil-
realisierungen ermöglicht.

Dazu wurde Hauptaufgabe 1 soweit vorangetrieben, daß
das Projekt in auf Einzelanwendungen bezogene Teilprojekte mit stabilen Schnittstellen untereinander
zerlegt werden konnte. Für diese Einzelanwendungen
wurden sodann Teilprojekte definiert, welche von den
einzelnen Partnern arbeitsteilig bearbeitet werden.

In Hauptaufgabe 2 wurden gewisse konzeptionelle und
technischen Vorgaben gemacht, welche die systemtechnische Integration sicherstellen.

Zu den drei Hauptaufgaben selbst wurden die Integra-
tionsprojekte

*   Fachliches Gesamtmodell
*   Basissystem
*   Software-Entwicklungsumgebung

definiert. Die Teilprojekte stehen in ständiger
Wechselwirkung mit den Integrationsprojekten.

2.1   FACHLICHES GESAMTMODELL/SYSTEMÜBERSICHT

Die Leistung des Systems PRIMOS wird zunächst durch
die Abgrenzung im betrieblichen Ablauf definiert
(Bild 1).

Bild 2 zeigt die Hauptfunktion des Systems PRIMOS
(funktionales Modell). Gemäß Teil 1 ist das System
PRIMOS abgestimmt auf die Anforderungen einer
Montageanlagenplanung im Baukastenprinzip.

Die hier dargestellte Übersicht mit hinreichend ver-
feinerten Informationsflüssen bildet nun die Grundlage für die Definition der Teilprojekte (je Hauptfunktion i. w. eines) und die dort stattfindende
weitere Spezifizierung und Umsetzung. Dabei führen
neue Erkenntnisse aus den Teilprojekten und der
Schnittstellenabsprache zwischen den Teilprojekten
immer wieder zur Fortschreibung des funktionalen
Gesamtmodells.

2.2 BASISSYSTEM

In Bild 3 wird die Struktur des Basissystems dargestellt.

Es besteht aus den Komponenten (Systemfunktionen)

1	MMK	(Mensch-Maschine-Kommunikation)
2	ALST	(Ablaufsteuerung)
3X	APMX	(Applikationsmodul X)
4	DBM	(Datenbankmodul)
5	MBS	(Methodenbausteine)
6	Hilfsfunktionen	(z. B. E/A-Funktionen für externe Geräte wie Drucker, Plotter, CAD-Bildschirm, usw.)

2.3 SOFTWARE-ENTWICKLUNGSUMGEBUNG

Es wird projektweit Vorgehensmodell und Methodik
(z. B. strukturierte Systemanalyse, Datennormalisierung nach CODD) des Softwareentwicklungssystems GUIDE
von der Firma GMO eingesetzt. Im Teilprojekt 7, über
welches im nächsten Teil berichtet wird, wurde das
System selbst durchgehend durch alle Phasen mit
Schnittstellen zu ORACLE eingesetzt.

Eine gute Einführung in die benutzten Methoden und
Vorgehensweisen bietet [2].

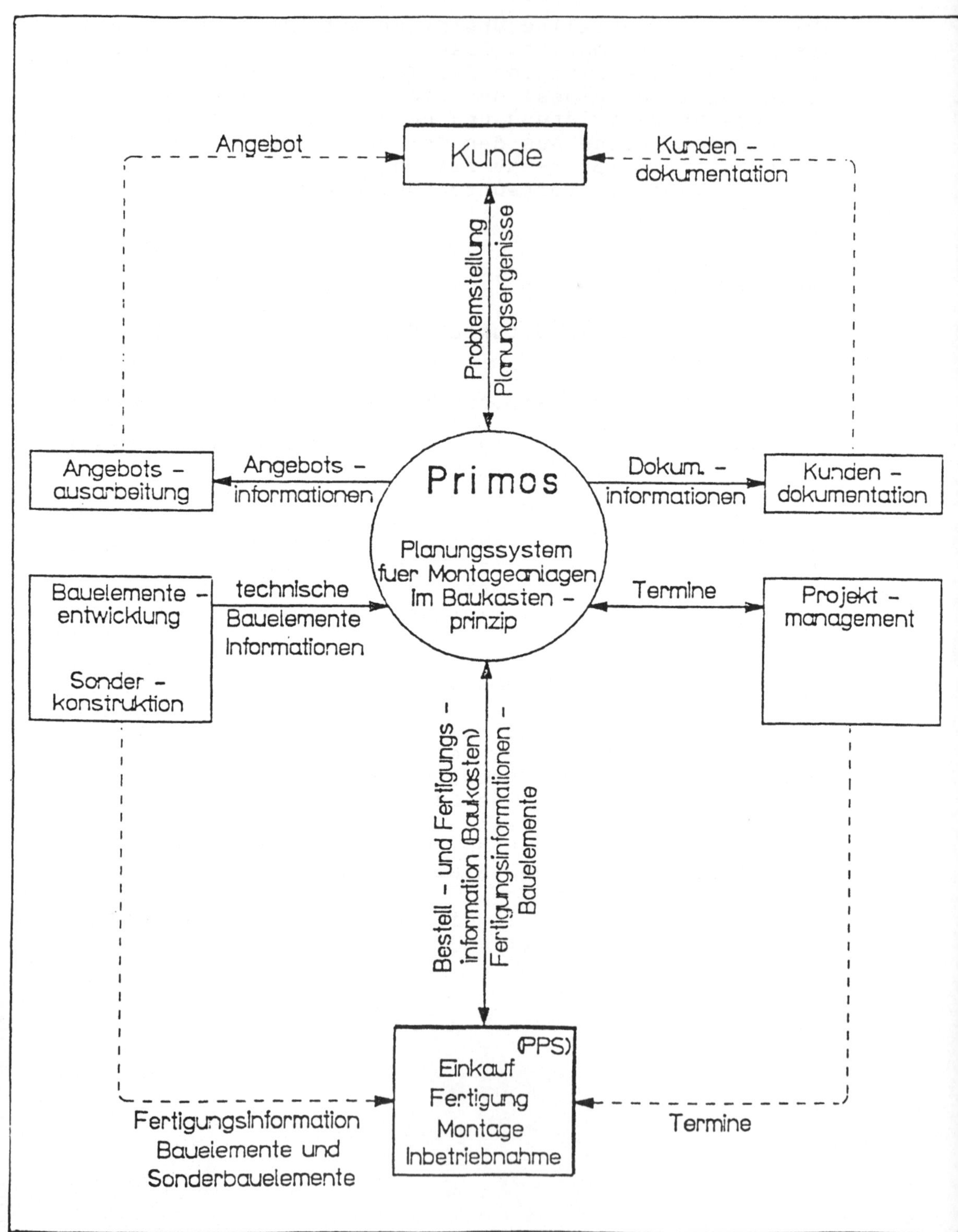

Bild 1: Schnittstellen des Systems PRIMOS

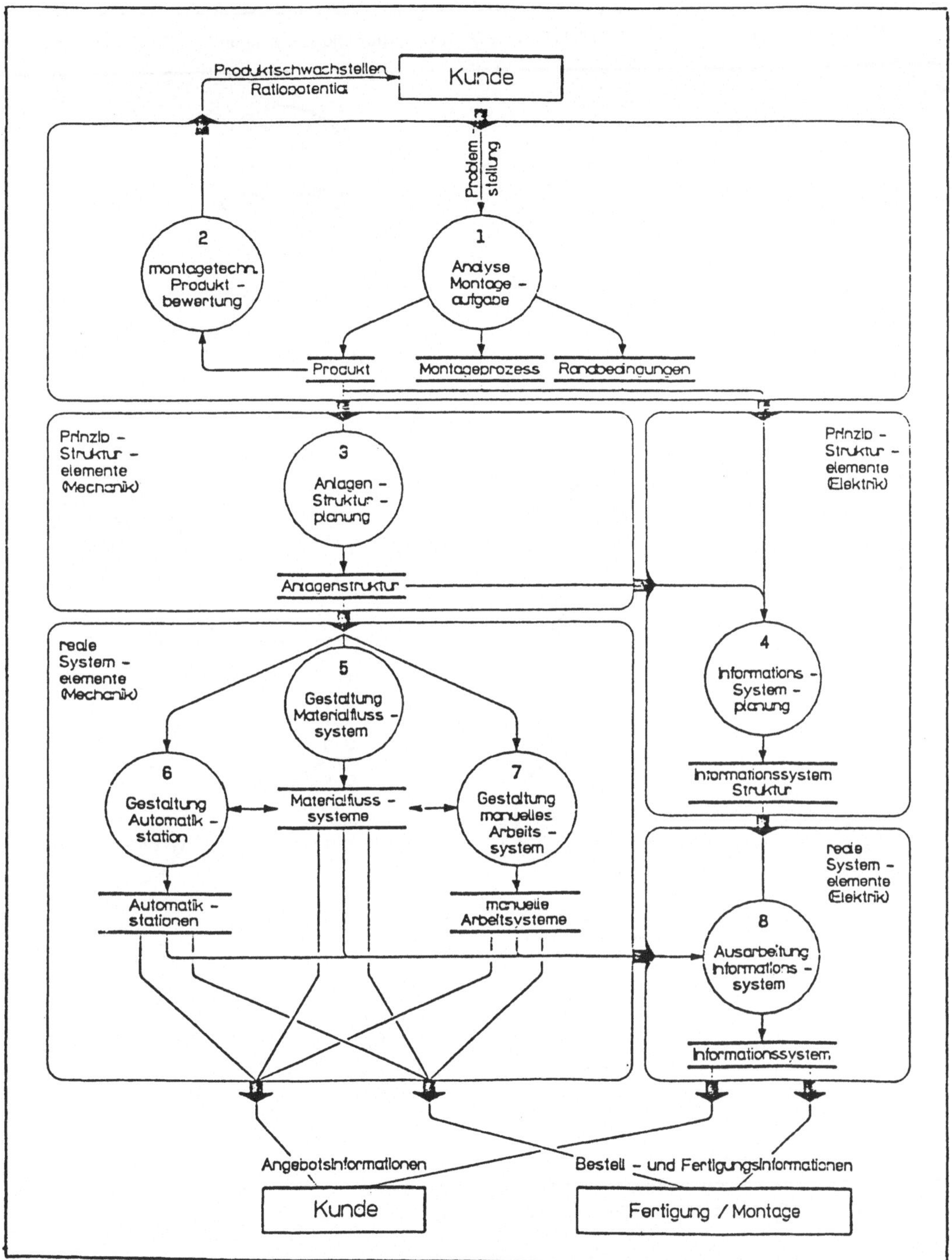

Bild 2: Hauptfunktionen des Systems PRIMOS

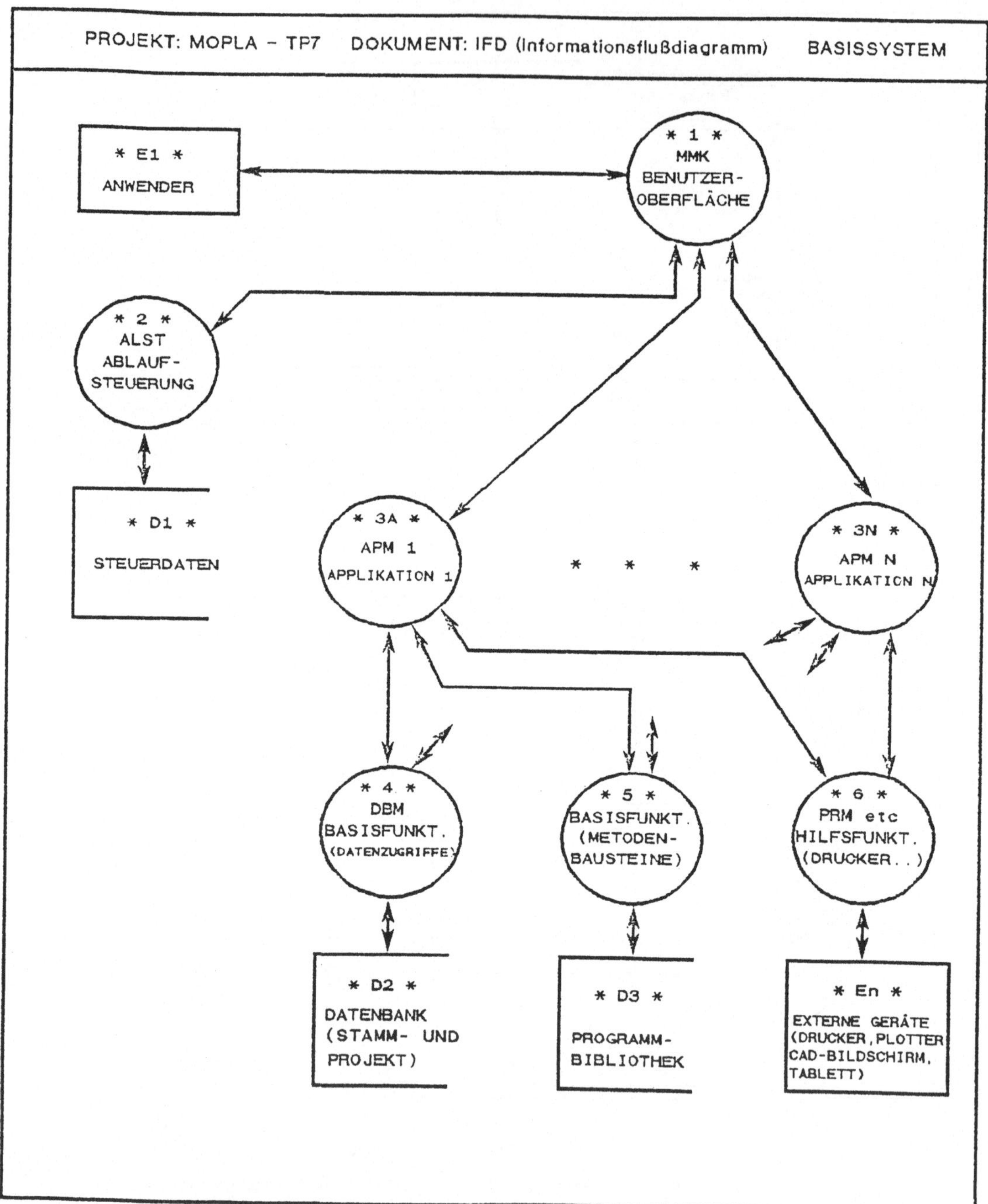

Bild 3: Struktur Basissystem PRIMOS

3. PLANUNG UND GESTALTUNG VON ANLAGENSTEUERUNGSSYSTEMEN

Eines der in Teil 2 dargestellten Projekte ist das
PRIMOS-TP7 'Planung und Gestaltung von Anlagen-
steuerungssystemen', welches die Firma IKOSS feder-
führend in Zusammenarbeit mit ROBERT BOSCH durch-
führt. In diesem Projekt wird das Produkt STsoft –
SOFTware zur Planung und Dokumentation von STeuerungssystemen entwickelt.

Ausgehend von einer steuerungstechnischen Beschreibung der Aktoren und Sensoren einer aus standardisierten bzw. neu konfigurierten Funktionseinheiten
zusammengesetzten Montageanlage wird eine umfassende
Steuerungssystemplanung in einzelnen, abgeschlossenen
Schritten unterstützt.

Mit STsoft können die Aufgaben

o   Planung der pneumatischen und elektrischen An-
     lageninstallation
o   Planung des SPS-Steuerschrank

und in einer zukünftigen Ausbauphase

o   Erstellung der Steuerungssoftware

durchgängig behandelt werden.

Mit Hilfe einer Datenbankanwendung können standardisierte mechanische und steuerungstechnische Anlagenkomponenten von beliebigen Herstellern als
Planungsstandards aufbereitet werden. Im Vergleich
zur freien Anwendung wird dadurch nochmals eine
wesentliche Erhöhung der Planungseffizienz ermöglicht.

STsoft enthält derzeit Planungsstandard für

o   BOSCH-FMS-Baueinheiten
o   BOSCH-elektrisches Steckinstallationssystem
o   BOSCH-Pneumatik-Elemente
o   BOSCH-SPS-Steuerungen

STsoft ist ein offenes und flexibles Programmsystem.
Der Anwender kann jederzeit eigene Planungsstandards
definieren und erstellen.

Funktionselemente können zu Funktionseinheiten (FUE)
zusammengefaßt werden. Die Funktionseinheiten werden
in der Regel analog zu den mechanischen Standard-
Baugruppen gebildet. Damit wird eine durchgängige
Mechanik- und Steuerungssystemplanung möglich.

Auf Basis der Definition für das Mechanik- und Steuerungssystem einer Anlage erfolgt dann die Steuerungssystemplanung entsprechend der systematischen Vorgehensweise unter Berücksichtigung der vordefinierten
Standards.

Das Programmsystem besteht aus folgenden Teilsystemem

o   Projektverwaltung
o   Funktionsschema definieren
o   Anlageninstallation planen
o   Steuerschrank planen

für den weiteren Ausbau sind die Funktionen

o   Funktions-/Ablaufbeschreibung erstellen
o   Steuerungssoftware erstellen

vorgesehen, wobei heute bereits die Schnittstellen
berücksichtigt sind (siehe Bild 4).

Entsprechend dem in Teil 2 beschriebenen Schema ist
die Grundlage des Systems ein fachliches Modell,
welches mittels eines Basissystems realisiert wurde,
mit Hilfe von spezifischen an die Aufgabe und das
Zielsystem angepaßten Software-Entwicklungsmethoden.

3.1   FACHLICHES MODELL

Das Fachliche Modell für das Teilprojekt 7 besteht
aus einem

o   Funktionalen Modell (Bild 5/6)

und einem

o   Datenmodell   (Bild 7 - für 1. Teilrealis.)

Dabei wird im funktionalen Modell die systematische
Vorgehensweise bei der Konstruktion des Steuerungssystem abgebildet (Konstruktionsfunktionen ein-
schließlich Datenaustausch zwischen Funktionen,
Speichern und externen Systemen).

Im Datenmodell sind in integrierter und normalisierter Form die den steuerungsrelevanten Teil des Anlagenmodells wiedergebenden Datenstrukturen sowie die für die konkrete Konstruktion benötigten spezifischen Daten konstanter Art enthalten.

Dies entspricht der Unterscheidung in

o   operationale Daten

und

o   informationelle Daten (z. B. Katalogdaten)

in [3], S. 48.

Funktionales Modell und Datenmodell sind in folgendem Sinne aufeinander bezogen.

o   Das Datenmodell beschreibt globale Struktur und
     Typ der zu speichernden Information

o   Das funktionale Modell beschreibt die auf dem
     Datenmodell durchzuführenden Manipulationen.

Damit ist das integrierte Datenmodell Kernbestandteil des Systems. Die funktionale Oberfläche optimiert nach Abgleich mit der Datennormalisierung die Konstruktionssystematik, hat aber weiterhin organischen Bezug zu der zugrundegelegten Vorgehensweise. Somit werden im System organisatorische Aspekte der verschiedenen am Projekt beteiligten Anwendergruppen und davon unabhängige Modellvorstellungen harmonisch integriert. Das führt natürlich zu einer großen Allgemeinheit des Systems.

3.2   BASISSYSTEM PROTOTYP

Im Rahmen von TP7 wurde zunächst ein Prototyp entwickelt, welcher einen Teil der Funktionalität und des Datenmodells des fachlichen Modells abbildet. Dabei wird die Funktionalität und das Datenmodell, im wesentlichen des Teils der 24V-Installationsplanung und des dafür erforderlichen Teils des Funktionsschemas, exakt abgebildet.

Das Basissystem bzw. die technischen Ausprägungen
seiner Komponenten haben als Kern das DB-System
ORACLE, welches aufgrund einer Datenbank-Marktanalyse
ausgewählt wurde (siehe [1]).

Hauptziele der Prototypentwicklung waren

o   möglichst rasche Bereitstellung der Funktionali-
     tät für die Pilotanwender zur Verifikation des
     fachlichen Modells

o   Erprobung von ORACLE als DB-Komponente für das
     Zielsystem und danach Festschreibung von ORACLE

o   Vorwegnahme und Erprobung der Methodik für die
     Gesamtentwicklung

o   weitere Spezifikation und danach Festschreibung
     der übrigen Basissystem-Komponenten.

Für die nicht der Datenbank zugehörigen Basissystem-
komponenten wurden zunächst bis zur Klärung der oben
angeführten Punkte Einschränkungen in Kauf genommen.
Nach Abschluß und Auswertung der Prototypentwicklung
wird das Ziel-Basissystem dann projektweit endgültig
festgelegt. Aus diesem Grund wurde auch weitgehend
hardware- und betriebssystemunabhängig auf dem IBM-PC
mit Portierungsmöglichkeit z. B. auf VAX bzw. UNIX-
Systeme entwickelt. Das haben wir zu erreichen versucht, durch Einsatz von portablen technischen Einheiten für MMK, ALST, DBM und DB, ausgelagerte
C-Applikationsmodule und ausgelagerte (hardwareab-
hängige) Methodenbausteine bzw. Utilities. Die Benutzung insbesondere von ORACLE-FORMS als MMK- bzw.
ALST-Tool, bedeutet eine gewisse Einschränkung der
Komfortatiblität der Benutzerschnittstelle.

Eine angemessene Funktionalität der Benutzeroberfläche unter einem hinreichend allgemeinen Konzept
ist jedoch mit den o.a. Restriktionen voll gegeben
und erlaubt Erweiterungen in Richtung auf

o   Flexiblere Bildschirmgestaltung (z. B. Window-
     Technik, Einbeziehung von Graphik)

o   Flexiblere Benutzersteuerung

Nachdem nunmehr die funktionale Akzeptanz des Systems
hergestellt ist, die technischen Risiken ausgeräumt
und konzeptionelle Überlegungen zum Basissystem ab-
geschlosen sind, können die noch offenen Detailfragen
insbesondere zur MMK bis Projektende "in Ruhe" gelöst
werden.

Insgesamt stellt das Prototyp-Basissystem (in geeig-
neter Interpretation) ein praktikable Umsetzung des
in 2.2 beschriebenen Basissystemkonzeptes dar. Das
Prototyp-Basissystem wird in Bild 8 dargestellt, der
Aufbau eines komplexen Applikationsmoduls unter
ORACLE und ORACLE-FORMS in Bild 9.

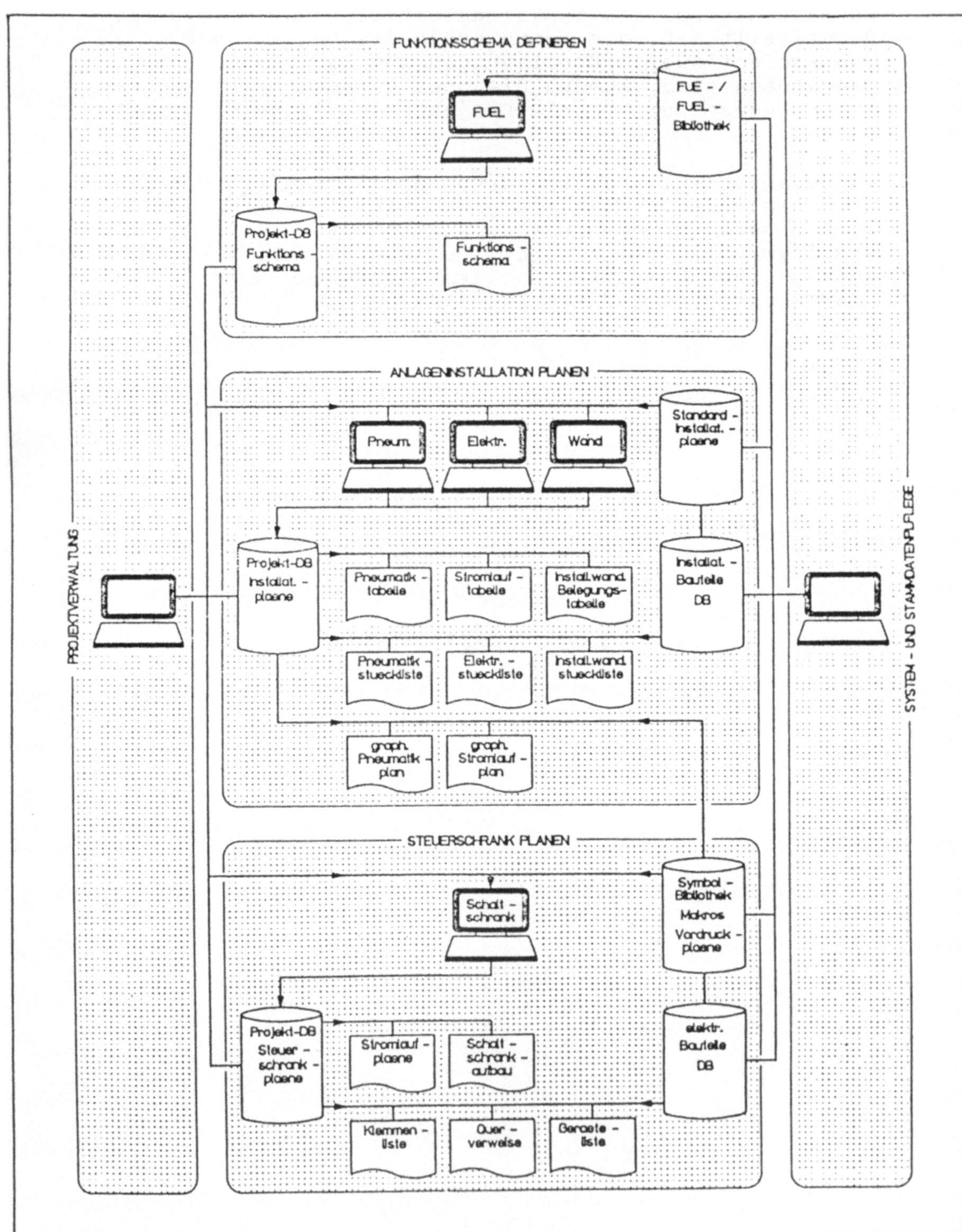

Bild 4: STsoft-Systemstruktur

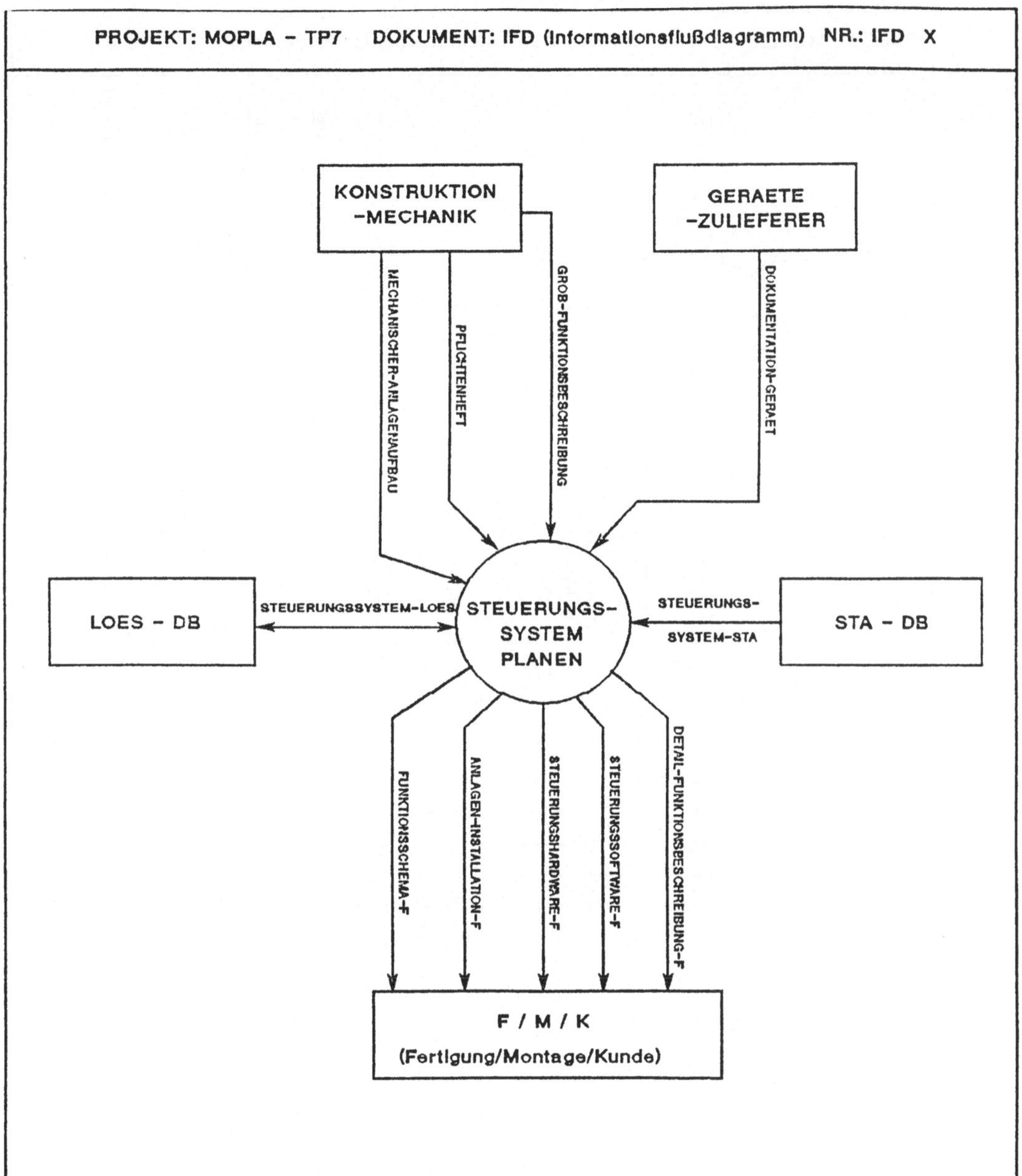

Bild 5:   Schnittstellen des Systems STsoft

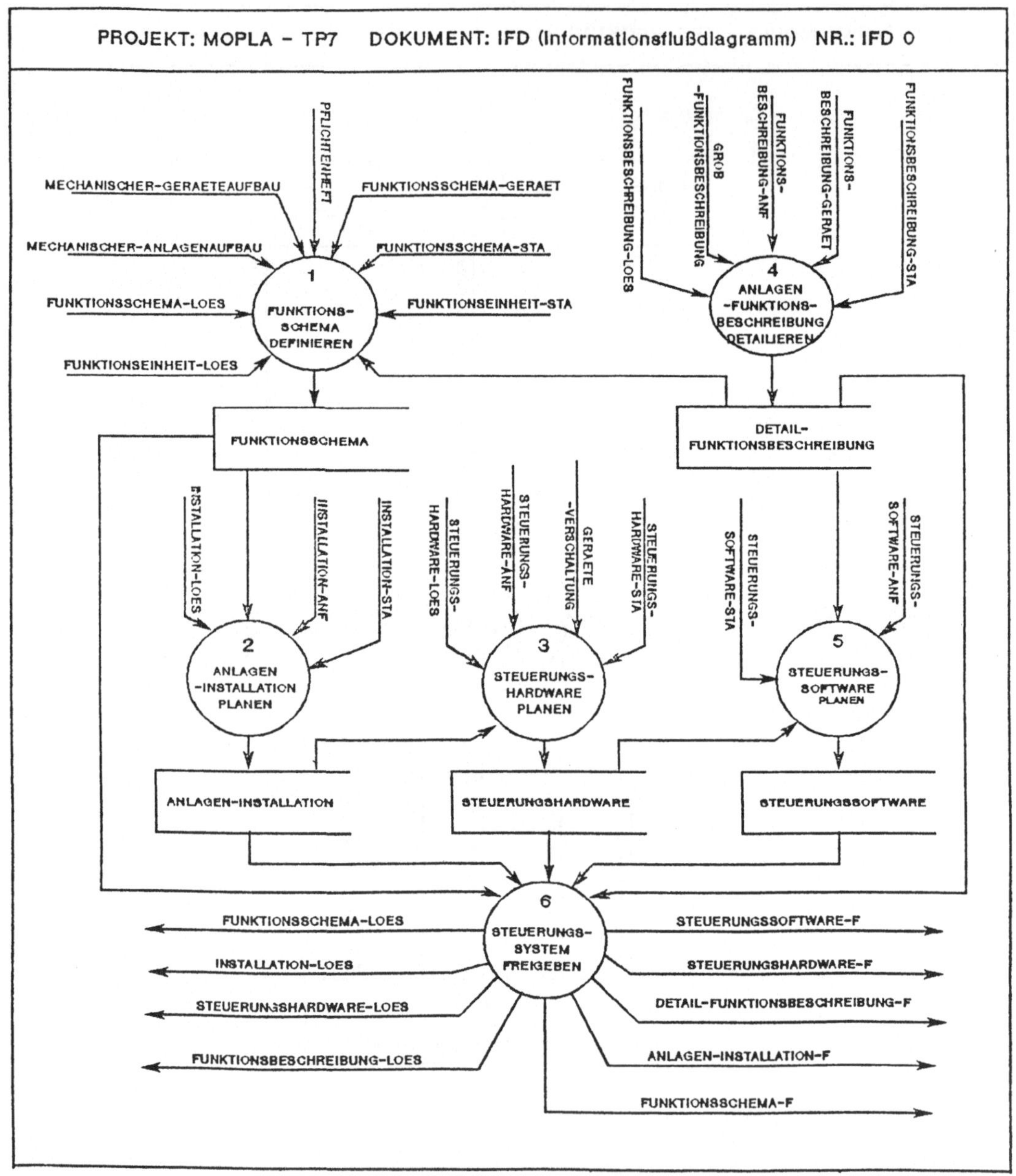

Bild 6:   Hauptfunktionen des Systems STsoft

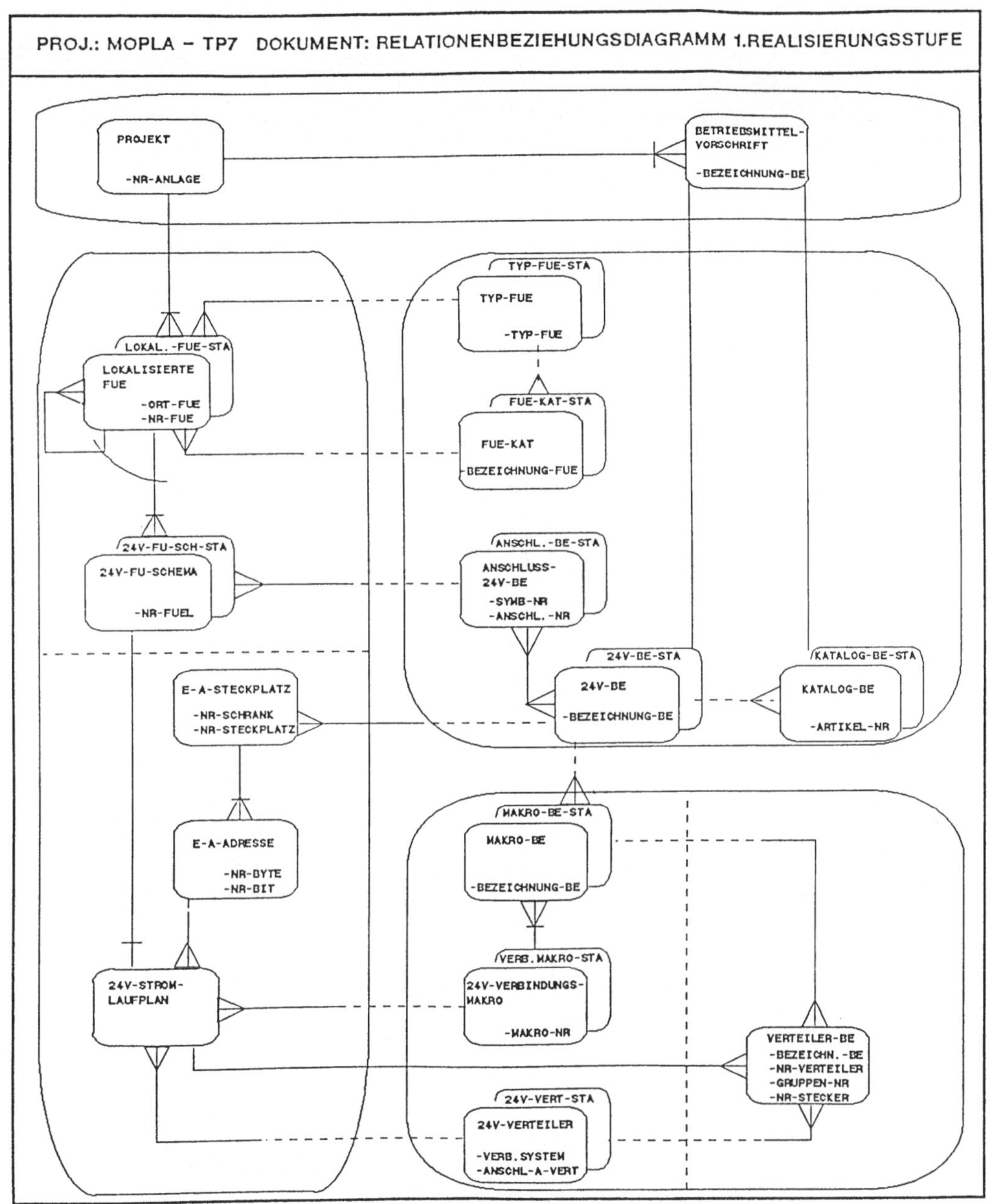

Bild 7:   Logisches Datenmodell des Systems STsoft
(1. Realisierungsstufe)

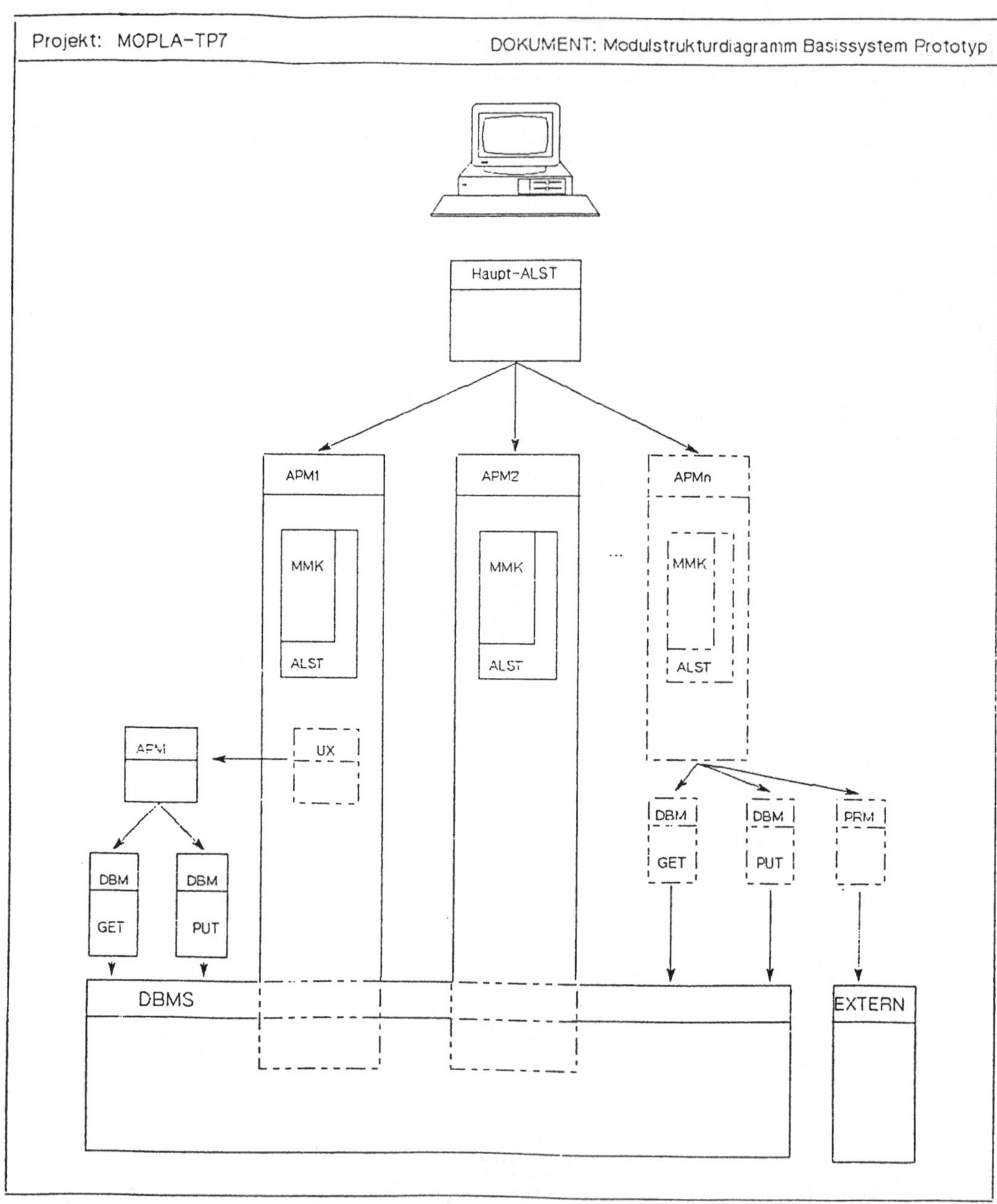

Bild 8:   Architektur Basissystem Prototyp

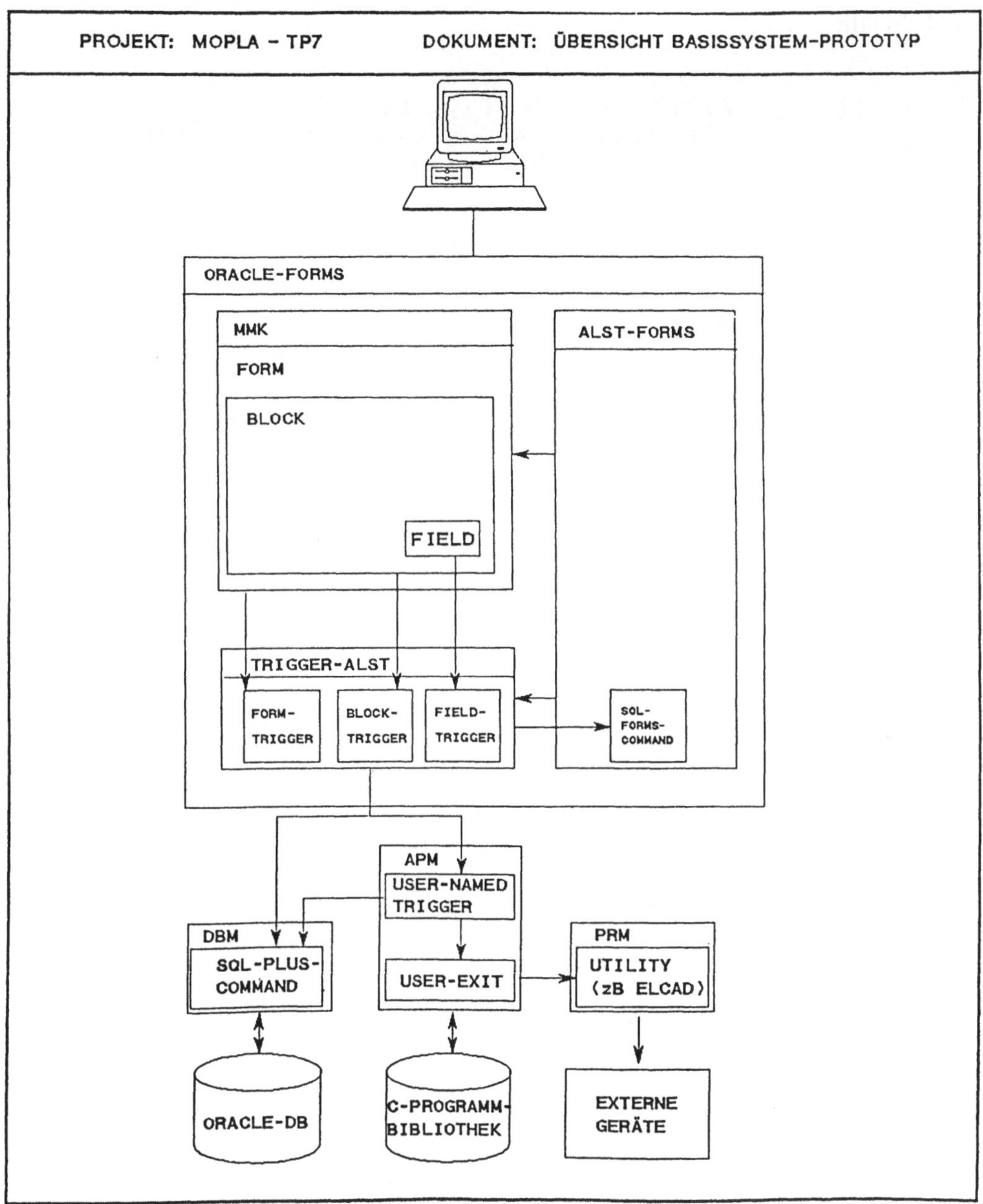

Bild 9:   ORACLE*FORMS-Applikationsmodul für das System STsoft

LITERATUR

(1)   Albrecht, R., Lay, K:
        Die Monageplanung als CIM-Komponente;
        CIM MANAGEMENT 4/86

(2)   DeMarco, Tom:
        Strucured Anaysis and System Specification;
        Prentice-Hall 1979

(3)   Eberlein, W:
        CAD-DAtenbanksystem; Springer-Verlag 1984

(4)   Encarnacao, J., Schlechtendahl, E.G.:
        Computer Aided Design; Springer-Verlag 1983

Eine Software-Produktionsumgebung zur Erstellung kommerzieller Anwendungssoftware für verteilte Systeme

Dietmar Eichstaedt, ADV/ORGA F.A. Meyer AG, Wilhelmshaven

Abstract

Moderne Hardwarearchitekturen und steigende Anforderungen der Benutzer von Anwendungssoftware erfordern neue Techniken bei der rationellen Softwareentwicklung. Im Rahmen des Förderprojektes UniBase wurde eine Software-Produktionsumgebung konzipiert und realisiert, die mit Hilfe integrierter Methoden und Werkzeuge den gesamten Prozess der Entwicklung und Wartung von komplexen Software-Produkten unterstützt. Im folgenden Beitrag werden die Anforderungen und Konzepte dargestellt, die eine moderne Software-Produktionsumgebung charakterisieren . Diese Anforderungen und Konzepte sind in der Entwicklung der Werkzeugkette ANIMOS, die von ADV/ORGA als Bestandteil von UniBase entwickelt wird, konsequent berücksichtigt und ergänzt worden.

Moderne Hardware-Infrastrukturen

In zunehmenden Maße werden in zentralen DV-Systemen intelligente Arbeitsplatzrechner (PC's,PS/2 oder UNIX-Workstations) als Endgeräte eingesetzt. PC's sind heute in Preiskategorien gerutscht, die denen "einfacher" Terminals entsprechen, gleichzeitig sind sie multifunktional am Arbeitsplatz verwendbar, als Ersatz z.B. für Schreibsysteme,

Tischrechner oder Telexgeräte. Dies wird dazu führen, daß einfache Terminals in der Zukunft durch Arbeitsplatzsysteme völlig verdrängt werden.

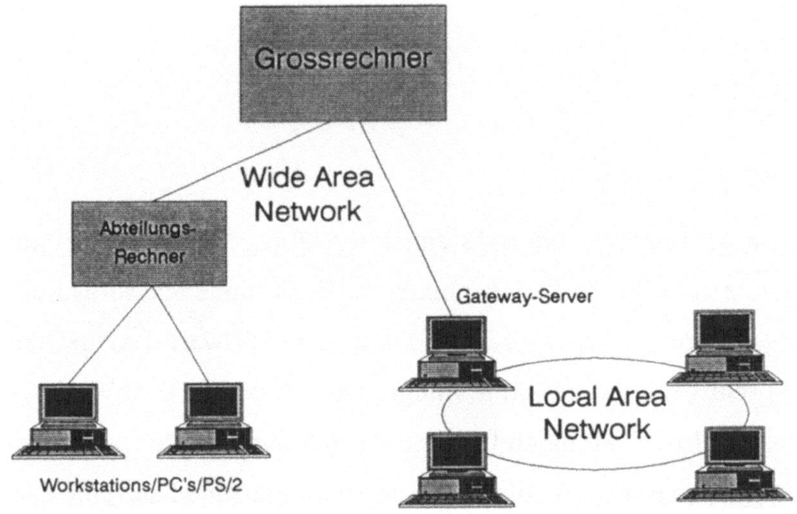

Abb 1. Mögliche Architekturen verteilter Systeme

Diese verteilte Intelligenz erfordert eine neue Software-Architektur, die es ermöglicht, die einzelnen Elemente einer Anwendung zu trennen:

- Benutzungsoberfläche (Dialog-Komponente)

- Prozeß (Anwendungs-Komponente)

- Daten-Organisation

Jede dieser Einzelfunktionen kann auf einer anderen Hardware-Komponente eines verteilten DV-Systems liegen. Da die Rechnernetze unterschiedlicher Technologie sein können, sind hier Schnittstellendefinitionen vorzusehen, die die Übertragung über nahezu beliebige Netze und Betriebsysteme ermöglichen.

Im Rahmen der ANIMOS-Entwicklung wurden Konzepte zur Entwicklungs- und Laufzeitunterstützung aller drei Teilkomponenten einer Anwendung erarbeitet. Die grundlegenden Ideen und Ansätze können hier nur grob erörtert werden.

User Interface Management System (UIMS)

Zur Entwicklung moderner Benutzungsoberflächen sind aufgrund der folgenden Überlegungen einige Grundprinzipien einzuhalten.

Bei dem WYSIWYG-Prinzip (What you see is what you get) wird dem Anwender in mehreren Fenstern z.B. Formulare, Tabellen,Texte oder Skizzen so gezeigt, wie er es von der manuellen Arbeit   am Schreibtisch gewohnt ist.

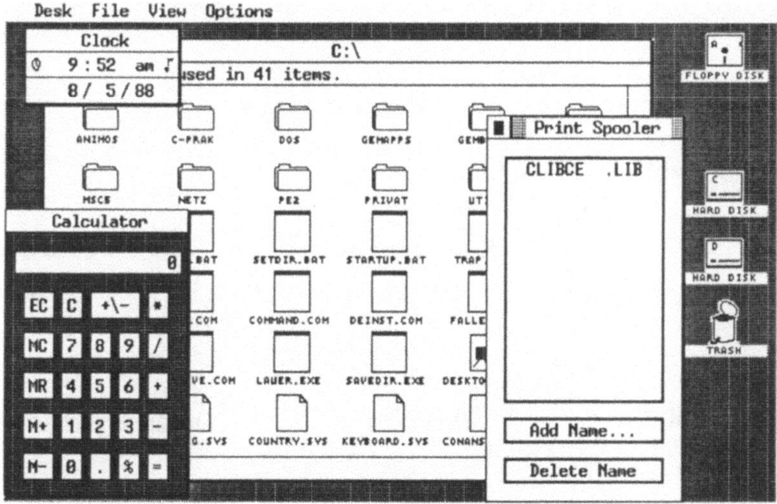

Das Desk-Top-Prinzip erlaubt das parallele Arbeiten an mehreren unterschiedlichen Vorgängen in verschiedenen Fenstern, ähnlich einem Sachbearbeiter der verschiedene Unterlagen und Hilfsmittel zur Erledigung seiner Aufgaben auf seinem Schreibtisch benötigt.

In der Vergangenheit wurde dem Standardsoftware-Anwender dessen Vorgehensweise durch das System vorgegeben. Die Software führt Dialoge mit den Benutzern, d.h. das Programm bestimmt welche Interaktionen zu einem bestimmten Zeitpunkt erlaubt sind und welche nicht, der Anwender wird in seinem Handeln geführt und kontrolliert. Künftige Anwendungssoftware wird mehr dem Werkzeuggedanken folgen, wo mit Hilfe moderner Interaktionstechniken der Benutzer den Dialog führt und bestimmt.

Bei der Betrachtung derzeitiger Softwaresysteme stellt man fest, daß trotz unterschiedlicher Zielsetzungen immer die gleichen Interaktionselemente bei der Bedienung und Anzeige verwendet werden. Solche Funktionen wie z.B. das Auswählen, Kopieren, Positionieren oder Rückgängig machen wurden bisher immer wieder individuell für jedes System neu "erfunden". Hierdurch folgt ein hoher Schulungsaufwand des Benutzers, da er sich bei jeder neuen Software auf eine neue Bedienung einstellen muß.

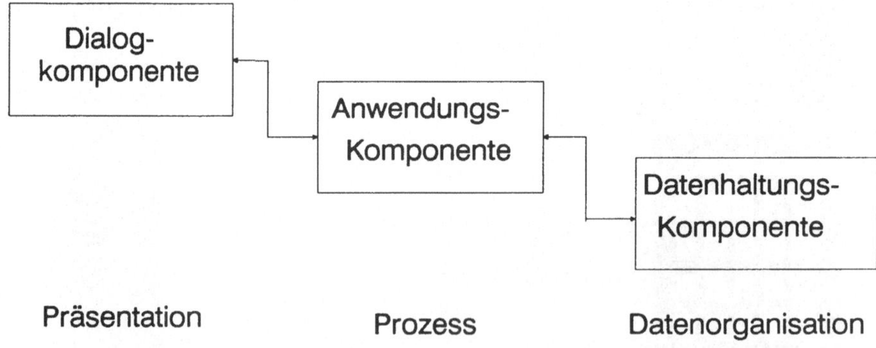

Abb 3. Das "PPD" - Modell

Es existiert also die Möglichkeit viele Elemente der Bedienung zu standardisieren. Dieses wird z.B. im SAA-Konzept (Standard Application Architecture) von IBM mit dem Teil "Common User Access" oder im CAE (Common Application Environment) der X-OPEN-Gruppe berücksichtigt, es gibt in diesen Konzepten Vorschläge zur Standardisierung solcher Softwaresysteme.

Bei den klassischen Dialogprogrammen stellt man fest, das ein sehr großer Teil eines Programmes der Benutzungsoberfläche gewidmet ist und der anwendungsspezifische Teil relativ klein ist.

Aus den genannten Gründen erscheint es sinnvoll die Dialogkomponente gänzlich aus den Programmen herauszulösen und ein Werkzeugsystem zur Verwaltung einer Benutzungsoberfläche zu konzipieren. Dadurch kann ein beträchtlicher Teil des Aufwandes zur Applikatioserstellung vermieden werden. Ein solches System, auch User Interface Management System (UIMS) genannt, muß folgende Anforderungen erfüllen:

- Kosten-Ersparnis bei der Entwicklung interaktiver Systeme

- Bessere Portabilität interaktiver Systeme

- Einheitlichere, konsistentere Benutzungs-Schnittstellen

- Unterstützung des Rapid Prototyping und einer iterativen Entwicklung von Benutzungs-Schnittstellen

- Erstellung/Änderung von Benutzungsoberflächen durch Nichtprogrammierer

Als charakterisierend für ein User Interface Management System sind die folgenden Punkte zu betrachten:

Es erfolgt eine Trennung zwischen der Dialog- und der Anwendungskomponente. Die Applikation ist völlig frei von Dialogelementen, der Dialog wird vollständig vom UIMS geführt und übergibt die aufbereiteten Daten über eine definierte Schnittstelle an die Anwendungskomponente. Durch diese Trennung ist es möglich, innerhalb einer verteilten DV-Umgebung, die Dialogkomponente auf einer intelligenten Workstation laufen zu lassen, während die Anwendungskomponente z.B. auf einem Abteilungsrechner oder einer zentralen DV-Anlage liegt.

Die Kommunikation zwischen Dialog- und Anwendungskomponente erfolgt auf der Basis von Abstraktionen. Hier wird ein objektorientierter Ansatz verwendet, d.h. die Anwendung stellt über die Schnittstelle Objekte dem UIMS zu Verfügung. Die Darstellung und Bearbeitung der Objekte wird durch das UIMS realisiert.Der Anwendung bleibt die Verwaltung der Objekte bezüglich der Präsentation verborgen.

Die Gestaltung eines Dialoges sollte durch ein interaktives Werkzeug möglich sein, damit eine großtmögliche Flexibilität der Benutzungsoberfläche erhalten bleibt. Dieses Werkzeug erlaubt dem Anwender ohne Programmierkenntnisse "seine" Benutzungsoberfläche selbst zu erstellen, ohne daß komplizierte Änderungen in bestehenden Quellprogrammen notwendig sind.Der entworfene Dialog wird in Form einer Resouce-Datei gespeichert die später während des Anwendungslaufes durch das UIMS gelesen und ausgeführt wird.

Die Steuerung des Dialogablaufes erfolgt durch das UIMS gemäß der interaktiv erstellten Dialogspezifikation. Die Informationen über die Dialogelmente werden vom UIMS aus der Resource-Datei gelesen und interpretiert. Es werden z.B.Fenster mit Menüleisten und Hilfefenstern aktiviert, genau in der Form wie sie vorher spezifiziert wurden. Die Dialogkomponente ruft die Anwendungskomponente als Funktionen auf, diese können in üblichen Programmiersprachen wie z.B. Cobol oder C codiert werden. Vorteil dieser Vorgehensweise ist, daß die fertige Benutzungsoberfläche mit Abschluß des Dialogdesigns zur Verfügung steht, es ist somit ein sehr schnelles Rapid-Prototyping möglich.Weiterhin sind Anpassungen der Benutzungsoberfläche sehr elegant möglich, ohne das die Anwendung komplizierte Compiler- oder Linkvorgänge durchlaufen muß.

Ein weiteres Hilfsmittel ist ein umfangreiches Formular-System, welches sowohl die Erstellung und Speicherung beliebiger Formulare als auch die Bearbeitung eines definierten Formulars erlaubt. Auch hier ist eine Schnittstelle vorhanden, die die Ergebnisfelder an eine dahinterstehende Applikation weiterreicht.

Syntaxorientierter System-/Programmentwurf

Welche Anforderungen sind an eine Software-Entwicklungsmethode zu stellen ?

Eine Software-Entwicklungsmethode soll den Entwickler sowohl in der Systementwicklung als auch in der Einzelprogrammentwicklung unterstützen und zu einer eindeutigen und nachvollziehbaren Lösung führen.

Sie muß eine Hilfestellung bieten, die den Entwickler von der Aufgabe bis zum Ziel begleitet, und durch eine methodische Unterstützung quasi eine Lösung garantiert.

Programme sollten unabhängig vom Programmierer sein, unterschiedliche Personen müssen zu annähernd gleichen Ergebnissen kommen, um den Aufwand für Wartungsarbeiten zu minimieren.

Das durch die Methode entstandene Programm sollte in sich schlüssig und selbstdokumentierend sein, um den zusätzlichen Dokumentationsaufwand so gering wie möglich zu halten.

Die Entwicklungsmethode ist durch Werkzeuge zu unterstützen, um den Aufwand, der durch den Methodeneinsatz entsteht, zu minimieren.

Selbst wenn nicht alle dieser Idealvorstellungen durch eine Methode erfüllt werden, so ist es dennoch heute für die Softwareindustrie kaum vertretbar, von den "intuitiven Programmierleistungen" einzelner Entwickler abhängig zu sein.

Im Rahmen der ANIMOS-Realisierung wird von ADV/ORGA eine Methode entwickelt, die die Vorteile bekannter Entwicklungsmethoden kombiniert und erweitert. Sie orientiert sich sehr stark an der JSD-Methode (Jackson System Development), aber auch andere Methoden wie z.B. SADT (Structured Analysis and Design Technic) nahmen Einfluß auf die Entwicklung.

Die Systementwicklungsmethode wird durch ein leistungsfähiges Werkzeug unterstützt. In der Hauptsache besteht das Werkzeug aus einem leistungsstarken Struktureditor, der die Notation der Entwicklungsmethode auf einfache Weise graphisch erstellen und Pflegen hilft.

Für den Einzelprogrammentwurf wurde eine Methode konzipiert die als Basis die JSP-Methode (Jackson Structured Programming) beinhaltet. Diese Methode wurde jedoch um einige wichtige Elemente erweitert, wie etwa die Rekursion oder die Implementation quasiparaller Prozesse. Ziel dieser Methode ist es, eine Vorgehensweise für die Einzelprogrammentwicklung zu entwerfen, die dem Entwickler eine unverzichtbare

Hilfestellung beim Design von Softwareprodukten gibt, und alle wichtigen Elemente der Programmierung berücksichtigt.

Die Werkzeugunterstützung zur Entwicklung der Einzelprogramme muß am umfassendsten sein, um den Entwurf von lesbarer und klar strukturierter Software zu gewährleisten. Während eines jeden Schrittes des Programmdesigns soll das Werkzeug eine unverzichtbare Hilfestellung bieten. Das beginnt mit der Definition von Input und Output des Programms, geht über die Komposition der Programmstruktur und dem Einbringen von Anweisungen und endet letztendlich mit der Generierung von Quellcode für das Zielsystem.Der Quellcode sollte automatisch aus der Programmstruktur durch das Werkzeug generiert werden. Zur Unterstützung verschiedener Zielsprachen und -systeme muß die Programmstruktur völlig unabhängig von der Zielumgebung sein. Um dies zu ermöglichen wird eine werkzeuginterne Darstellungsform (Pseudocode) gewählt, die dann durch verschiedene Generatoren den Quellcode für die gewünschten Zielprogrammiersprachen und Zielsysteme erzeugt.

<u>Datenorganisation in verteilten Systemen</u>

Ein wichtiges Kriterium der Datenorganisation ist die weitestgehende Portabilität bezüglich der vorhandenen Datenbank-Systeme. Um dies zu erreichen ist es sinnvoll, eine standardisierte Datenbank-Manipulations-Sprache zu wählen. Als Standard für relationale Datenbanken hat sich SQL (Standard Query Language) herauskristallisiert, z.B. im SAA-Konzept. In der Praxis sind jedoch noch viele nichtrelationale DB-Systeme im Einsatz. Zur Steuerung dieser Systeme sind Schnittstellen erforderlich, die SQL-Befehle auf die real vorhandene Datenbank abbilden.
Innerhalb von ANIMOS wurde hier ein SQL-Zugriffsinterpreter konzipiert, der zusätz-

lich zur Unterstützung verschiedener DB-Systeme den Zugriff über verschiedene Netze erlaubt. Hierdurch ist es z.B. möglich, die Anwendungskomponente auf einer Workstation zu halten, während die Datenspeicherung auf einem zentralen System erfolgen kann.

Zum komfortablen Erstellen von SQL-Befehlen dient ein interaktives Werkzeug. Durch einen menuegeführten Dialog mit einfachen Ankreuz- und Auswahlmöglichkeiten werden SQL-Befehle generiert, die wahlweise entweder direkt ausgeführt werden können oder in Programme eingebunden werden.

Als weiteres Hilfsmittel für den Datenbank-Betrieb steht ein portables, aktives Software-Dictionary zur Verfügung. Die Anforderungen an ein solches Software-Dictionary als Voraussetzung für eine breite Anwendbarkeit als Systemprodukt sind durch folgende Punkte zu charakterisieren:

Es sollte eine größtmögliche Portabilität hinsichtlich der zu unterstützenden Datenbanksysteme, der vorhandenen Systemsoftware und der existierenden Hardware-Architekturen gewährleistet sein.

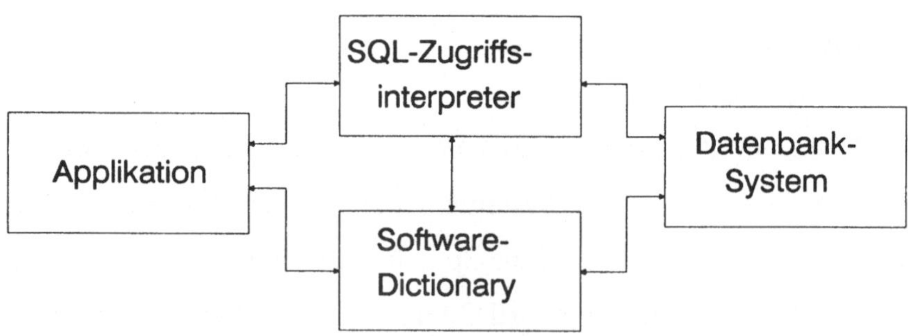

Abb 4. ANIMOS-Datenbankbetriebs-Werkzeuge

Das Design einer Datenbank sollte durch Werkzeuge unterstützt werden, sowohl für relationale, hierarchische und Netzwerk-Datenbanksysteme. Alle entstehenden Metadaten wie Namen, Größen, Typen usw. müssen automatisch in die Metadatenbank aufgenommen werden.

Der Entwurf einer Datenbank erfolgt innerhalb von ANIMOS nach dem Verfahren nach Bonczek, Holsapple und Whinston und wird durch ein graphisches Werkzeug unterstützt, welches direkt die Metadaten für das Software-Dictionary erzeugt und dort einstellt. Weitere Hilfsprogramme erlauben das automatische Anlegen von Datenbanken aus den Einträgen der Metadatenbank heraus.

Zusammenfassung

Der wichtigste Aspekt der entstandenen Konzepte besteht in der Verlagerung von Software, die sonst individuell jedesmal gebaut werden müßte, in den System-Software-Bereich. Sehr deutlich wird dieser Trend bei dem User Interface Managment System, mit dessen Hilfe der Anwendung jegliche Dialogführung abgenommen wird. Aber auch der Betrieb der Datenbank wird mit Hilfe intelligenter Schnittstellen und durch Einsatz eines zur Laufzeit aktiven Softwaredictionarys sehr viel komfortabler, ohne jedoch die Applikation stark zu belasten.

Mit ANIMOS steht eine Werkzeugfamilie zur Verfügung, die die dargestellten Konzepte realisiert und alle technischen Bereiche der Software-Entwicklung unterstützt:

- Benutzungsoberflächen-Implementierung incl. Dialogsteuerung

- Graphischer System- und Programm-Entwurf

- Graphischer Datenbank-Entwurf nach der Entity-Relationship-Modelling-Methode

Für die Laufzeitunterstützung der Anwendungssoftware sind weitere ANIMOS-Komponenten vorgesehen:

- Datenbank-Zugriffsgenerator zur menuegeführten Generierung von SQL-Befehlen

- Datenbank-Zugriffsinterpreter (Schnittstellen) zur Umsetzung von SQL-Befehlen auf alle gängigen, auch nicht-relationale Datenbank-Systeme, inclusive Unterstützung verteilter Systeme

- Aktives, portables Software-Dictionary

Geplant ist die durchgängige Unterstützung der Betriebssyteme MS-DOS, OS-2 und UNIX auf der Workstation-Seite, sowie alle gängigen Host-Betriebssysteme der IBM und Siemens-Welt.

Literaturverzeichnis

W. Hübner, G.Lux-Mülders, M. Muth
THESEUS - Die Benutzungsoberfläche der UniBase-Softwareentwicklungsumgebung
Springer-Verlag, 1987

Systems Application Architecture Library
International Business Machines Corporation, 1987

Michael A. Jackson
System Development
Prentice-Hall, 1982

Michael A. Jackson
Principles of Program Design
Academic Press, 1975

Robert H. Bonczek, Clyde W. Holsapple, Andrew B. Whinston:
Micro Database Management
Academic Press, 1984

Jackson System Development mit Speedbuilder

Eine toolgestützte Methode zur Spezifikation und Implementierung verteilter Systeme

Wolfgang George und Christiane Kapteina
c/o ExperTeam GmbH Eupener Straße150, 5000 Köln 41

Zusammenfassung

Die Systementwicklungsmethode Jackson System Development (JSD) dient zur Spezifikation von Systemen in Form kommunizierender sequentieller Prozesse sowie der Implementierung derartiger Systeme. Ausgangsbasis für die eigentliche Systemspezifikation ist dabei ein Modell des systemrelevanten Realitätsausschnitts. Die Beschreibung dieses Modells ist der erste Schritt der Systementwicklung nach JSD.

Summary

Jackson System Development (JSD) ist a method for the specification of systems in terms of communicating/cooperating sequential processes (CSP). It also tackles the implementation of such systems. As a basis for the specification task, a real world model is used, which is developed at the begin of a JSD project.

Hinweis:

Alle Abbildungen sind mit Hilfe der Jackson-Tools Speedbuilder und JSP-TOOL erzeugt worden.

1.   Überblick

Jackson System Development (JSD) ist eine Systementwicklungsmethode, die in den Jahren 1978-1982 von Michael A. Jackson und John R. Cameron (Michael Jackson Systems Ltd, London) erarbeitet wurde. Die schon vorher bekannte Programmentwurfsmethode Jackson-Strukturierte-Programmierung (JSP) wurde dabei integraler Bestandteil von JSD. Grob kann eine Systementwicklung nach JSD in drei Phasen eingeteilt werden:

*   Modellbildung
*   Spezifikation
*   Implementierung

Die Entwicklung eines Modells wird bei JSD als separate Phase der eigentlichen Systemspezifikation vorangestellt. Dabei lautet die wesentliche Fragestellung: "Welche Aspekte der Realität sind für das neue System relevant?". Dieser expliziten Beschreibung der "realen Welt" wird nach Meinung der JSD-Väter bei traditionellen Systementwicklungsmethoden zu wenig Bedeutung beigemessen.

2.   Die JSD-Entwicklungsphasen und ihre Unterstützung durch die Jackson-Tools Speedbuilder und JSP-TOOL

2.1   Modellbildung

In der Phase Modellbildung werden diejenigen Ereignisse (Vorgänge, Aktionen) definiert, die in der bestehenden oder - wie z. B. bei einem Embedded System - zu schaffenden Realität für das zu entwickelnde System relevant sind.

Beispiele hierfür sind

- bei einem Verwaltungssystem für eine Leihbibliothek
  - Buch erwerben
  - Buch verkaufen
  - Ausleihfrist verlängern
  - Buch zurückgeben
  - Buch zum Binden ausliefern
- bei einer Liftsteuerung
  - Knopf drücken zur Lift-Anforderung
  - Ankommen des Lifts an einem Stockwerk
  - Verlassen eines Stockwerks durch den Lift

Diese Ereignisse werden exakt definiert, so daß eine gemeinsame Verständigungsbasis zwischen Softwarespezialisten und Auftraggebern (z. B. Fachbereich) geschaffen wird. Außerdem werden die Ereignisse einzelnen Objekten (Entities, Entitäten) zugeordnet, die diese Ereignisse ausführen (oder an denen die entsprechenden Ereignisse/Aktionen ausgeführt werden).

Speedbuilder unterstützt das Erfassen dieser Informationen auf eine sehr kompakte, weitgehend redundanzfreie Weise. Alle Systembestandteile werden in der Speedbuilder-Spezifikationsdatenbank systematisch anhand eines vom Werkzeug generierten Rasters beschrieben.

Systembestandteile, die an anderer Stelle bereits beschrieben sind, werden von Speedbuilder automatisch referenziert und entsprechend gekennzeichnet.

Aus diesen einzelnen Beschreibungen kann man mit der Report-Funktion von Speedbuilder die unterschiedlichsten Dokumente erzeugen (vgl. Abb. 1 und 2).

```
LIFT.EN;1.6

ENTITY LIFT
   REFERENCE LIFT
   CLASSIFICATION
   SUMMARY
      Im vorliegenden System zu steuernder Lift.
   NARRATIVE no
   IDENTIFIER
      VARIABLE LIFT-NR
         TYPE LIFT-NR
   ACTION-LIST
      ACTION ANKOMMEN
      ACTION VERLASSEN
   CONSTRAINTS
      Die Variable Stockwerk-Nr hat den Wertebereich 0 ...
      top. Bei zwei aufeinanderfolgenden Stockwerken, die der
      Lift besucht, darf die Stockwerk-Nr maximal um 1
      differieren.
   STRUCTURE-LINK
   PROCESS-LINK
```

Abb. 1: Eingaben in Speedbuilder

```
Entity: LIFT                                                    Classification:

Summary: Im vorliegenden System zu steuernder Lift.


Identifier: LIFT-NR                        State Vector: AKTUELLES-STOCKWERK
                                                         VORHERIGES-STOCKWERK


Action                Attributes              Definition
------                ----------              ----------
ANKOMMEN              STOCKWERK-NR            Ankommen des Lifts an einem bestimmten Stockwerk m von
                      LIFT-NR                oben oder von unten. Ankommen ist definiert als das
                                             Erreichen des Bereiches +- 15 cm um die Ruheposition
                                             eines Stockwerks.
                                             Ankommen heißt nicht notwendigerweise, daß der Lift an
                                             diesem Stockwerk anhält.


Action                Attributes              Definition
------                ----------              ----------
VERLASSEN             STOCKWERK-NR           Verlassen eines bestimmten Stockwerks m durch den Lift
                      LIFT-NR                nach oben oder nach unten. Der Lift verläßt den Bereich
                                             +- 15 cm um die Ruheposition eines Stockwerks.
                                             Beachte, daß keine Richtung angegeben ist.
```

Abb. 2:   von Speedbuilder generierte Dokumentation; hier: Beschreibung zum Objekt "Lift"

Bei der Modellbildung in JSD wird ein besonderes Gewicht auf die Beschreibung dynamischer Aspekte des relevanten Realitätsausschnitts gelegt. So wird für jedes Objekt ein sogenanntes Objektstrukturdiagramm erstellt, das die zeitlichen Beziehungen zwischen den Ereignissen/Aktionen eines Objektes definiert.

Als Darstellungstechnik für Objektstrukturdiagramme dienen die von JSP her bekannten Jackson-Baumdiagramme (zur Erinnerung: "*" kennzeichnet wiederholtes Auftreten einer Komponente, "o" kennzeichnet, daß Komponenten Alternativen darstellen, keine Kennzeichnung haben Komponenten, die zeitlich nacheinander - von links nach rechts zu interpretieren - auftreten).

Zur Erfassung dieser Objektstrukturen wird das Werkzeug JSP-TOOL benutzt. Aus der Objektbeschreibung in Speedbuilder kann man über "STRUCTURE-LINK" JSP-TOOL unmittelbar aufrufen. Die erfaßten Strukturen sind Bestandteil der Speedbuilder-Spezifkationsdatenbank und werden wie die übrigen Teile der Systembeschreibung verwaltet.

```
BUCH.EN;1.1

ENTITY BUCH
    REFERENCE BU
    CLASSIFICATION PHYSISCH
    SUMMARY
        Ein Buch in der Bibliothek.
    NARRATIVE no
    IDENTIFIER
        VARIABLE IDENTIFIER
            TYPE BUCH-ID
    ACTION-LIST
        ACTION ERWERBEN
        ACTION BIND-EINLIEFERN
        ACTION BIND-AUSLIEFERN
        ACTION NORM-AUSLEIHEN
        ACTION VERLAENGERN
        ACTION RESVN-AUSLEIHEN
        ACTION ZURUECKGEBEN
        ACTION VERKAUFEN
        ACTION EINLIEFERN
        ACTION AUSLIEFERN
    CONSTRAINTS
    STRUCTURE-LINK
    PROCESS-LINK
```

Abb. 3: Eingaben in Speedbuilder

```
Diagram:
```

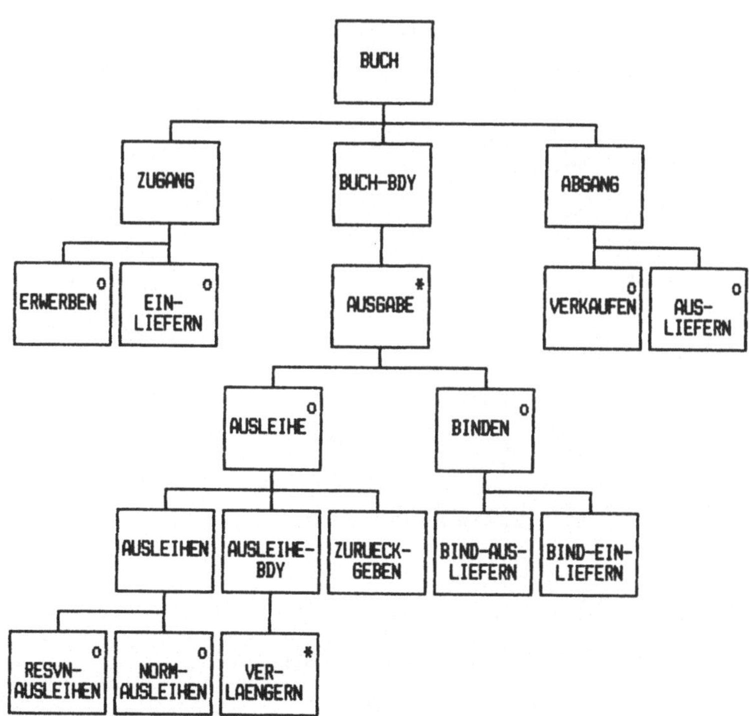

Abb. 4:   mit JSP-TOOL erstellte Objektstruktur

Zur Beschreibung eines Objekts gehört auch die Festlegung der Objektattribute, die in der Folgephase als lokale Variablen der Objektprozesse deren sogenannten Statusvektor (state vector) bilden.

Die Objektprozesse werden ähnlich wie Objekte und Aktionen mit Speedbuilder beschrieben.

Über "STRUCTURE-LINK" ruft man, ähnlich wie bei der Objektbeschreibung, das Werkzeug JSP-TOOL auf und beschreibt den Porzeßalgorithmus in Form von Jackson-Baumdiagrammen.

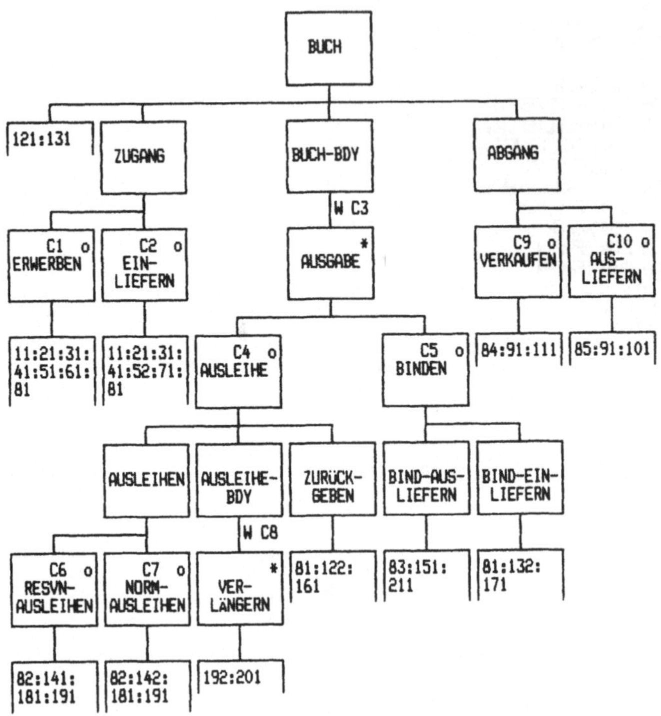


```
Operation List:                                          Condition List:

80.[  0]        *WO                                        C1.[  1]      ERWERBEN
81.[  4]          SET WO TO IN-BIBL                        C2.[  1]      EINLIEFERN
82.[  2]          SET WO TO AUSGELIEHEN                    C3.[  1]      AUSLEIHEN OR BIND-AUSLIEFERN
83.[  1]          SET WO TO BUCHBINDEREI                   C4.[  1]      AUSLEIHEN
84.[  1]          SET WO TO VERKAUFT                       C5.[  1]      BIND-AUSLIEFERN
85.[  1]          SET WO TO IM-AUSTAUSCH                   C6.[  1]      RESVN-AUSLEIHEN
90.[  0]        *AUS-DATUM (IF WO = VERKAUFT OR IM-AUSTAUSCH)  C7.[  1]  NORM-AUSLEIHEN
91.[  2]          STORE AUS-DATUM                          C8.[  1]      VERLÄNGERN
100.[  0]       *NACH-BIBL (IF WO = IM-AUSTAUSCH)          C9.[  1]      VERKAUFEN
101.[  1]         STORE NACH-BIBL FROM AUSLIEFERN.ZIEL-BIBL  C10.[  1]   AUSLIEFERN
110.[  0]       *BETRAG (IF WO = VERKAUFT)
111.[  1]         STORE BETRAG FROM VERKAUFEN.VK-PREIS
120.[  0]       *N-LEIH
121.[  1]         SET N-LEIH TO ZERO
122.[  1]         ADD ONE TO N-LEIH
130.[  0]       *N-BIND
131.[  1]         SET N-BIND TO ZERO
```

Abb. 5: mit JSP-TOOL erstellte Prozeßstuktur

2.2   Spezifikation

Die Spezifikation des zu entwickelnden Systems erfolgt bei JSD in Form eines Netzwerks kommuni-
zierender/kooperierender sequentieller Prozesse (CSP). Ein derartiges Netz wird zunächst graphisch
mit Systemspezifikationsdiagrammen (SSDs) entworfen (vgl. Abb. 6).

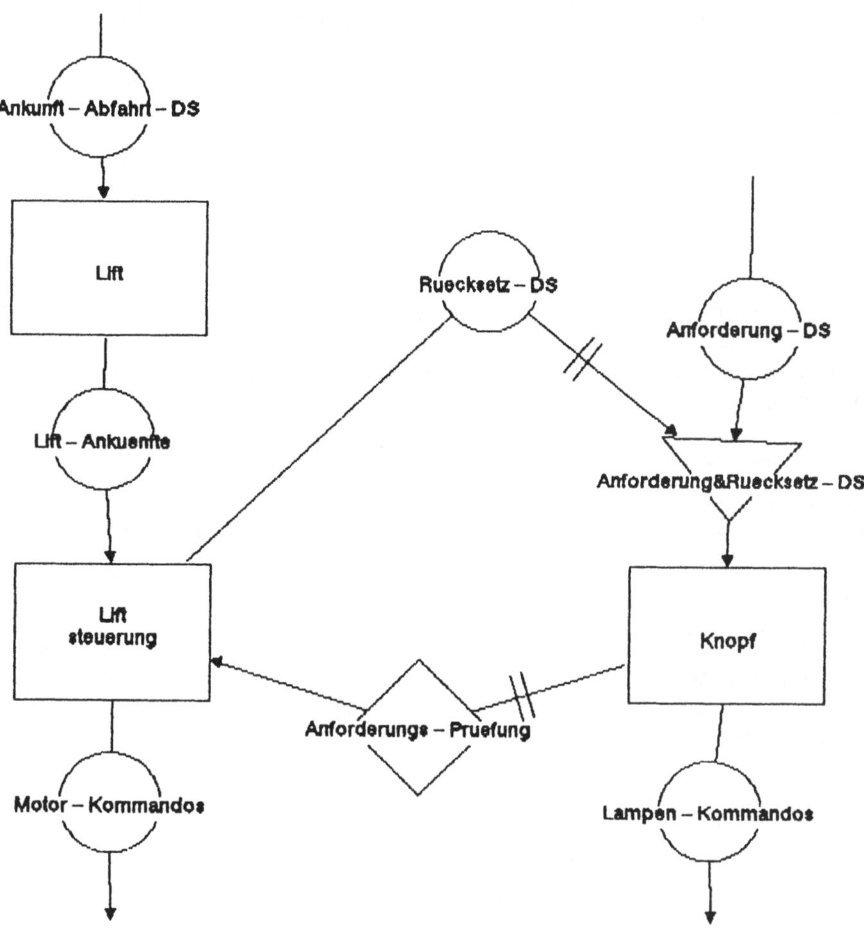

Abb. 6:   mit Speedbuilder erstelltes Systemspezifikationsdiagramm zum Prozeß
"Liftsteuerung"

Speedbuilder verfügt über einen graphischen Netzwerkeditor, der das Erstellen solcher Diagramme interaktiv am PC ermöglicht. Das Werkzeug läßt nur im Sinne der Notation formal korrekte Netze zu. Außerdem erfolgt eine kontinuierliche Konsistenzprüfung sowie auf Wunsch ein automatischer Update von dieser graphischen Ebene in die Ebene der textlichen Beschreibung in der Speedbuilder-Spezifikationsdatenbank.

Die Rechtecke im Systemspezifikationsdiagramm repäsentieren Prozesse (genauer gesagt Prozeß-klassen), Kreise repräsentieren Datenströme, Rauten Zustandsvektorverbindungen und Pfeile die Richtung des Datenflusses.

Prozesse tauschen untereinander Nachrichten aus, indem sie Datenströme schreiben bzw. lesen. Der Zustandsvektor eines Prozesses ist der Sammelbegriff für alle Daten, die zu einem Prozeß gehören. Unter Zustandsvektorinspektion versteht man einen Read-only-Zugriff eines Prozesses auf die Daten eines anderen.

Wir beginnen eine Spezifikation nach JSD mit einem Prozeß für jedes Objekt (in unserem Beispiel-system Lift und Knopf). Dann werden die Datenstrom- und Zustandsvektorverbindungen festgelegt. Die Algorithmen bestehender Prozesse werden entworfen und neue hinzugefügt.

Das Entwerfen der Prozeßinterna erfolgt dabei wiederum von Speedbuilder aus über "STRUCTURE-LINK" mit JSP-TOOL.

Es gibt drei Hauptgründe für das Hinzufügen neuer Prozesse:

a)   Das Sammeln von Eingaben, die durch Ereignisse/Aktionen in der Realität ausgelöst wurden. Diese Eingaben werden geprüft und an den geeigneten Objektprozeß weitergeleitet.

b)   Das Generieren von Aktionen, die für das System relevant sind, aber nicht in der Realität vorkommen.

c)   Das Durchführen von Berechnungen und das Produzieren von Ausgaben.

Lift-Ctr ist ein Beispiel für b) und c), wobei "Rücksetzen einer Anforderung" eine durch Lift-Ctr generierte Aktion ist. Beispiele für a) sind Knopf-Poller in Abb.7 und dialogführende Komponenten in kaufmännisch-administrativen Anwendungen.

Für eine komplette Spezifikation werden meist viele Teilnetze in SSD-Form beschrieben. Zwischen diesen Teilnetzen bestehen keine hierarchischen Beziehungen. Vielmehr liegen alle Teilnetze auf der gleichen Ebene und werden durch gemeinsame Elemente verbunden.

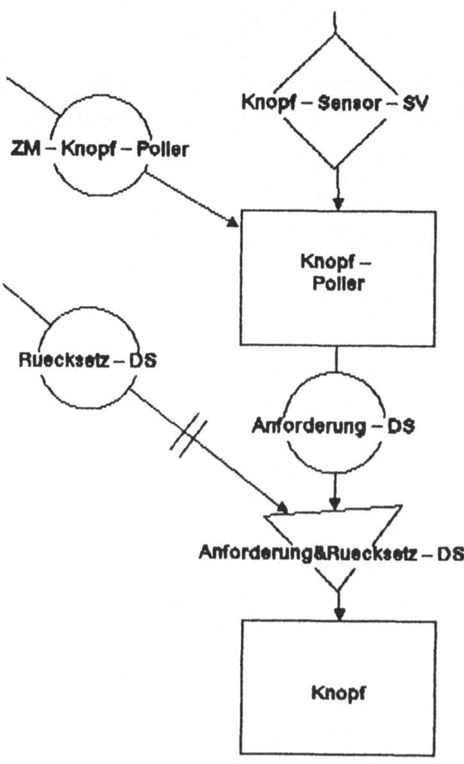

Abb. 7:   mit Speedbuilder erstelltes SSD zum Prozeß "Knopf-Poller"

In den SSDs der Abb. 6 und 7 sind die gemeinsamen Elemente die Prozeßklasse Knopf und deren Eingabedatenstrom.

Bei Anwendung von JSD versucht man, Verbindungen zwischen Prozessen, die keine Objektprozesse sind, zu vermeiden oder wenigsten zu minimieren; d. h. diese Prozesse kommunizieren nur über den Objektprozeß miteinander. Unter Beachtung dieser Regel kann man ein großes Netzwerk als Menge von Teilnetzen beschreiben, die lediglich Objektprozesse gemeinsam haben. Das Gesamtnetzwerk ist dann die Vereinigung der Teilnetze. Diese Technik erlaubt es, mehr noch als bei der Verwendung normaler hierarchischer Zergliederungstechniken, die Komplexität des Systems unter Kontrolle zu halten.

Neben der Spezifikation des Systems in Netzwerkform erfolgt der Entwurf der einzelnen Prozesse in Form strukturierter Programme. Die verschiedenen Bestandteile der Spezifikation eines Prozesses sind am Beispiel von Knopf in Abb. 8 und 9 in Ausschnitten wiedergegeben.

von Speedbuilder erzeugte Prozeßbeschreibung:

Prozess: KNOPF	Referenz :	Klassifikation :

Zusammenfassung : Knopf unterstützt das Konzept der "Anforderungsgruppe".
Dahinter verbirgt sich eine Gruppe von Anforderungen
des Lifts (Knopfdrücken), die durch einen Stop des
Lifts am angeforderten Stockwerk befriedigt
(zurückgesetzt) werden. Knopf schaltet die dem
entsprechenden Knopf in der Realität zugeordnete Lampe
mit Hilfe von Lampenkommandos.

Identifikator :

STOCKWERK-NR	: STOCKWERK-NR
KNOPFART	: KNOPFART
LIFT-NR	: LIFT-NR

Statusvektor :

ANFORDERUNG	: BOOLEAN

Eingabe-Liste :

Lokaler Name	Datenstrom	Ref	Schreiber	Daten-Inhalt		Bemerkungen
	LIFT-ANF-DS					
ANFORDERUNG-&-RÜCKSETZ-DS	ANFORDERUNG-DS	ANF-DS	KNOPF-POLLER	KNOPF-DRUCK STOCKWERK-NR KNOPFART LIFT-NR	: STOCKWERK-NR : KNOPFART : LIFT-NR	
ANFORDERUNG-&-RÜCKSETZ-DS	RÜCKSETZ-DS	RS-DS	LIFTSTEUERUNG	KNOPFDRUCK-ERLEDIGT STOCKWERK-NR KNOPFART LIFT-NR	: STOCKWERK-NR : KNOPFART : LIFT-NR	
RESET&ANFORDERUNG-DS	LIFTANFORDERUNG-DS					
RESET&ANFORDERUNG-DS	RUECKSETZ-DS		LIFTSTEUERUNG			

Ausgabe-Liste :

Datenstrom	Ref	Leser	Daten-Inhalt	Bemerkungen
LAMPEN-KOMMANDOS	LK-DS		EIN AUS	

SV-Zugriffs-Liste :

SV-Zugriff	Ref	Inhaber	SV-Untermenge	Zugriffspfad	Bemerkungen

Abb. 8:   von Speedbuilder generierte Dokumentation; hier: Prozeßspezifikation "Knopf"

Prozeßentwurf mit JSP-TOOL:

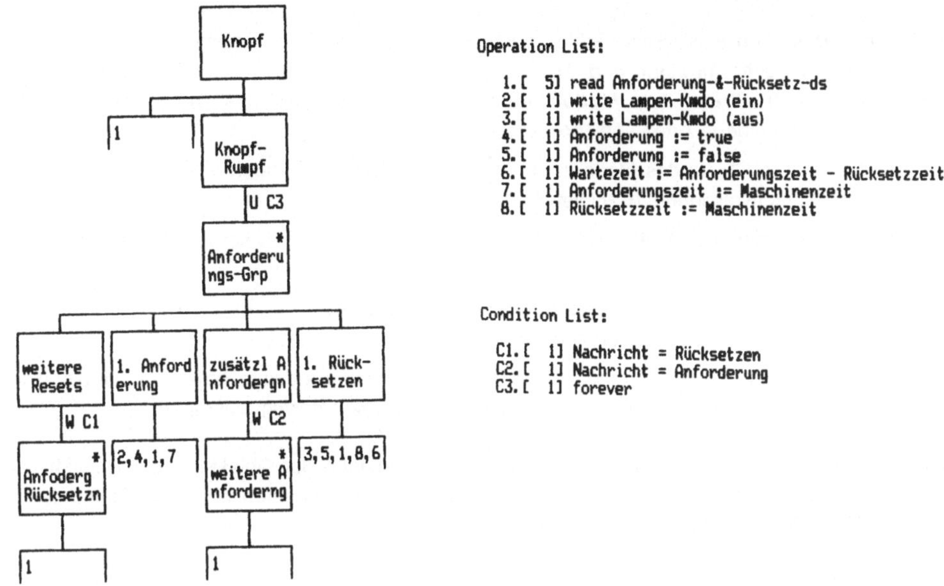

Abb. 9:   mit JSP-TOOL erstellte Prozeßstruktur

von JSP-TOOL generierter Pseudocode:

```
Knopf            SEQ
                     DO  1  : read Anforderung-&-Rücksetz-ds
   Knopf-Rumpf       ITR U (  C3): forever
    Anforderungs-Grp SEQ
       weitere Resets    ITR W (  C1): Nachricht = Rücksetzen
         Anfoderg RücksetznSEQ
                     DO  1   : read Anforderung-&-Rücksetz-ds

         Anfoderg RücksetznEND
       weitere Resets    END
       1. Anforderung    SEQ
                     DO  2  : write Lampen-Kmdo (ein)
                     DO  4  : Anforderung := true
                     DO  1  : read Anforderung-&-Rücksetz-ds
                     DO  7  : Anforderungszeit := Maschinenzeit
       1. Anforderung    END
       zusätzl AnfordergnITR W (  C2): Nachricht = Anforderung
         weitere AnforderngSEQ
                     DO  1   : read Anforderung-&-Rücksetz-ds

         weitere AnforderngEND
       zusätzl AnfordergnEND
       1. Rück-setzen    SEQ
                     DO  3  : write Lampen-Kmdo (aus)
                     DO  5  : Anforderung := false
                     DO  1  : read Anforderung-&-Rücksetz-ds
                     DO  8  : Rücksetzzeit := Maschinenzeit
                     DO  6  : Wartezeit := Anforderungszeit - Rücksetzzeit
       1. Rück-setzen    END
    Anforderungs-Grp END
   Knopf-Rumpf       END
Knopf            END
```

Aus einem solchen Prozeßentwurf läßt sich mittels der Codegeneratoren von JSP-TOOL automatisch Programmcode in einer der gängigen Programmiersprachen wie beispielsweise C, COBOL, PASCAL, PL/I oder RPG III generieren.

Fassen wir die Besonderheiten einer Spezifikation nach JSD an dieser Stelle zusammen. Ein nach JSD spezifiziertes System ist sehr modular und änderungsfreundlich. Dies resultiert einerseits aus der vorgeschalteten expliziten Phase der Modellbildung und andererseits aus der Verteilung der Systemleistungen auf verschiedene Arten von Prozessen:

a) Objektprozesse (pro Objekt des Modells einer), die im System den Status des jeweiligen Objekts in der Realität nachvollziehen (Beispiele: Lift, Knopf);

b) Eingabeprozesse, die die Objektprozesse mit dem nötigen Input versorgen (Beispiel: Knopf-Poller);

c) Funktionsprozesse, die die Systemausgaben generieren und die eigentlichen Automatisierungsaufgaben übernehmen (Beispiel: Lift-Ctr).

Die Eingabeprozesse verkapseln die Verbindung zur Input liefernden Hardware bzw. in kaufmännisch-administrativen Systemen die Dialogführung bzw. die Zugriffe auf Batch-Bewegungsdaten.

Die Objektprozesse repräsentieren mit ihren lokalen Daten den Zustand der Objekte in der Realität. Sie sind typischerweise die Treiberprozesse in technischen Anwendungssystemen bzw. die Stammdatenpflegeroutinen in kaufmännisch-administrativen Systemen.

Die Funktionsprozesse dienen zur Befriedigung des Informationsbedarfs des Benutzers bzw. zur Automatisierung.

Die hier skizzierte Vorgehensweise, zunächst ein Modell als abstrakte Beschreibung der Realität zu entwickeln, auf dieser Basis einen ersten Teil des Systems zu spezifizieren und erst danach Systemteile zur Spezifikation von Funktionen zu ergänzen, findet ihre Begründung in folgenden Beobachtungen:

- Das einmal konzipierte Modell ist stabiler als die vom Anwender gewünschten Funktionen. Das Modell ist ein Abbild der Realität. Es ändert sich nur, wenn sich die Realität selbst ändert. Das ist in der Regel seltener als der sich wandelnde Informationsbedarf des Anwenders, der ständig neuen Erfordernissen angepaßt werden muß.

- Ein JSD-Modell ist ein Gerüst für ein ganzes Spektrum denkbarer Funktionen. Es ist einfacher, zunächst dieses Gerüst zu definieren, als im einzelnen die Systemausgaben zu beschreiben, die der Benutzer wünscht.

- Das Modell beschreibt die Welt des Benutzers (oder zumindest einen Ausschnitt davon). Das ist allemal ein guter Ausgangspunkt.

Der Werkzeugverbund Speedbuilder/JSP-TOOL bietet für die Phasen Modellbildung und Spezifikation umfassende Unterstützung.

2.3 Implementierung

Als Ergebnis einer JSD-Spezifikation liegt ein System vor, das prinzipiell ausführbar ist.

Eine direkte Implementierung mit realen Prozessoren könnte beispielsweise mit Hilfe von Transputern in Occam erfolgen.

Häufig sind solche extrem verteilten Implementierungen ineffizient. Die Gesamtanzahl der Prozesse läßt sich jedoch, falls nötig, durch JSD-Implementierungstechniken reduzieren. Die wichtigste Technik in diesem Zusammenhang ist die Programminversion, die einen Prozeß in eine Subroutine transformiert. Diese kann dann von beliebigen anderen Prozessen über eine Parameterschnittstelle aufgerufen werden. Dabei repräsentiert jede Parameterübergabe einen Satz des Eingabedatenstroms. Eine andere Technik erlaubt es, eine Prozeßklasse durch eine einzelne Subroutine und die entsprechende Anzahl von Zustandsvektoren zu implementieren.

Noch extremer als bei technischen Anwendungen sind die Mengenverhältnisse in der Regel bei kaufmännisch-administrativen Anwendungen. Gibt es in einer Bibliothek 100.000 Exemplare des Objekts Buch, so geht die Spezifikation von 100.000 Exemplaren der Prozeßklasse Buch aus. Die direkte Implementierung eines solchen Systems mit realen oder virtuellen Prozessoren wäre sehr unökonomisch. Deshalb spielen bei kaufmännisch-administrativen Systemen die obengenannten JSD-Implementierungstechniken eher noch eine größere Rolle als bei technischen Anwendungen, wo zunehmend Implementierungsumgebungen, die Parallelität und verteilte Systeme unterstützen, zur Verfügung stehen.

Ein entscheidender Vorteil der Methode JSD ist, daß auf der Basis einer JSD-Spezifikation jeder beliebige Grad von Parallelität und Verteiltheit für die Implementierung realisierbar ist: die JSD-Spezifikation geht immer von völliger Parallelität aller Prozesse aus - die Transformation der Spezifikation in die Implementierung führt also höchstens zu einer Reduktion der Parallelität und Verteiltheit.

Diese Transformation bei der Systementwicklung wird z. Z. noch nicht vom Speedbuilder unterstützt.

Ein weiterer Bestandteil der Implementierungsphase von JSD ist die Entwicklung eines relationalen Datenmodells und der physische Datenentwurf. Die mit JSD erstellte Spezifikation liefert dazu das Rohmaterial, nämlich die lokalen Daten der Prozesse. Nach formalen Regeln läßt sich aus diesen Prozeßzustandsvektoren ein Datenmodell ableiten, das dann wie üblich als Basis für den physischen Datenentwurf dient.

Da im Speedbuilder-Raster auch Beschreibungselemente wie VARIABLE und DATA TYPE vorgesehen sind, kann man alle Informationen zur Datenbasis ebenfalls mit Speedbuilder verwalten.

Die Erfahrung hat gezeigt, daß auch eine parallel zur Modellbildung und Spezifikation nach JSD durchgeführte Datenmodellierung sinnvoll sein kann. Die Ergebnisse beider Ansätze ermöglichen dann eine abschließende Konsistenzprüfung.

3. Prinzipien von JSD

Als wesentliche Prinzipien von JSD bleiben festzuhalten:

- Die Modellbildung in der Systementwicklung erfolgt vor der eigentlichen Spezifikation, da hierdurch eine höhere Wartungs- und Änderungsfreundlichkeit erwartet wird;

- Die Spezifikation eines Systems ist von der Implementierung strikt getrennt;

- JSD bietet durch die Unterteilung der Systementwicklung eine Reihe klar voneinander abgegrenzter Phasen und seine speziellen Implementierungstechniken einen sicheren Weg von der Spezifikation zur Implementierung.

4. Vergleich von JSD mit konventionellen Systementwicklungsmethoden

Ein Vergleich von JSD mit konventionellen top-down-orientierten Methoden wie z. B. SADT (Ross), Structured Analysis (de Marco), Structured Design/Composite Design (Constantine, Yourdon, Myers) u. ä. läßt eine Reihe von Unterschieden erkennen.

Die konventionellen Ansätze fordern die Trennung von Anforderungsdefinition (externem Verhalten) und Software-Entwurf (interner Struktur) eines Systems. Bei JSD existiert diese Trennung nicht. Es wird vielmehr für nötig gehalten, die Fragen des "Was ist zu tun?" und "Wie wird es erreicht?" miteinander zu verquicken.

JSD trennt die problemorientierte Struktur der Spezifikation strikt von Implementierungsüberlegungen. Bei den konventionellen Ansätzen liefert der Systementwurf die Moduln, die das gewünschte externe Verhalten bewirken sollen. Aber eine derartige Systemstruktur muß auch zur Implementierungsumgebung passen und die Performance-Restriktionen erfüllen. Dazu muß der Entwickler problem- und implementierungsorientierte Aspekte gleichzeitig berücksichtigen.

Bei konventionellen Ansätzen erfolgen Systemdesign und Moduldesign (Programmieren im Großen und Kleinen) nacheinander. Es müssen jedoch in beiden Phasen sowohl Fragen der funktionsorientierten Zergliederung als auch solche der Performance und der Ressourcennutzung gleichzeitig beachtet werden.

Bei JSD sind alle Fragen, die mit den Funktionen des Systems zu tun haben, mit der Spezifikation abgeschlossen. Fragen der Ressourcennutzung werden ausschließlich in der Implementierungsphase betrachtet.

Bei der Entwicklung von kaufmännisch-administrativen Systemen hat dies dazu geführt, daß auf der Basis ein und derselben Spezifikation sowohl zentrale als auch verteilte Implementierungen möglich waren.

Bei dem Vergleich mehrerer Spezifikationsmethoden am Beispiel der Entwicklung eines Musik-Synthesizers war JSD die einzige Methode, bei der beim Übergang von einer Ein- zu einer Zweiprozessorlösung keine Änderungen an der Spezifikation erforderlich waren.

Bibliographie

Jackson, Michael A.:	System Development. Prentice Hall, Englewood Cliffs, N.J. 1983.
Jackson, Michael A.:	Principles of Program Design. Academic Press, London 1975. in deutsch: Grundsätze des Programmentwurfs. S. Toeche-Mittler Verlag, Darmstadt 1979.
Cameron, John R.:	JSP & JSD: The Jackson Approach to Software Development. IEEE Computer Society Press 1983.
Cameron, John R.:	An Overview of JSD. In: IEEE Transactions on Software Engineering. Vol. SE-12/2 (Febr. 1986) S. 222 ff.
Dorn, Anton; Schaefer, Richard:	Spezifikation einer Anwendung aus der Versicherungswirtschaft - ein Projekterfahrungsbericht. In: Tagungsband zum Treffen der Jackson Method User Group - deutschsprachiger Teil - Köln Nov. 1983 (unveröffentlicht).
George, Wolfgang:	Jackson-System-Development (JSD): Systementwurf durch Modellierung von Objekten und Ereignissen der Realität. In: Proceedings der GI/ACM-Fachtagung Modellierung und Konstruktion bei der Entwicklung von Informationssystemen. Tutzing 1984, S. 277 ff.
Renold, André:	Parallele Echtzeitprogrammierung: Erfahrungen mit verschiedenen Entwurfsmethoden. In: Entwurf großer Software Systeme, Hrsg. von Morgenbrod, Horst und Remmele, Werner. Teubner, Stuttgart 1985, S. 94 ff.
Zave, Pamela:	The Operational Versus the Conventional Approach to Software Development. In: Comm. ACM Vol. 27/2 (Febr. 1984) S. 104 ff.

How to Support the Development of Distributed Object Oriented Applications

L. Heuser°, A. Schill*, H. Frank °, M. Mühlhäuser* *

Project DOCASE
°Digital Equipment GmbH, CEC Karlsruhe
*University of Karlsruhe, Institute for Telematics
D-7500 Karlsruhe, F.R. Germany

Abstract

The need for distributed applications is growing dramatically due to the fact that state-of-the-art software cannot keep pace with the capabilities of "networked workstations". New techniques are investigated to design distributed applications in a well-structured, object oriented way. In addition transparency in object oriented approaches hides underlying communication protocols. However, supporting the development of such applications is lacking in appropriate techniques and methodologies. The *DOCASE* project proposes a methodology, which enables the programmer to develop his application starting with the design phase, and accompanies him through the subsequent stages of the software life cycle.

Keywords: Distributed Applications, Distributed Programming, Design Support, Object Oriented Approach, CASE.

1 The Need for Distributed Applications

During the last decade a revolutionary approach towards networked workstations arose. Today, we recognize that the cycles of hardware development are much faster than those of software engineering, so there is a huge gap between the power of exisiting *workstations* or *networks* and the capability of software to use their facilities (e.g. by parallel or distributed processing). Distributed applications are needed to fill this gap, but support for their development is just at the beginning [MÜH88].

Distributed systems, which are the basic platform for distributed applications, are defined as a dynamically varying number of distinguished processor sets. That means that two sets never share the same memory. Today, distributed applications can be divided into two classes. In the first category the applications use *distributed databases* [MOH84], where remote data is taken by local operations. The members of the second class are those which use the *remote procedure call* (RPC) [BIR84] for distribution abstraction. RPC offers the advantage of hiding remote operations through unique procedure interfaces. Both methodologies provide only a subset of the required functionality summarized below:

- Comunication transparency

- Location transparency

- Shared access of transient and persistent data

---

*random sequence of authors

- Transparency of data access

- Transparent services

- Concurrent or cooperative work of distributed processes

- Full resource sharing

- Reliable processes

- Data and service availability

In summary we can say that the classes of distribution concepts mentioned above don't fulfil the listed requirements. Therefore new approaches have to be investigated providing the additionally required features. In section 2, the *object oriented* approach is described, which supports higher levels of abstraction and transparency. Combining it with the above mentioned concepts of RPC or distributed databases leads to new categories of applications.

2 Objects for Structuring Distributed Applications

New methodologies are investigated [HEU88] to support the development of **object oriented** distributed applications. The object oriented approach provides all the features [WEG87], which are needed for *reusability, maintainability*, and *extensibility*, as listed below:

Data abstraction - allows to provide data structures without describing their implementation. *Sets* are examples where the application does not have to know if the *set elements* are stored either in arrays or in doubly-linked lists, for example. Using the first implementation results in the fact, that "is-set-member" relations are defined within the *set* data structure, whereas the other solution uses pointers as part of the *set elements*. Figure 1 and Figure 2 show these examples. They are written in Trellis/Owl[1] [OBR87], an object oriented language, and present only the relevant parts of the specification.

Information Hiding - results from data abstraction, so data can only be accessed through well-defined operations of the specific object. This concept is based on the *abstract data type* methodology. Direct data access is prohibited by the system. Data consistency and access synchronization can be easily specified by using this kind of data abstraction. For example, transactions are embedded into operations or monitors are used within objects, where only the object itself is able to define the access control. The client objects, which invoke an operation, have not to be concerned with these mechanisms. So *information hiding* protects both the client object and the server object.

Types and Subtyping - allow to reuse operations and data structure. For example, all cars can be described by the type *car* and the operations are able to work on all instances of the type *car*. A subtype of *car* is *DKW*, which describes DKW cars as specialization. In the context of *subtyping* the concept of **inheritance** is introduced. *Inheritance* enables the programmer to use all operations and data structure of the "supertype"[2]. The *subtyping* mechanism is flexible, that means new subtypes can be added easily.

Operation Invocation - is done in a uniform way. That means every object provides a uniform interface through its operations and a caller gets access to its information or service by invoking one of these operations. Invocations are performed by uniform message-passing which allows to extend the communication to *remote invocation* [DEC86].

```
type_module Set[T: Type]
!
!   A Set is a mutable Collection, whose elements are unique (each element
!   occurs at most once) and occur in the Set in no particular order.
!


----------------------------- hidden area  -----------------------------


component me.data: Array[T]
    ! storage for the set elements
component me.size: Integer
    ! number of elements in the set


end type_module


----------------------------- hidden area  -----------------------------
```

Figure 1: Implementation of a *Set* as array

This paper introduces enhancements of distributed application support extending the possibility of defining different *levels of abstraction* (cf. section 3), or modeling the *functional* behaviour of the application (cf. section 4).

The functional dimensions of distributed object oriented applications are not yet well investigated. *Cooperation* of the different parts of the application is mostly implicitly described rather than explicitly defined. In addition the complexity of *interaction* grows dramatically with the number of nodes or active components in a distributed system. As a result no control mechanism exists which would be able to guarantee the correct run of an algorithm. Transcations [CAL87] don't solve this problem because they are used at a relatively fine-grained consistency level, dealing with short term *atomic* actions on persistent data. Algorithms need more functionality to provide the required services.

3   Development Support Starting with the Design Phase

In the past, software engineering has lacked coupling the *requirements gathering* and *design phases* with the software *implementation* phase. The specification was done mostly informally, using non-computerized tools. The emerging CASE efforts [IEE88] made it possible that software specifications, especially graphical ones, became available on-line. Yet, automating and computer-assisting the transition from *requirements into specification* or *between specification*

---

[1]Trellis is a trademark of Digital Equipment Corp.

[2]Supertype is the opposit of subtype

```
type_module Set[T: Type]
!
!   A Set is a mutable Collection, whose elements are unique (each element
!   occurs at most once) and occur in the Set in no particular order.
!


---------------------------- hidden area ----------------------------


component me.first: Element[T]
    ! pointer to the first set element
component me.last: Element[T]
    ! pointer to the last set element
component me.size: Integer
    ! number of elements in the set


end type_module

---------------------------- hidden area ----------------------------


type_module Element[T: Type]
!
! Element describes an entity of a set
!

---------------------------- hidden area ----------------------------


component me.data: T
    ! storage for the set elements
component me.successor: Element[T]
    ! pointer to the next element
component me.predecessor: Element[T]
    ! pointer to the previous element


end type_module

---------------------------- hidden area ----------------------------
```

Figure 2: Implementation of a *Set* using a doubly-linked list of *Elements*

and implementation is still in its early days.

Requirements gathering suffers from the gap of non-computable, application oriented requirements and software oriented requirement statements. For guaranteeing the conformance of user requirements and existing implementations provable, computer-assisted transformation steps have to be defined. As a basis of correct requirement transformation a poweful, wide-spectrum specification language is necessary. Especially a "natural" behaviour of the language is required for enabling the programmer to define the relationships between requirements and top-level specification. Wide-spectrum specification language and code transformation [BAU82] seem to be the most promising approaches. Such languages allow the specification of a system at different levels of abstraction, from top-level design to a level which can be easily translated into source code. This approach has several advantages:

- A *uniform* formalism takes place during the main period of development independent from the current level of abstraction.

- Transformation steps which lead from one level of abstraction to another can be computer-assisted, where the computer-assistance can even assure verified transformation steps (assuring that if the software was fulfilling its specification before applying a transformation, it will do so afterwards).

- Transformation from the *bottom level specification* into the *implementation* is easy and can be automated or at least reduced to a non-creative task. This way maintenance and evolution of the program can be deferred to the specification level, fulfilling a very important requirement in software engineering (because maintenance and evolution at source code level easily leads to a mismatch of specification and implementation).

- Using a widespectrum specification language, it becomes evident that optimization tools could reflect their optimization actions in the specification. Allowing generally valid optimization rules to be fed back from a specific installation into the software evolution cycle guarantees the conformance of specification and running versions.

- For the raw design, formal, constructive wide-spectrum specification languages can obviously be complemented by a graphical representation. This can be used as a basis for building a corresponding top-down graphical design aid (in the sense of a CASE tool): the top-level structuring rules and structure elements as well as the refinement steps offered (at least for higher levels of the design) can easily be graphically supported.

Combining the wide spectrum design language with the *object oriented* approach results in a powerful medium for describing the application in a more "real world" terminology. Actually, *levels of abstraction* and *uniformity*, as required in wide-spectrum specification languages, are main concepts in the "object" world. The natural view of "objects" and their decomposition as specialization has to be supported in early stages of application development. In section 4 a methodology is introduced which combines the following main design features: a) *Data abstraction*, b) different *levels of abstraction* and *transparency*, and c) *top-down approach*, if required.

4 DOCASE - A Support Environment

In the previous sections the need for distributed object oriented applications and their development support has been described. The capabilities of objects and their groundrules present new ways of software structuring. Nevertheless, today current approaches fail in providing an appropriate *level of abstraction*. *Abstraction* supports the early stages of the software life cycle and makes specific features explicit to the application programmer in an integrated way. Examples are higher level *communication, mobility* or *cooperation* constructs as described in the following sections.

DOCASE, which stands for "Distribution and Objects in CASE", is a project that deals with these specific support problems for distributed object oriented applications mentioned in this paper. It is a joint project between the Campusbased Engineering Center (CEC) Karlsruhe of Digital Equipment GmbH and the Institute for Telematics at the University of Karlsruhe. One goal of the project is to achieve a uniform way of describing application features like *cooperation* of "autonomous" parts, *mobility* of objects in distributed systems, *communication patterns*, *structural* and *dynamical* behaviour. In addition to that *requirements engineering* is integrated enabling the system to support the programmer as early as possible.

4.1 Requirements Engineering

Requirements Engineering is the actual start of the development of an application and the terminology mainly used is natural language mixed with application specifics. Natural language in the sense of description language is object based, that means *objects* represent things and activities. Natural language is fit to describe the looks and behaviour of objects and the connections between objects.

For the goal of building an object oriented software system, the application, this seems to be optimal. But there is the problem that *not all* objects perfectly fit to describe "real world" are fit to describe a software model. So what is needed to support the development of object oriented applications is not only support mechanisms for the design and decomposition of a software model but also the support for the transformation of an object based description of the "real world" model into a software model without losing the object benefits.

With the DOCASE architectural concept we want to support the synergy between the object based natural language and the object oriented software system that models the application. This will be achieved by designing a specification language that is fit to support the early design steps as well as the later ones and that can be seen as the connection between the natural language and final implementation language (cf. section 4.2). On top of this language a requirements transformation support can be added through interactive classfication of requirements into special transformation units to get transformed into the specification language and build the framework of the software model. The semantic of the specification language covers the specific needs of an object oriented model and can therefore lead the developer during the decomposition of the specification. Added specification possibilities to control performance within a distributed system and runtime information that can be fed back into the specification complete the DOCASE architecture to cover: support for requirements engineering and the transformation to the first design model, semantic support during the refinement of the design specification, and optimization support for performance aspects. All of this is based on objects within a distributed environment and on the semantics that are added to the objects (cf. section 4.2).

4.2 The DOCASE Design Foundation

To develop a distributed object oriented application, DOCASE is providing a number of generic design objects. These objects form a class hierarchy exploiting inheritance. Objects generated from this class hierarchy represent a particular design. They form an arbitrary instance hierarchy describing the overall top-down view of the designed system. The advantage of the explicit toplevel hierarchy is that all CASE tools (graphical design aids, runtime visualization tools, etc.) can exploit it. In the following, the different design object classes will be introduced.

The highest level class is the *system component*. It is an abstract class with different concrete subclasses.

We distinguish between *configured elements* and dynamically *generated elements*. Configured elements are created, deleted and modified by special *configuration operations*. This way, explicit knowledge of their existence is related to the system and can be used by tools. At design time, statements about their initial instance population can be made. Generated elements are manipulated by usual object oriented invocations not being recorded by special tools. They are only known by their class at design time, but not as instances.

This distinction of configured (intuitively 'visible', more 'static') objects and generated (intuitively 'short-living', more 'dynamic') objects has proven in our software engineering expertise to be very close to a software designer's way of thinking.

As the third major class of design elements, we introduce *relation objects* in order to represent static and dynamic relations between other objects. The explicit and separate expression of interobject relations is one of the key issues of the DOCASE foundation.

Configured Elements

Configured elements are divided into *subsystems, basic objects* and *interface objects.*

A *subsystem* is a functionally coherent entity of a distributed object oriented application. It is the major building block to represent the logical structure of the overall application. Subsystems can be nested and are thus able to represent the system components at different levels of abstraction. For more details see section 4.4.

At a lower level of abstraction, a subsystem consists of a number of *basic objects*. The class of basic objects is an abstract class having several concrete subclasses, which describe *active* and *passive* entities.

Generated Elements

As *generated elements* we offer objects with associated *threads* of control (basically introducing fine-grained parallelism) and *data* objects. Data objects represent the principle elements of the logical 'data flow' in the system.

Relation Objects

Relation objects are divided into different kinds of relations. A *communication* relation describes communication between a number of other objects. Examples range from simple point-to-point to complex *n-party* interactions among more than two objects. *Migration* describes the relations between a shared object and its potential accessors with respect to object movement. This relation is used for mobility decisions, e.g., to make objects local to their sharers. *Cooperation* describes complex, long-duration interactions between different autonomous parts (usually subsystems) of the application system. Both migration and cooperation will be described in detail in this chapter.

The DOCASE design methodology provides the framework for any kind of interobject relation. As respective sections of the DOCASE project (e.g., modelling tools, reliability support) will be integrated, these kinds of relations will be refined.

4.3 Communication Optimization Using Object Mobility

Most distributed object oriented systems [ALM85, BLA87, DEC86, BEN87] support *object mobility*. Objects can *move* dynamically to different locations at runtime. This section reviews object mobility and proposes a higher-level object placement control based on migration facilities.

Distributed object oriented systems enable *fine-grained* mobility. That is, the units of migration are objects of arbitrary size ranging from single data objects to large objects with associated threads. As opposed to that, the grain of mobility of *process migration* are the heavyweight processes with its address space. Objects are moved between address spaces representing *logical nodes*. After migration, all further invocations to an object are redirected to the new location by the system. So migration remains transparent for other objects. Objects can be related strongly by attaching their references in order to create units of mobility. The main goals of object migrations are to hide underlying mechanisms of data transmission, to colocate interacting objects in order to reduce remote communication and to perform load balancing by moving larger units of work.

In current systems, the application programmer must explicitly specify when to move an object. While all other operations, especially method invocations, provide distribution transparency, distribution becomes evident by the need for controlling object migrations. This is leading to higher complexity during software development and maintenance. Moreover, dynamic information available to the system cannot be exploited for migration decisions. Therefore, we are proposing a higher level of abstraction by automating object placement.

A higher level control of object placement should be based on information about application behaviour rather than on direct calls to mobility operations. To realize this approach, we introduce a special *control layer* having a conceptual view of the application objects and their relationships. All objects relevant to distribution are represented in this layer. As opposed to current systems, relationships between them are made explicit and are typed. Additionally, mobility and placement restrictions can be specified and static descriptions of object clusters can be given.

Treatment of object mobility during application development is divided into two major steps. In a first phase, application behaviour is analysed by monitoring creation and deletion of objects and relationships and gathering measures of communication intensity associated with an object relationship. This way, typed relationships can be weighted and behaviour information can be added to them. Basic changes of relationships can also be hidden by higher-level operations such as the transfer of control over an object from one referencing object to another. A further example of a more abstract construct would be a one-step instantiation of complex interobject relationships by associating a number of objects with a predefined cluster object describing these typed relationships.

At runtime, the *a-priori knowledge* about application behaviour gathered during the previous phase is then combined with dynamically monitored information including active object invocations and current relationships. Based on a heuristic evaluation of this information, appropriate object migrations can be performed. This approach exploits the conceptual view of an application provided by our design methodology. Most important, information provided at design time is maintained and exploited at runtime. The software engineer may use familiar notions of objects and relationships while it is a task of the system to handle the more complex aspects of distribution. We are currently doing the detailed design of the control layer and are working on migration heuristics.

4.4 Object Cooperation and Algorithm Control System

Algorithms and *cooperation* exist in every computer system, mostly implemented via processes. These active entities compete for resources, such as CPU time, peripherals, and storage. New approaches arose at the time when distributed systems were introduced. Extensions to the classical process models are now under investigation to obtain better descriptions of the active entities. Such extensions allow the distribution of a sequential process and the interaction of concurrent distributed processes.

Definition and Terms

Valuable classifications of object oriented programming languages are available but for the introduction of cooperation we need further control constructs. Therefore the following terms and definitions, which arise from the needs of developing relations of cooperation in large distributed object oriented systems, are introduced.

ComProc - A *complex procedure* describes the dynamic properties and constraints of interactions between different applications, different users (humans or machines) in a real world environment.

Example:

The production of goods, eg. a car, involves many kinds of applications like *developing environment, production planning & control system, calculation applications, marketing analysis* or *quality assurance*. These applications implicate different kinds of *application programmers* specialised on topics related to the target application areas. Usually none of them is concerned with the overall *functional behaviour* of the integrated distributed environment.

Analysing "real world" procedures results in the identification of the following **ComProc**[3] characteristics:

- A *ComProc* consists of a *hierarchical* set of *sequential, concurrent* or *distributed activities* (see below).

- A *ComProc* can be a subset of a superimposed ComProc. That means, *ComProcs* are decomposable into a hierarchy of variable height.

- A *ComProc* coordinates its components through *precedence order* and *time constraints*.

- A *ComProc* can be declared as "stable" by including *reliability* properties.

- The success and the correctness of a *ComProc* is application-defined.

- A *ComProc* is an abstract entity which is not related to a specific configuration. That means, its existence is independent from the availability of a specific node in the distributed environment, so it survives each shutdown or net partition. We would define this characteristic as the *long-living* paradigm for functional behaviour.

- A *ComProc* doesn't have to be completely designed. New *activities* or subprocedures can be added dynamically. We call this the *uncompleteness* paradigm.

Activity - An *activity* describes the functional and cooperative behaviour of **one** subsystem (see below) related to *one* overall ComProc during a period. An *activity* is embedded into its environment, which consists of the input/output information, the local state of the subsystem and the global state of the related ComProc. This definition differs from others (Trellis, Comandos [HOR87]) in which DOCASE *activities* are used in a higher level of abstraction, and *not* as a construct for active entities mostly existing only for a *short* time. Our definition conforms to real world activities, for example the design of a piece of software. Activities have a well-defined initial state and also a well-defined final state[4], they describe the transformation done by the activity. The following 7-tupel defines the representation of an activity:

---

[3] COMplex PROCedure

[4] Error states and timeouts can be described as well-defined final states if the related conditions can be identified.

$$A = (CP,SS,I,S(CP),S(SS),ALG,O)$$

CP: The superimposed ComProc
SS: The underlying subsystem
I: Input data of the activity
S(CP):   Actual state of the superimposed ComProc
S(SS):   Required state of the underlying subsystem
ALG: The basic algorithm of the activity on SS
O: Output data of the activity

Each state of an activity can be described by taking the relevant instances of each 7-tupel component. For an overall cooperative description, DOCASE needs the initial and final state of an activity at a given stage of execution. The final state could be either calculated by the programmer or computed by the system depending on the life-cycle phase.
Activities differ from "active" objects like the DOCASE *independent object* in the complexity of the functional behaviour. They define tasks which might involve several basic components of a *subsystem* rather than one "active" entity.

Subsystem - A DOCASE *subsystem* is defined by the following *main* characteristics:

- A *subsystem* is an abstract entity, which consists of a set of *related* objects.
- These objects are called *configured elements* because they are parts of the configuration and related to the *subsystem* through *configuration operations*.
- Objects of a *subsystem* can be distributed, so subsystems are no "local" entities.
- At least one server or independent object is associated with a *subsystem*. Therefore *subsystems* can be declared as "active" entities.
- A *subsystem* provides service information about its current configuration and its *internal state*.

Subsystem-Activity relations are the basic platform for the integration of structural and functional behaviour. Through these relations the system, including tools, can support the integrated development of distributed applications and their functional behaviour without using a monolithic approach. *Subsystem-Activity relations* are the main building blocks of distribution for *ComProcs* or in other words: Distribution of *ComProcs* occurs through distribution of the underlying applications.

After describing the major components of *cooperation* and the underlying structure we introduce paradigms, which define the characteristics of *ComProcs* as mentioned above. For the sake of space the introduction is very brief but sticks out the foundation of each paradigm.

Long-living Paradigm - Looking at real world procedures we find that their duration covers days, months or years. Getting into a deadlock (no *activity* could be started as part of the ComProc) does not imply a restart from the beginning, rather a return to the latest checkpoint where status was saved. Two different reasons for deadlocks exist, one is the situation that a specific subsystem cannot accomplish its activity because of unsatisfied requirements, and the other is interruption of the information or physical links. Both result in reorganizing and restructuring the ComProc which is achieved by activating known or computable alternatives. In contrast to reliability (see below), we define that a *long-living* procedure doesn't need to be *stable*, which means, that the requirements do not have to be fully accomplished.

Reliability Paradigm - To prevent crashing of critical *ComProcs* reliability concepts have to be defined. According to [BEL86] we introduce an abstract behaviour which can be mapped to different implementations dependent on the application requirements, like replicated computing or checkpointing with rollback approaches.

Success Paradigm - A *ComProc* is *successful*, if the output of *activities* satisfies the predefined goals. This property is a measure for the complexity of reconfigurating a ComProc, if the goals are not achieved. It enables the programmer to describe levels of success by weightings.

$$0 \leq weight_i \leq 1, \qquad \sum_{i=1}^{n} weight_i = 1 \qquad n : \# \ of \ boolean \ expressions$$

For example printing a document might be an activity which could have failed but the superimposed *ComProc* is still successful. The weightings are timed with "boolean expressions" which describe the dependency of the different ComProc entities.

Uncompleteness Paradigm - A *ComProc* is a dynamic entity which normally cannot be described completely. In contrast to the decomposition of the application structure the functional behaviour depends on constraints which might disable the programmer from defining a complete description of a *ComProc*. An example is the addition of new subsystems in the structure, which provide new services required from an overall procedure.

Stage of Execution - The execution of a ComProc can be divided into several distinguished phases. We call them *stages of execution* [ELR82]. During each stage several related activities are accomplished. Time constraints are part of the stage of execution descriptions. Several stages of execution can exist in parallel but like transactions they have to be serialised.

Algorithm Control System

An *Algorithm Control System* (ACS) enables the programmer to define functional behaviour of the application. The buiding blocks are splitted in those, which describe superimposed controlling, *ComProc*, and those, which embed the *basic algorithm, activities*. With these entities a progammer can define application oriented active components like *tasks, planning management* or *office control management*. These *algoritms* based on *ComProcs* and *activities* are system supported through the ACS. The programmer in this way is only concerned with the application dependent features, like document processing or job floor control, and *not* with reliability of distributed processes, controlling of cooperating active entities. Because of the object oriented approach existing algorithms could be easily integrated through the ComProc hierarchy concept.

Future work on the ACS will be centered around its architecture including ComProc and *activity* management. The paradigms mentioned above have to be investigated and integrated to fulfil the requirements on the described characteristics of ComProcs and *activities*.

4.5   Future Directions of DOCASE

In the next steps an overall architecture has to be investigated for classifying DOCASE and positioning it against existing CASE environments. This architecture will help to position the different features described above within the DOCASE environment and to assure their integration into it. Building a basic platform for tools by using the design components mentioned in section 4.2 enables the integration of additional tools related to the user interface layer and storage mechanisms.

5   Conclusions

We examined the need of distributed applications and their favoured structure, the *object oriented* approach. Supporting the early phases of the software life cycle enables the programmer to hide implementation details. To achieve this goal a project, *DOCASE*, was presented which covers main features for supporting the development of distributed object oriented applications. Requirements engineering and system supported design objects present computer aided software engineering in the very first phases of the life cycle. Object mobility and algorithm control system assist the programmer in handling specific application requirements in a more abstract way.

At the moment, example prototypes are under development exploiting characteristics of the investigated features. Future work centers around the architecture, the design foundation and specific topics of the features presented in section 4.

The authors thank Ursula Hugger and Paul Tallett for their fruitful suggestions and recommendations.

References

[ALM85] G. Almes, A. Black, E. Lazowska, J. Noe
The Eden System: A Technical Review
IEEE Trans. on Software Engineering, Jan. 1985

[BAU82] Bauer, F.L.
From specifications to machine code: program construction through formal reasoning
Proc. 6th Intl. Conf. SW Engineering, Tokyo 1982, pp. 84-91

[BEL86] Belli, F., Echtle, K., Görke, W.
Methods and Models of Fault Toleranz
Informatik-Spektrum, Springer, Vol.9, No.2, pp. 68-82, German

[BEN87] Bennett, J.K.
The Design and Implementation of Distributed Smalltalk
OOPSLA '87 Proceedings, ACM 1987

[BIR84] Birrell, A.D., Nelson, B.J.
Implementing Remote Procedure Calls
ACM Transactions on Computer Systems, Feb. 1984

[BLA86] Black, A., Hutchinson, N., Jul, E., Levy, H.
Object Structure in the Emerald System
OOPSLA '86 Proceedings, ACM 1986

[CAL87] Calton, P., Jerre, D.N.
Design and Implementation of Nested Transactions in EDEN
Proc. 6th Symp. on Reliability in Distributed Software and Database Systems, 1987

[DEC86] Decouchant, D.
Design of a Distributed Object Manager for the Smalltalk-80 System
OOPSLA '86 Proceedings, ACM 1986

[ELR82] Elrad, T., Francez, N.
Decomposition of Distributed Programs into Communiation Closed Layers
Science of Computer Programming, Vol. 2, No. 2, 1982, pp. 155-173

[HEU88] Heuser, L., Schill, A., Mühlhäuser, M.
Development Support for Distributed Object Oriented Applications
Technical Report, CEC, Digital Equipment GmbH, 1988

[HOR87] Horn, C.
COMANDOS: Object-Oriented Architecture
ESPRIT Project 834, Sept. 1987

[IEE88] Special Issue on CASE
IEEE Software, March 1988

[MOH84] Mohan, C.
Recent and Future Trends in Distributed Data Base Management
Proceedings on New Directions for Database Systems, New York, 1984

[MÜH88] Mühlhäuser, M.
Software Engineering For Distributed Applications: The DESIGN Project
Proc. IEEE 10th Intl. Conference on Software Engineering
Singapore, April 1988

[OBR87] O'Brien, P., Halbert, D., Kilian, M.
The Trellis Programming Environment
OOPSLA '87 Proceedings, ACM 1986

[WEG87] Wegner, P.
Dimensions of Object-Based Language Design
OOPSLA '87 Proceedings, ACM 1987

Informationsflußanalyse, eine methodische Vorgehensweise zur Funktions-, Informations- und Leistungsanalyse komplexer Systeme

F.H. Kaufmann, Siemens AG, München

Abstract:

Die Informationsflußanalyse ist eine Methode für die Spezifikation und den Entwurf von Mensch-Maschinensystemen, wie wir sie im Bereich der Wirtschaft als Org-DV Systeme und im Bereich der Technik als Steuer- und Kontrollsysteme finden. Schwerpunkt dieser Ausarbeitung ist die Darstellung der Vorgehensweise bei der Erstellung von Pflichtenheften und Leistungsbeschreibungen in Form von konsistenten Modellen, die aus einfachen grafischen Elementen und Datendarstellungen in Tabellen bestehen.
Die Modelle stellen Funktionen und Informationen in einer Weise dar, die DV-gestützt geprüft werden kann (Verifikation).

Die formale Darstellung mit der grafischen Entwurfssprache von CADOS[R] ermöglicht es ein Modell soweit zu verfeinern, daß es automatisch in ein ablauffähiges Simulationsmodell umgewandelt werden kann oder ein Softwaresystem daraus generiert werden kann.

1. Anwendungsbereich und Ziele der Informationsflußanalyse

Die Informationsflußanalyse stellt methodisch eine Weiterentwicklung der strukturierten Analyse für dynamische Systeme dar, die von diskreten Ereignissen (Eingangsdaten, materielle Objekte, Steuerinpulse) angestoßen werden und innerhalb einer bestimmten Zeit reagieren müssen.

Typische Beispiele bei denen die Methodik bereits eingesetzt wurde sind:

o Dialogsysteme in Wirtschaft und Verwaltung
o Systeme der Produktionssteuerung und Logistik
o Führungssysteme für Luft- und Raumfahrt
o Technische Systeme und Automaten

Die Informationsflußanalyse verbindet die Gedanken der strukturierten Analyse mit der objektorientierten Sichtweise der Entity-Relationship-Analyse

In Ergänzung zur strukturierten Analyse werden die Zeit und die Mengenverhältnisse in die methodische Betrachtung einbezogen.

Die Entity Relationship-Analyse wird in Ergänzung zur Funktionsanalyse zur Strukturierung und Modellierung der Daten herangezogen.

Die Informationsflußanalyse umfaßt in einer integrierten Methodik die

o Kommunikationsanalyse (Ermittlung von Informationsflüssen zwischen den Systemkomponenten)
o Funktionsanalyse (Abgrenzung und Verfeinerung von Funktionen)
o Informationsanalyse (Definition von Datenobjekten und deren Beziehung)
o Leistungsanalyse (Zeitverhalten in Abhängigkeit vom Informationsfluß)

eines Systems.

Der Schwerpunkt dieser Ausarbeitung liegt bei der Vorgehensweise in den Phasen von der Istanalyse bis zur Leistungsbeschreibung (Vorgabe für die Realisierung) von Hard- und Softwaresystemen. Auf die Simulation und die Generierung von Softwaresystemen wird hier nicht eingegangen.

Die Informationsflußanalyse hat das Ziel, durch Einführung von zusätzlichen Kriterien und Prioritäten bei der Strukturierung

- die dynamischen Schwerpunkte und Engpässe eines Systemes herauszuarbeiten,
- möglichst zielführend die gewünschte Detailierungsstufe zu erreichen,
- bei Restrukturierungen bzw. Änderungen des Systemmodelles den Auf-wand gering zu halten,
- Redundanzen und Verfeinerungen an der falschen Stelle zu vermeiden
- die Vorgehensweise eindeutiger zu machen. Damit wird sie besser planbar, stärker zielorientiert und besser erlernbar.

Zur Darstellung der Methode wird die Spezifikationssprache GRAPES 85 (grafische Entwurfssprache für Systeme) verwendet, die im Analyse und Entwurfswerkzeug CADOS [R] (Computer Aided Design für Organisatoren und Systemingenieure) zur Anwendung kommt.

Die Methodik und die Darstellung der Modelle sind jedoch grundsätzlich unabhängig von einem Werkzeug. Bei überschaubaren Systemen kann sie auch mit Papier und Bleistift betrieben werden.

Bei komplexen Systemen ist die Unterstützung durch ein erprobtes Werkzeug von großem Wert, vorallem wenn es die Möglichkeit bietet, das erstellte System nicht nur zu verwalten, sondern auch auf Konsistenz und Vollständigkeit zu prüfen und die Modelldatenbank nach vielfältigen Gesichtspunkten auszuwerten (Verwendungsnachweise). Im Bild 1-1 sind die verfügbaren Komponenten von CADOS [R] dargestellt /1/.

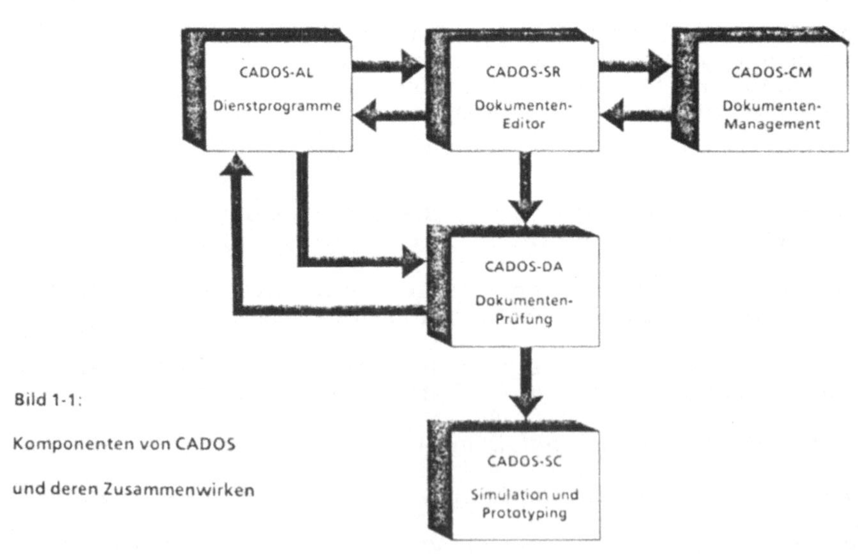

Bild 1-1:

Komponenten von CADOS

und deren Zusammenwirken

CADOS [R] Eingetragenes Warenzeichen der Fa. Siemens AG, München

2. Systemsicht und Darstellung in Grapes 85

2.1 Makrobetrachtung

System

Ein System besteht aus Komponenten, die über Informationsflüsse miteinander kommunizieren. Diese Systemsicht nennen wir eine Makrobetrachtung, weil nicht der Ablauf eines Einzelereignisses im System betrachtet wird, sondern die mittleren Flüsse der Komponenten.

Komponente

Eine Komponente repräsentiert einen oder mehrere Prozesse. Die Komponenten sind die Prozessträger. Eine Komponente wandelt einen oder mehrere Eingangsflüsse in eindeutig zuordenbare Ausgangsflüsse um (Transformation).
Ein Ausgangsfluß ist um die Durchlaufzeit durch die Komponente gegenüber dem Eingangsfluß verschoben (Bild 2.1-1).
Bei kommerziellen Systemen steht die Transformation von Datenobjekten (Eingangsdokumente in Ausgangsdokumente) im Vordergrund. Bei technischen Systemen steht vielfach der Algorithmus der zeitlichen Verschiebung im Mittelpunkt der Betrachtung.

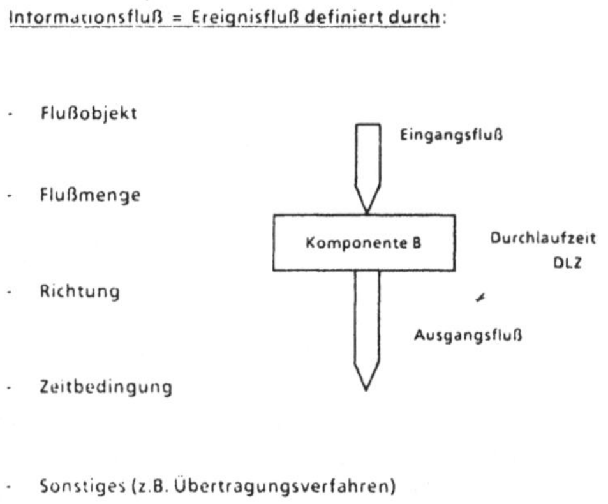

Bild 2.1-1:   Komponente als Flusswandler

Kenngrößen der Informationsflüsse

Informationsflüsse entstehen dadurch, daß die Prozesse Datenobjekte senden bzw. empfangen.
Ein Informationsfluß ist durch folgende Angaben definiert:

- Ein Flußobjekt.
  Dies ist der Datentyp, der die Klasse von Objekten charakterisiert, die im Fluß zusammengefaßt sind.
- Eine Richtung.
  Sie ist gekennzeichnet durch den Interaktionsweg bzw. die Kommunikationspartner.
- Die Flußmenge.
  Die Anzahl von Datenobjekten die in der Zeiteinheit über die Schnittstellen fließen.
- Die Zeitbedingung.
  Dies ist die Übertragungszeit auf der Schnittstelle.
- Sonstige Angaben, z. B. Übertragungsverfahren usw. (Optional).

2.2 Darstellung des Kommunikationsverhaltens

Kommunikationsdiagramm

Die Systemkomponenten und ihre Kommunikation über Schnittstellen wird bei Grapes 85 in einem Kommunikationsdiagramm als Block-Diagramm (SBD = Schematic Bloc Diagramm) dargestellt.

Bild 2.2-2 zeigt die oberste Ebene eines Erfassungssystemes, das im Rahmen einer Leistungsbeschreibung spezifiziert werden soll. Seine externen Kommunikationspartner sind das Dialogterminal mit dem Erfasser und der Drucker.
Das Erfassungssystem ist ein geschlossenes System.

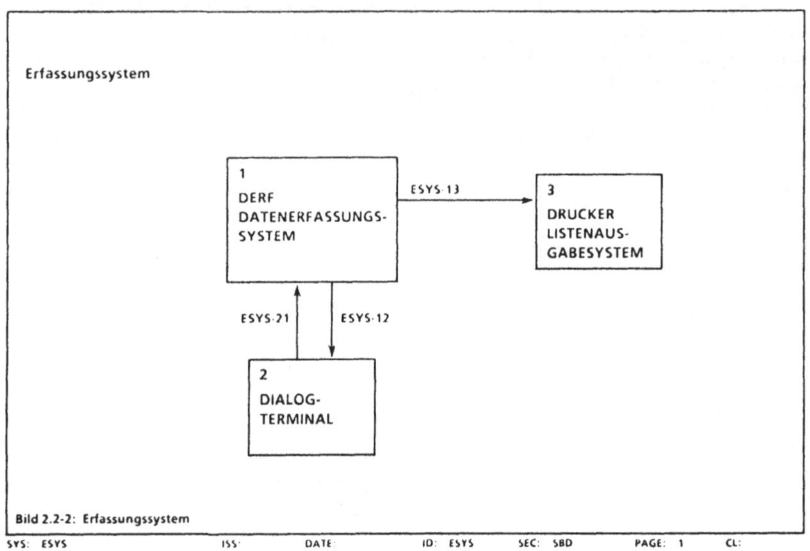

Die Informationsflüsse, gekennzeichnet durch das Flußobjekt (Datentyp) und die Flußmenge (Anzahl/Zeiteinheit), fließen in "Kanälen" auf den Schnittstellen zwischen den Komponenten in Pfeilrichtung.
Die Informationsflüsse fließen mit gleichmäßigem Durchsatz (Anzahl Objekte/Zeiteinheit), der dem zeitlichen Mittelwert entspricht. Die Komponenten transformieren (pumpen) die Eingangsflüsse in die Ausgangsflüsse und bewirken eine mittlere zeitliche Verschiebung. Diese zeitliche Verschiebung ist die Antwortzeit der Komponente.
Es wird nicht das Einzelereignis betrachtet, sondern die mittleren Flüsse.

* **Das Kommunikationsdiagramm mit seinen Flüssen stellt da-** *
* **her eine Makrobetrachtung dar.** *

Parametertabellen für Komponenten und Schnittstellen

Eine Komponente repräsentiert laut Definition einen oder mehrere Prozesse.

Bei den Prozessen handelt es sich je nach Aufgabenstellung um die Darstellung des dynamischen Ablaufes einer

- organisatorischen Einheit
- funktionellen Einheit
- technischen Einheit.

Diese Prozesse und damit die Komponente transformieren Eingangsflüsse in Ausgangsflüsse, die durch Durchlaufzeiten zeitlich verschoben werden.

Die Prozesse bearbeiten die Datenobjekte, die ihnen auf externen oder internen Schnittstellen zufließen. An externe Schnittstellen fließen beispielsweise die Eingangsdaten vom Terminal zu oder es werden vom Prozess Listen erzeugt, die am Drucker ausgegeben werden.
Interne Schnittstellen führen zu den Dateien, auf die die Komponente zugreift, und zu anderen Komponenten.

Ziel der Informationsflußanalyse ist es, diese Informationsflüsse und damit die Komponenten bezüglich ihres Datenbedarfs möglichst genau festzulegen, da sich bei datenorientierten Systemen erst daraus die nötige Transformation und damit der Prozessablauf ergibt.
In der Praxis bedeutet dies das Analysieren bzw. Entwerfen von

- Dokumenten
- Listen
- Masken
- Menüs,

ein Vorgang, der sehr zeitaufwendig ist, der aber auch zu einer verarbeitungsgerechten Gestaltung der Datenobjekte führt.
Wir nennen dies den Vorgang der Formatisierung der Datenobjekte. Dieser Schritt wird, zusammen mit der nötigen Abstimmarbeit, vielfach unterschätzt. Basis einer Abschätzung sind die Anzahl der verschiedenen Datenobjekte, die in den internen Parametertabellen festgehalten werden.

Bild 2.2-4 zeigt die Darstellung der Informationsflüsse in der internen Parametertabelle des Erfassungssystemes.

GRP	Beschreibung (DIM)	Name	Wertebereich	Einheiten, Bedeutung
	<Informationsflüsse>			[Min., max. Zeichenzahl] Informationsfluß, Kommentar
	Erfassungsdatei (5000)	SESATZ	(ALL)	[100,200] 30/Stunde gleichzeitig Fluß vom Terminal
	Maskendatei (112)	SMASK	(ALL)	[50,300] 30/Stunde gleichzeitig Fluß vom Terminal
	Listen (15)	SLIST	(ALL)	[600,800] 70/Tag normal im Maximum 90/Tag Fluß zum Drucker
	<Entscheidungsbedingungen> Dokumentart	DOKART	(1. 2, 3.)	= Dokumententyp A = Dokumententyp B = Dokumententyp C
	Maximaler Wert	MAXWERT	(100. 200. 300.)	für Dokumententyp A für Dokumententyp B für Dokumententyp C

Bild 2.2-4: Informationsflüsse und Entscheidungsparameter

SYS: ISS: DATE: ID: SEC.   PAGE: CL:

2.3 Das Metamodell

Markieren der Komponenten mit Merkmalen

Durch die Beschreibung der Informationsflüsse und Bedingungen (Bild 2.2-4) in den Parametertabellen und die Dokumentation der Zeitverschiebung im Komponentenblock wird eine Komponente festgelegt (Makrosicht).

Damit sind aber im allgemeinen nicht alle Parameter einer Komponente beschrieben. Sie ist in den meisten Fällen noch durch eine Zahl von anderen Merkmalen gekennzeichnet, je nachdem unter welchen Aspekt eine Komponente oder ein System betrachtet wird. Derartige Aspekte sind z. B.:

Organisation und Planung

- Verantwortlichkeit für eine Komponente
- Bearbeitungszustand
- Bearbeitungsaufwand
- Fertigstellungstermin
- Zugehörigkeit zu einer technischen oder organisatorischen Einheit

Technische Leistungsanforderungen und Einschränkungen

- Mengenangaben
- Numerische Grenz- bzw. Sollwerte aller Art

Realisierungsangaben

- Abmessungen
- Gewichte
- Materialbeschreibungen

Referenzierung zum Anforderungskatalog

Bevor man ein Systemmodell entwickeln kann, muß ein Anforderungskatalog vorliegen, der zumindest in Schlagworten die Grundanforderungen enthält.

Jede Anforderung bekommt eine eindeutige Bezeichnung, die zur Referenzierung verwendet werden kann.

Metainformationen

Wir nennen die angeführten Merkmale "Metainformationen", sie gehören in der Regel nicht zum fachlichen Modell, sie berücksichtigen zusätzliche Bedingungen und Einschränkungen.

Um ein System nach den Metainformationen auswerten zu können, müssen die Komponenten mit den Aspekten markiert werden.
Dies geschieht in den Parametertabellen der zugehörigen Prozesse bzw. Subprozesse. Die Merkmale werden in Form von

- numerischen Konstanten (Organisation und Planung, Leistungsangaben und Realisierungsangaben)
- logischen Variablen mit den Werten 'TRUE' und 'FALSE' (Referenzierung von textuellen Spezifikationen)

in die Parametiertabelle eingebracht.

<u>Auswertung</u>

Ein Werkzeug zur Modelldarstellung muß Dienstfunktionen haben um die Markierungen in einem Modell entsprechend auswerten zu können.

Sehr wirksam in dieser Richtung sind Standardauswertungen der Modelldatenbank, wie

- Verwendungsnachweise für Konstante und Variable
- Verwendungsnachweise für Prozesse und Subprozesse.

Wir nennen ein Modell, das alle im life-cycle eines Zielproduktes nötigen Daten und Beziehungen enthält ein <u>Metamodell</u>.

2.4   <u>Mikrobetrachtung</u>

<u>Der Informationsfluß als Ereignisfluß</u>

Bei der Mikrobetrachtung wird der Ablauf eines einzelnen Ereignisses im System betrachtet. In einem ereignisgesteuerten System werden die Prozesse durch Objekte angestoßen. Ein Ereignis tritt dann ein, wenn ein Objekt einen Prozeß anstößt.
Es ist durch
- das Objekt
- den Zeitpunkt und
- den betroffenen Prozeß

gekennzeichnet. Im Bereich technischer Prozesse werden die Ereignisse "Stimuli" genannt, die entsprechenden Ausgangsobjekte der "Response" (Stimulus-Response Prinzip).

Ein Prozeß kann durch Ereignisse verschiedenster Natur ausgelöst werden:

- Produktivobjekte, das sind Objekte die in den nachfolgenden Prozeßschritten bearbeitet werden (Materialien, Dokumente usw.).

- Steuerobjekte, das sind Zeitsignale, Aufrufparameter, Promptinginformationen, usw.

- Bedingungs- bzw. Zustandswechsel (Steuer- bzw. Kontrollsysteme)

In Anlehnung an die Informationstheorie werden die Ereignisse, die einen Prozeß auslösen (= vom Prozeß "verstanden" werden) als Information bezeichnet.

Ereignisse sind gekennzeichnet durch den Typ (Flußtyp) und eine Wahrscheinlichkeit des Auftretens. Sie sind statistische Phänomäne im Sinne der Informationstheorie von Shannon /6/.

Der Ereignisfluß wird daher INFORMATIONSFLUSS genannt. Er transportiert die Information zum Starten eines Prozesses.

Er ist identisch mit dem Informationsfluß auf den Schnittstellen. Die Informationsflüsse werden von Prozessen erzeugt und stoßen ihrerseits wieder Prozesse an (Prozessinteraktion).

2.5   Darstellung des dynamischen Verhaltens

Bei der Mikrobetrachtung wird der zeitlich/logische Ablauf der Bearbeitung beschrieben, dem die Eingangsobjekte einer Komponente unterliegen.
Bild 2.5-1 zeigt ein Prozessdiagramm.
Es wird der Ablauf für ein Eingangsobjekt beschrieben. Die Schleife bedeutet, daß dieser Zyklus bei jedem Eingangsobjekt neu beginnt.
Die Pfeile geben im Sinne der Informationsflußanalyse die Richtung der Ereignisflüsse an, die die Subprozesse zum Ablauf bringen.

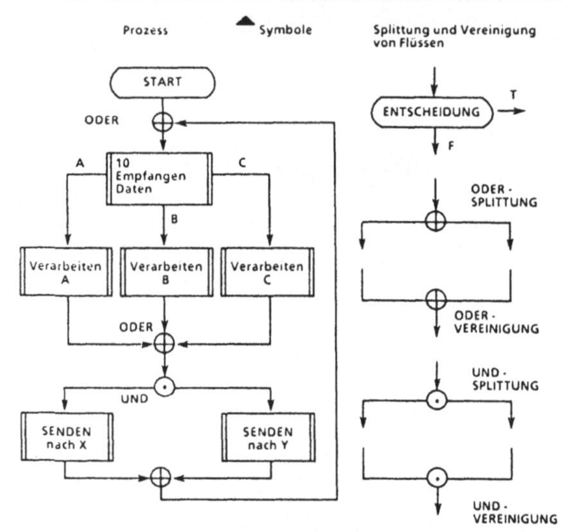

Bild 2.5-1: Symbolsatz für grafische Darstellung von dynamischen Abläufen

Die Daten, die der Prozess braucht bzw. die zugehörigen Flüsse wurden in einer zum Prozess bzw. der Komponente gehörenden internen Parametertabelle (Bild 2.2-4) beschrieben.
Die einzelnen Prozesschritte stellen Aufrufe von Subprozessen (Teilabläufe, Unterprogramme) dar, die mehrfach im System verwendet werden können. Will man ein System exakt beschreiben, so werden diese Subprozesse, genannt PPD (Predifined Process Diagramm), mit der nonprozeduralen Spezifikationssprache GRAPES 85 bis auf Codeebene in ihrem zeitlichen und algorithmischen Verhalten beschrieben. Sie ermöglicht die Darstellung paralleler Prozesse und kennt folgende Darstellungselemente:

- Ein/Ausgabesymbole mit denen beliebig komplexe Übertragungsprozeduren für die Schnittstellen aufgebaut werden können.

- Verzögerungselemente, die zur Darstellung des Zeitverbrauches der Algorithmen dienen.

- Algorithmische und logische Operationen
  (Arithmetische-, Boolsche-, Vektoren-, Matrizzen-, Mengen-, Zeichenoperationen).

- Verzweigungssymbole
  (Entscheidungssymbole und Symbole für die Zusammenführung bzw. Splittung von Flüssen).

- Eine Datendarstellung mit einem Typkonzept, wie es moderne Programmiersprachen (PASCAL, Ada) aufweisen.

Mit GRAPES 85 können beliebige Probleme exakt spezifiziert werden. Das bedeutet, daß so dargestellte Systeme mit CADOS auch auf Vollständigkeit und syntaktische Richtigkeit geprüft und automatisch in ein ablauffähiges Simulationsmodell umgesetzt werden können. Es erfolgt dabei eine automatische Umsetzung des Modelles in Ada-Source-Code, der kompiliert wird und als Simulationsmodell ablauffähig ist.

Wenn eine so spezifizierte Komponente eine Softwarekomponente darstellt, können sie auch direkt in ablauffähige Ada-Komponenten umgesetzt werden.

Will man Algorithmen nicht bis ins letzte Detail in GRAPES 85 spezifieren, weil man beispielsweise als Zielsprache COBOL oder C hat, so begrenzt sich die Modellierung im wesentlichen auf die Darstellung von
o Kommunikationsdiagrammen
o Parametertabellen
o Prozessdiagrammen mit
        - Subprozessaufrufsymbole
        - Verzweigungssymbole (UND, ODER, Entscheidung) (Bild 2.5-1).

Wir beschränken uns im weiterem auf diesen Satz von Darstellungssymbolen und damit auch auf diesen Grad der Feinheit der Darstellung.
Die Praxis zeigt, daß man damit beliebige Problemstellungen im technischen und kommerziellen Bereich ausreichend exakt beschreiben kann.
Der Vorteil dieser Beschränkung liegt darin, daß dieser Satz von Symbolen

- von Organisatoren und Technikern leicht erlernt und nach Schulung auch zur Formulierung ihrer Aufgabenstellung eingesetzt werden kann,
- die Darstellungen vom Manager bis zum Wartungstechniker nach kurzer Einführung gelesen werden kann.

2.6   Das vollständige Modell

Um die Anforderungen an ein System zu definieren, müssen auch seine Schnittstellen zur Umwelt erfaßt werden.

Dies geschieht am besten in der Weise, daß man die Kommunikationspartner des Systems mitbetrachtet, die die externen Ereignisse an das System senden und dadurch die Systemprozesse anstoßen.

Ein Modell (Bild 2.6-1) entsteht dadurch, daß man

- ein Zielsystem (zu untersuchendes System) mit seinen Kommunikations-
  partnern in einem Kommunikationsdiagramm darstellt. Damit wird das Kom-
  munikationsverhalten des geschlossenen Gesamtsystems beschrieben.

- die Informationsflüsse auf den Schnittstellen in Parametertabellen nach
  Objektart (Datentyp), Flußmenge und Übertragungszeit feststellt.

- für die einzelnen Komponenten (Prozeßträger) die Prozesse definiert.
  Die Datenobjekte, die von den Komponenten benötigt werden, legt man in
  internen Parametertabellen fest.
  Dasselbe gilt auch für Implementierungs-, Design, Referenz- und sonstige
  Informationen.

- Das Zeitverhalten des Systemes ergibt sich aus dem Zeitverbrauch der Informationsflüsse (Übertragungszeit) und dem Zeitverbrauch der Komponenten
  (Zeitraum zwischen Eingabeereignis und Ausgabeereignis = Durchlaufzeit).

Ein Modell ergibt sich als Kombination der Makro- und Mikrobetrachtung.

Das dynamische Modell der obersten Ebene stellt die Aufgabenstellung des
Systemes dar.

Es werden die Eingangsflüsse vorgegeben und die erwarteten Ausgangsflüsse
spezifiziert.

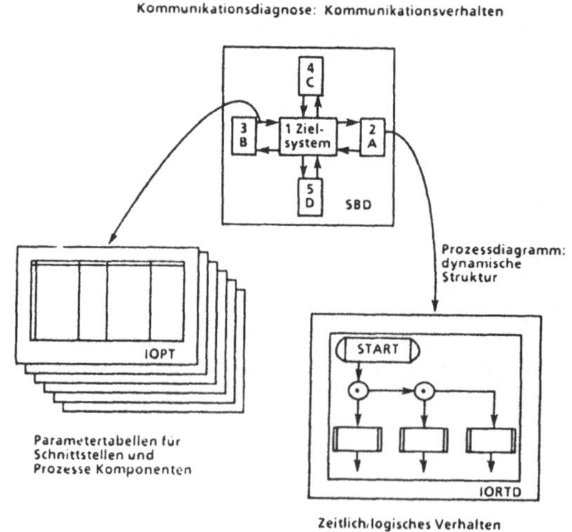

Bild 2.6-1: Modelldarstellung durch formale Beschreibung des
Kommunikationsverhaltens und des zeitlich/logischen Ablaufs

2.7   Die Strukturierung eines Systemes mit DOMINO-Steinen

Ein Kernproblem der Analyse und Darstellung von Systemen mit formalen, nicht grafischen Mitteln ist die geringe Anschaulichkeit.
Bild 2.7-1 zeigt die Strukturierung eines Systemes aus der Sicht der Informationsflußanalyse.

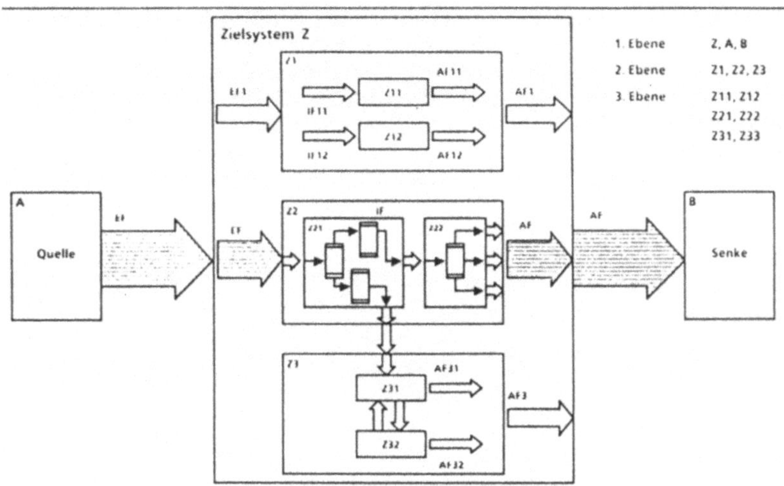

Bild 2.7-2: Prozessdiagramme und Kommunikationsdiagramme als DOMINO-Steine

Eine Flußquelle A erzeugt einen Eingangsfluß EF für das Zielsystem Z, das als Zielobjekt (Resultat) den Ausgangsfluß AF hervorbringt.
Die Strukturierung erfolgt so, daß der Eingangsfluß nach bestimmten Regeln gesplittet und über Komponenten entsprechenden Ausgangsflüssen zugeordnet wird.

Die Splittung von Flüssen führt zu einer Parallelisierung, also einer Abspaltung von unterschiedlichen Flüßen (Flußobjekt, Zeitzyklen) entsprechend einer Zerlegung des Zielsystemes in die Komponenten Z1, Z2.
Die Zerlegung der Komponente Z2 in hintereinandergeschaltete Teilkomponenten Z21 und Z22 nennen wir eine Sequentialisierung (Hintereinanderschalten) von Komponenten bzw. Flüssen.

Durch die Parallelisierung (Splittung) und Sequentialisierung von Flüssen werden die Komponenten in Teilkomponenten zerlegt, die parallel oder sequentiell Flüsse bearbeiten.
Die Darstellung des Prozessablaufes in einer Komponente kann als weitere Verfeinerung der Flußdarstellung innerhalb einer Komponente angesehen werden. Das zeitlich/logische Hintereinander der Transformationen, die auf den Eingangsfluß ausgeübt wird, um daraus den Ausgangsfluß zu machen, wird damit dargestellt.
Kommunikationsdiagramme und Prozessdiagramme zeigen die Transformation von Flüssen.

Durch die Strukturierung wird die ursprünglich leere Fläche des Zielsystemes systematisch mit Flüssen und Pumpen bzw. Verteilerstationen (Komponenten) beschrieben. Durch diese Vorstellung wird eine zweidimensionale Systemdarstellung erreicht, die anschaulich ist und ohne viel Abstraktion auskommt. Die Kommunikationsdiagramme und Prozessdiagramme werden als DOMINO-Steine, die immer kleiner und feiner werden in ein ebenes Mosaikbild eingefügt. Die Kommunikations- und Prozessdiagramme sind diese DOMINO-Steine, die im System CADOS editiert, verwaltet und formal geprüft werden.

* Wesentlich für den Analysator ist es, sich dieses Bild bei der Strukturierung*
* eines Systemes vor Augen zu führen. Die heutigen Systeme liefern leider   *
* dieses Übersichtsbild noch nicht, sondern die einzelnen DOMINO-Steine.   *
* Die Informationsflußanalyse gibt die Regeln für die systematische   *
* Vorgehensweise beim Zerlegen von Flüssen in parallele und sequentielle   *
* Teile und damit Komponenten.   *

3.   Konzeptionelles Datenschema

Ein konzeptionelles Datenschema entsteht in der klassischen Vorgehensweise dadurch, daß eine sogenannte "Miniwelt" als Untersuchungsfeld abgegrenzt wird und die Datenobjekte und deren Beziehungen in dieser "Miniwelt" untersucht werden. Diese Miniwelt ist in unserem Fall das Zielsystem, das im CADOS-Kommunikationsdiagramm abgegrenzt und durch die zu bearbeitenden Informationsflüsse definiert wird.

Im Rahmen der Analyse wird durch die Prozesse und die Informationsflüsse ein dynamisches Modell dieser Miniwelt erstellt. Durch die Definition der Objekte und die Bestimmung ihrer Merkmale (Antragsteller hat Name und Adresse, Antragsunterlagen haben identifizierende und beschreibende Merkmale) wird die Basis für das Datenmodell gelegt. Welche Merkmale bei einem Objekt vorhanden sein müssen, ergibt sich aus den vorhandenen und geplanten Verarbeitungen.

Ein konzeptionelles Datenschema, dargestellt in einen Datenstrukturdiagramm ist somit eine Darstellung der Beziehungen der Datenobjekte auf Grund der vorhandenen oder geplanten Verarbeitung.

* **Durch die Informationsflußanalyse werden Funktionsanalyse**   *
* **und Daten bzw. Informationsanalyse integriert abgewickelt.**   *
* **Die Informationsflüsse zwischen Verarbeitungsprozessen und**   *
* **Datenverwaltungssystem stellen den Datenbedarf der Kompo-**   *
* **nenten dar, der aus Dateien gedeckt wird. Die Informationsflüsse** *
* **enthalten die Datenstruktur und die Ansprechhäufigkeit. Dieser**   *
* **Datenbedarf ist die Basis für die Datenmodellierung, er stellt die**   *
* **"Benutzersichten" der Anwendungen bzw. Komponenten dar.**   *

* **Im Bild 3-1 ist der Zusammenhang zwischen konzeptionellen**   *
* **Datenschema, Benutzersichten und technischer Sicht für die**   *
* **Speicherung gezeigt.**   *

Bild 3-1: Drei Ebenen von Datenstrukturen

Die Datenbeziehungen werden parallel zur Funktionsanalyse entwickelt. Sie stellen neben Kommunikationsdiagrammen und Prozessdiagrammen ein wirksames Mittel dar, die Erkenntnisse über Funktionen und Daten zu ergänzen. Zur Darstellung von Datenstrukturdiagrammen verwendet man die Kommunikationsdiagramme von CADOS in einem getrennten Modell.

Das konzeptionelle Datenschema stellt ein eigenständiges Beziehungssystem dar, das parallel zum Systemmodell entwickelt wird.

Die Blöcke stellen im konzeptionellen Datenschema Objekte (Entities) dar, die Interfaces kennzeichnen die Beziehung.

Die gegenseitigen Beziehungen werden durch zwei getrennte Interfaces dargestellt.

Wenn es sich um eine 1:N Beziehung handelt wird dem Interfacebezeichner N angefügt. Bei einer 1:1 Beziehung wird dem Interfacebezeichner nichts angefügt.

Bei der Datenmodellierung wird nach der Methodik der Entity-Relationship-Analyse /4/ vorgegangen. Bild 3-2 zeigt das Datenmodell einer Topebene.

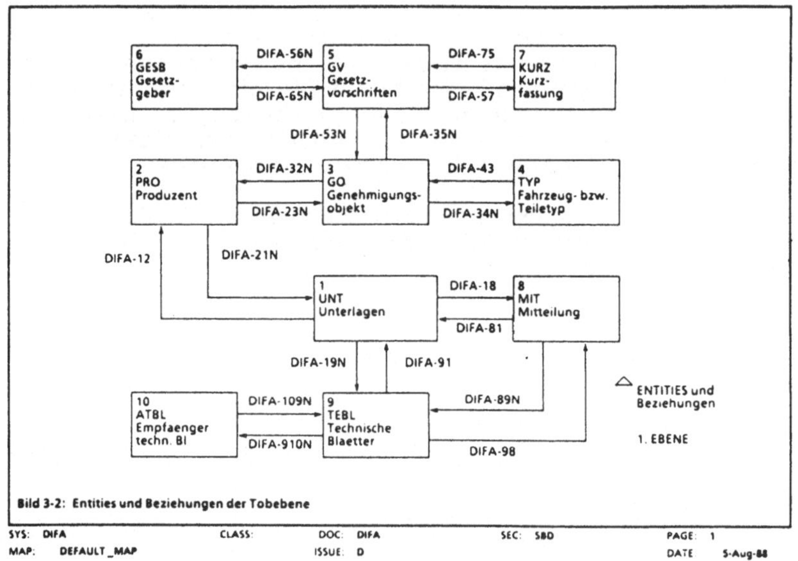

Die spezielle Form der hierarchischen Auflösung der Objekte und Beziehungen ist ein Teil der Methodik der Informationsflußanalyse.

*** Das Resultat ist ein konzeptionelles Datenschema, dessen unterste Ebene ***
*** nur noch Objekte enthält, die als Tabellen einer relationalen Datenbank ***
*** in normalisierter Form in die Parametertabelle beschrieben sind. ***

4. Methodik der Verifikation und Validierung

4.1 Statische Verifikation

Prüfung auf korrekte Darstellung, Vollständigkeit und Konsistenz

Der Dokumentenprüfer von CADOS[R] ermöglicht es

- den formal richtigen Aufbau (Syntax und Semantik) eines Systemmodells,
- die formale Konsistenz und Vollständigkeit zu prüfen.

Die Korrektheit eines Modelles wird durch einen Diagnoseablauf überprüft und folgende Fehler beispielsweise gemeldet:

o Semantische Fehler
- ungültige Parameternamen
- illegale Zeichen
- illegale Datendefinitionen

o Syntax Fehler
- illegale Symbole in einem Plan
- unzulässige Verknüpfung von Symbolen

o Cross-Reference Fehler
- Parameter sind referenziert aber nicht definiert
- falsche Referenzierung von Subprozessen

o Konsistenz-Fehler
- Parametername mehrfach definiert
- widersprüchliche Definition der Datenflußrichtung
- widersprüchliche Ein/Ausgabedefinitionen
- Verwendung typfremder Operatoren

o Vollständigkeitsfehler
- fehlende Prozeßpläne und Parametertabellen
- fehlende Parameter bzw. falsch oder unvollständig beschriebene Parameter
- nicht verbundene Schnittstellen und Komponenten
- unvollständig beschriebene Schnittstellen

Die Überprüfung auf Vollständigkeit und Konsistenz erfolgt in folgenden Stufen:

- Pro erzeugte Seite bzw. Plantyp
  (Strukturplan, Prozeßplan, Parametertabellen)

- Pro Systemebene (Dokument)

- Für das ganze System

Verifikation von Informationsflüssen und Metainformationen durch statisches Tracing

Von besonderer Bedeutung für die Verifikation von Informationsflüssen ist die Möglichkeit,
- jeden konstanten Wert
- jedes Datenobjekt
- jeden Parameter,

der in den Parametertabellen definiert ist, über alle Systemebenen zu verfolgen.

Die Data-Dictionary-Funktion von CADOS ermöglicht es, einen Parameter nach
Verwendung in
- Schnittstellen
- Komponenten
- Prozessen
- Subprozessen

pro Systemebene auszuwerten.

Damit ist es möglich
- Informationsflüsse
- Leistungswerte für die Implementierung
- Konstruktions, Material- und Qualitätsmerkmale
- Referenzinformationen für funktionale Anforderungen, Standards, oder
  sonstige Spezifikationen (Sicherheit, Test usw.)

über alle Systemebenen zu verfolgen.

Die Voraussetzung für ein DV-gestütztes Verfolgen von Informationsflüssen ist
die Definition bzw. Referenzierung der Informationsflüsse in den Parametertabellen der Schnittstellen und in den Parametertabellen der Prozesse bzw.
Subprozesse.
Das Prinzip des Verfolgens von Informationsflüssen ist in Bild 4.1-1 gezeigt.

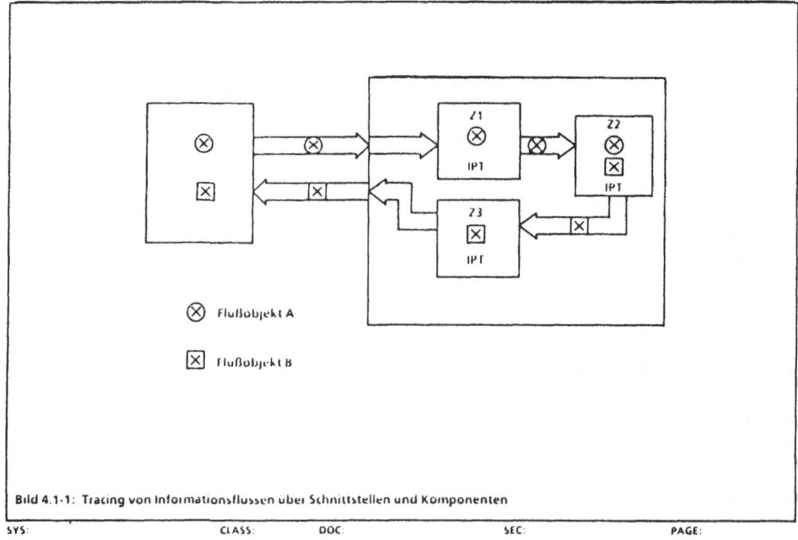

Bild 4.1-1: Tracing von Informationsflüssen über Schnittstellen und Komponenten

In gleicher Weise können in den internen Parametertabellen Metainformationen
wie
- Leistungswerte für die Implementierung
- Konstruktions-, Material- und Qualitätsdaten
- Referenzinformationen auf übergeordnete Anforderungen oder Standards

in Form von Konstanten oder Variablen hinterlegt und in Verwendungsnachweisen über alle Systemebenen nachgewiesen werden.

4.2 Dynamische Verifikation durch Simulation

Prinzip der dynamischen Verifikationen

Die dynamische Verifikation erfolgt durch Simulation.
Durch Simulation kann das

- funktionale Verhalten
- das Zeitverhalten
- das Leistungsverhalten unter Last

überprüft werden.

Funktionssimulation

Durch eine Funktionssimulation wird das algorithmische Verhalten eines Systemes
simuliert. Die Voraussetzung dafür ist, daß alle Algorithmen eines Systemes in
ausreichender Feinheit spezifiziert sind.

Leistungssimulation

Unter Leistungssimulation verstehen wir die Simulation des Zeitverhaltens unter
Lastbedingungen. Wenn im Informationsfluß Komponenten mit begrenzter
Kapazität liegen kann es zur Bildung von Warteschlangen kommen. Eine andere
Ursache für die Bildung von Warteschlangen ist im organisatorischen Bereich das
Fehlen von Teilinformationen zur Weiterbearbeitung eines Vorganges. Im
Bereich der Produktion tritt dieser Effekt ein, wenn ein benötigter Bestandteil
fehlt oder wenn es aus Qualitätsgründen zur Nacharbeit kommt.

Bei der Leistungssimulation müssen nicht die Funktionen selbst sondern ihr Zeitverbrauch bzw. die Reaktionszeit simuliert werden. Der Aufwand ist im allgemeinen wesentlich geringer als bei einer Funktionssimulation.

Systeme, die über 3 Stufen des Dokumentenprüfers von CADOS

- Analysis   (pro Seite)
- Compilation (pro Ebene)
- Integration   (gesamtes System)

statisch verifiziert wurden, können in ADA-Source-CODE umgesetzt, compiliert
und über den Simulation-Compiler zum Ablauf gebracht werden (Bild 4.2-2).

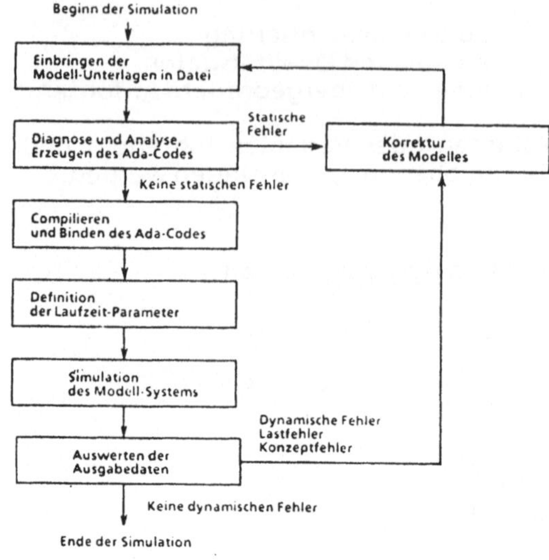

Bild 4.2-2: CADOS-Dynamische Kontrolle (DK)

Prototyping durch Simulation

Wurden entsprechend den Methoden der Informationsflußanalyse Funktions-
und Leistungsverhalten modelliert, so erhält man einen Prototyp des Systemes,
dessen Verhalten getestet werden kann.

Der Simulation-Compiler unterstützt

- die Fehlersuche in einem Modell durch einen Dialog-Ablaufverfolger, der es
  ermöglicht den Ablauf an einem beliebigen Punkt zu unterbrechen und sämtliche Werte von Variablen anzusehen bzw. zu verändern.

- Er unterstützt die Auswertung der Ablaufinformation des Modelles durch
  Utilities, die den Anschluß von individuellen Auswerteroutinen gestatten.

Durch die Möglichkeit, sich als Benutzer im Dialog direkt in den Simulations-
prozess einzuschalten und zu reagieren, können Dialogsysteme wirklichkeitsnah
simuliert werden.

4.3   Prototyping und Generierung

Mit dem CADOS-CODE-Generator kann aus einer vollspezifizierten Komponente
direkt ein Softwaresystem generiert werden. Als erster CODE-Generator steht ein
ADA-Codegenerator zur Verfügung. Eine wesentliche Fehlerquelle, die perso-
nelle Codierung wird ausgeschaltet, der entstehende Code ist streng konsistent
mit der Spezifikation. Das entstehende Softwaresystem stellt einen Prototyp dar,
der in vielen Fällen noch optimiert werden muß.

Traceability

Die Verfolgbarkeit zwischen Modell und Ada-Code und zurück ist durch folgende
Zuordnungen möglich:

> GRAPES 85-Sektionen werden eigenen Ada-Compilierungseinheiten zugeord-
> net.

> GRAPES 85-Namen gehen über in ähnliche Ada-Namen.

> GRAPES 85-Symbole finden sich wieder in Ada-Labels, die Modellseite und
> Symbol wieder geben.

Fehleranalyse

Voraussetzung für die Codegenerierung ist der erfolgreiche Test des Systemes
durch den Dokumentenprüfer über die Stufen

- Analyse
- Compilation
- Integration

Die dynamische Verifikation durch Simulation ist sehr zu empfehlen, um logische
Fehler auszuschalten.

Validierung am Zielsystem

Durch die Umsetzung von CADOS-Systeme in Ada-Code ist der entstehende Code
auf Systemen mit gültigen Ada-Compiler ablauffähig.

Damit ist man in der Lage Systeme auf der Workstation unabhängig vom Host zu
erstellen und kann sie anschließend beliebig portieren.

Zur Validierung wird das generierte System auf das Zielsystem übertragen, dort
optimiert und mit den spezifierten Testdaten auf Übereinstimmung mit den
Anforderungen überprüft.

4.4 Grundsätze des methodischen Vorgehens bei der Strukturierung:

Ziel der Informationsflußanalyse ist ein methodisches Vorgehen, in dessen Mittelpunkt eine "Konzentration auf das Wesentliche" durch Gewichtung nach Informationsflüssen und Bearbeitungsintensität steht.

Die wichtigsten Schritte der Methodik können folgendermaßen zusammengefaßt werden:

1.) Aufbau eines Systemmodelles nach der Methode Outside-In.

2.) Zusammenfassung der externen Informationsflüsse durch Abstraktion.

3.) Zuordnung zu wenigen typischen Systemprozessen die mitteinander über Informationsflüsse gekoppelt sind:

- verschiedene Eingangsflüsse
- verschiedene Ausgangsflüsse
- keine Rückkoppelungsbeziehungen zu den übrigen Systemprozessen
- unterschiedliche interne Daten.

4.) Aufbau eines Grundmodelles durch Sequentialisierung und Parallelisierung.

5.) Stufenweise Konkretisierung der Zeitanforderungen.

6.) Verifikation des Grundmodelles.

7.) Erweiterung des Grundmodelles zum Gesamtmodell.

8.) Verifikation des Gesamtmodelles.

4.5 Situation bei der Werkzeugunterstützung /1/

Die Werkzeugunterstützung bei CADOS umfaßt heute bereits folgende Schritte:

Automatische Verkettung von Funktionen, Daten und Merkmale über alle Ebenen der Verfeinerung bzw. Strukturierung.

Automatische Prüfung der Datenkonsistenz.

Data-Dictionary, mit Verwendungsnachweisen und Tracing-Informationen für Daten und Prozesse.

Automatische Umsetzung des Systemmodelles in ein ablauffähiges Simulationsmodell.

4.6 Ausblick

Bei professioneller Anwendung der Informationsflußanalyse und der Werkzeugunterstützung kann man bei komplexen Projekten mit

- wesentlichen Einsparungen durch rechtzeitiges Aufdecken von Inkonsis-
tenzen, Unklarheiten, Unvollständigkeiten

- wesentlicher Verbesserung der Qualität der Spezifikation der Produkte

und damit mit einer starken Minderung des Zeit- und Kostenrisikos rechnen.

Einen weiteren Schritt in Richtung Produktivitätssteigerung stellt die automatische Umsetzung der formalen Modelle in ablauffähige Software dar.

Die technischen Mittel dafür werden ständig verbessert. Eine Breitenwirkung
wird man damit allerdings erst erzielen können, wenn es gelingt, den Stand und
die Möglichkeiten der Methoden und Werkzeuge auf der Ebene des
Managements und im Fachbereich deutlich zu machen. Wie jeder Fortschritt
bedeutet der Einsatz der modernen Methoden

- das Lösen von konventionellen Vorstellungen und
- eine gewisse Anfangsinvestition.

Gewonnen wird dadurch Professionalität, Sicherheit und geringere Kosten.

Literaturverzeichnis

/1/   CADOS, Computer aided Design für Organisatoren und Systemingenieure,
       Produktschrift 1985 Siemens AG, München

/2/   Groh, H. Lutz K.:
       Outside-in statt Top-Down, Siemens date report 19, (1984) Heft 3

/3/   De Marco, T., Structured Analysis and System Specification, Yourdon Inc.,
       New York, 1979

/4/   Chen P. Entity-Relationship approach to Information Modelling and
       analysis, North Holland, 1981

/5/   Kaufmann, F. H..
       Informationsflußanalyse, Systemanalyse und Entropie zeitkritischer
       Systeme. Siemens AG, München Januar 1987

/6/   Shannon, C.E., A mathematical theorie of Communication, Bell System.
       Techn. ./. 27 (1948)

P P S 3

Projektplanungs- und Steuerungssystem

Peter Christgau
Industrieanlagen-Betriebsgesellschaft mbH
8012 Ottobrunn (München)

I n h a l t

Kurzfassung

PPS3 unterstützt die Projektplanung, -Steuerung und -Überwachung in ihrer ganzen Breite. Es bietet praxisorientierte und theoretisch fundierte Funktionsmoduln, interaktive Eingabe im Laien- und Expertenmodus, flexible Listenausgabe und Schnittstellen für die graphische Ausgabe von Struktur-, Netz- und Balkenplänen. Das System ist einsatzfähig auf Personal-Computern bis hin zum Großrechner. Eine SQL-Version befindet sich in der Testphase.

PPS3 - Projektplanungs- und Steuerungssystem
- Einleitung -

1. Einleitung

Projekte verlassen häufig den gegebenen Kosten- und Zeitrahmen
oder verfehlen die Erwartungen an Leistung oder Qualität. Es
mangelt nicht an Beispielen, die bei dieser Gelegenheit gerne
zitiert werden: vom Turmbau zu Babel bis zu den Investitionsrui-
nen der Gegenwart. Auch Entwicklungsprojekte in der Informatik
sind gelegentlich betroffen.

Die Probleme des Projektmanagements sind nicht neu, aber sie
verschärfen sich: Die beschleunigte technische Innovation verkürzt die Produktzyklen und verstärkt den Termindruck. Der wachsende technische Inhalt der Produkte selbst sowie die fortschrei-
tenden Fertigungstechniken schaffen immer komplexere und umfang-
reichere Projektstrukturen.

Durch die zunehmende Spezialisierung auf anspruchsvolle Marktseg-
mente werden auch kleinere und mittlere Unternehmen von dieser
Entwicklung erfaßt. Ähnliches gilt für Fachabteilungen in Großun-
ternehmen oder Behörden, die eigenverantwortlich Teilprojekte
bearbeiten.

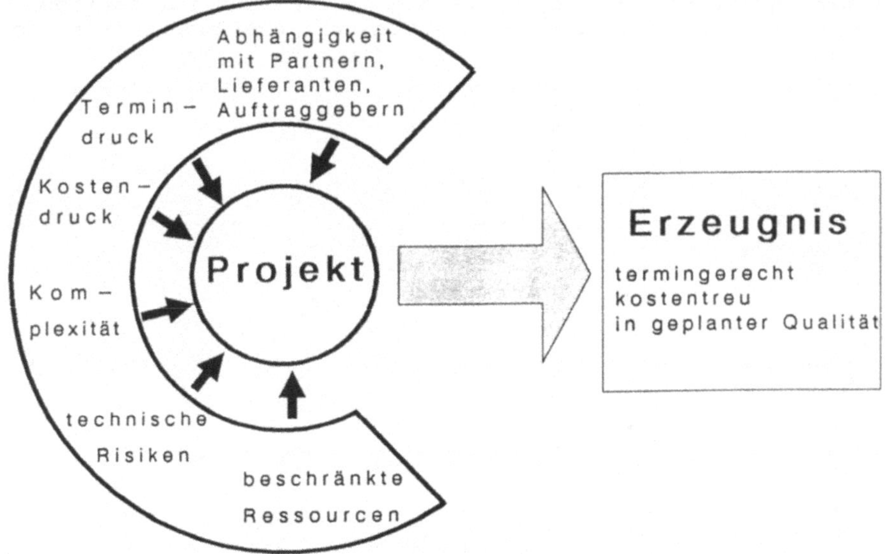

Abb. 1: Projektmanagement: Ziele und Einflüsse

Im militärischen Bereich wurden - wie auch in der Raumfahrt -
frühzeitig DV-gestützte Informationssysteme für das Projektmanagement eingesetzt. Das im Auftrag des Bundesamts für Wehrtechnik
und Beschaffung (BWB) von der Industrieanlagen-Betriebsgesellschaft entwickelte System PPS3 berücksichtigt die Erfahrungen des
Auftraggebers im Management umfangreicher Rüstungsprogramme. Es
wird als Standardsoftware auch der zivilen Wirtschaft und Verwaltung angeboten.

PPS3 - Projektplanungs- und Steuerungssystem
    - Entwicklungsziel und -richtung -

---

2. Entwicklungsziel und Entwicklungsrichtung

Die Software für das Projektmanagement soll nach wie vor die
bewährten Verarbeitungsalgorithmen wie Netzplantechnik bereit-
stellen, sie soll aber heute auch stärker die Aspekte der Manage-
mentinformation sowie der Projektkontrolle und -verwaltung berücksichtigen. Für die Unterstützung des Managements sind die
Daten der Detailplanung auf höhere und übersichtlichere Ebenen zu
aggregieren.Die Anforderungen der Verwaltung sind im Detail sehr
organisationsspezifisch und können oft nicht mit Standardsoftware
befriedigt werden.

Möglich ist es allerdings, ein offenes System zu ergänzen durch
z. B. ein Verzeichnis der Projektdokumentation oder eine Termin-
überwachung für Verwaltungsvorgänge. Schnittstellen zu anderen
Informationssystemen wie betriebliches Rechnungswesen, Qualitäts-
kontrolle o.a. sollen durch möglichst redundanzfreie Speicherung,
Schlüsselverweise und einheitliche und mächtige Werkzeuge leicht
realisierbar sein und sich im praktischen Einsatz bewähren.

Wesentliche Forderungen sind auch die Interaktion für häufige
und gelegentliche Benutzer und die Qualität und Aufbereitung der
Ergebnisse.

PPS3 - Projektplanungs- und Steuerungssystem
- Modellbildung in PPS3 -

---

3. Modellbildung in PPS3

3.1 Ansatz und Grundstrukturen

Der erste Schritt, ein Projekt zu planen besteht darin, es in
Teilaufgaben zu zerlegen. Diese hierarchische Struktur ist der
Projektstrukturplan (PSP). Er ist das zentrale Ordnungsschema der
Projektplanung und -Steuerung. Auf der untersten Ebene des Struk-
turplans sind Arbeitspakete zu definieren, die mit Eckdaten für
Zeit und Kosten abschätzbar sind.

An dieser Stelle beginnt die weitere Zerlegung des Projekts in
Vorgänge. Dies sind Einheiten, welche mit ihrem definierten An-
fangs- und Endzustand in logischer und zeitlicher Abhängigkeit zu
anderen Vorgängen stehen.

Diese zahlreichen Abhängigkeiten bestehen darin, daß ein einzelner Vorgang nur begonnen werden kann, wenn die Erzeugnisse anderer Vorgänge fertiggestellt sind und werden "Anordnungsbeziehungen" genannt.

In diesem Modell des Netzplans wird also der Projektablauf als
gerichteter Graph mit den Vorgängen als Knoten und den Anordnungsbeziehungen als Kanten dargestellt.

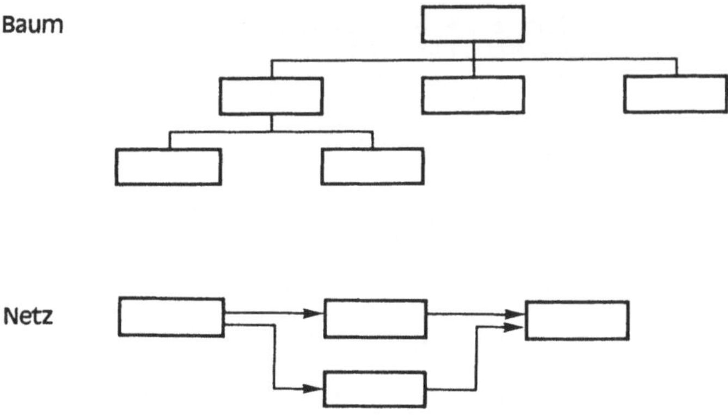

Abb. 2: Grundstrukturen in PPS

PPS3 - Projektplanungs- und Steuerungssystem
- Modellbildung in PPS3 -

Wichtige Datenfelder der Vorgänge sind:

Eingabe:

Name (Primärschlüssel)
Beschreibung (freier Text)
Funktionsträger (Verweis zur Organisationsstruktur, s.u.)
Dauer
Terminvorgaben,
Fix- und Ist-Termine

Ausgabe:

frühester Anfangs-/Endtermin
spätester Anfangs-/Endtermin
Pufferzeiten (geben an, inwieweit der Vorgang verschoben werden kann, ohne das Projekt zu verzögern).

Die Anordnungsbeziehungen werden im wesentlichen beschrieben durch:

Vorgänger, Nachfolger — Name der inzidierten Vorgänge (Vorgang, dessen Ergebnisse vor Beginn des Nachfolgers vorliegen müssen)

Typ — gibt an, ob Anfang oder Ende der betreffenden Vorgänge inzidiert werden

minimaler/ maximaler Zeitabstand — gibt eine einzuhaltende Wartezeit (mögliche Vorziehzeit) zwischen zwei Vorgängen an

Somit sind die beiden Grundstrukturen

Baum (z.B. Projektstrukturplan)

und

Netz (Netzplan mit Vorgängen und Anordnungsbeziehungen)

für das Projektmanagement bestimmend, siehe Abbildung 2.

Die zu Beginn dieses Abschnitts eingeführte Baumstruktur wird auch angewendet für die Aufbauorganisation von Behörden oder Unternehmen ("Organisationsstruktur"), für detaillierte Phasenmodelle der Projektdurchführung oder für meist standardisierte Erzeugnisstrukturen, z.B. einheitlich bezeichnete Baugruppen für alle Kraftfahrzeuge.

PPS3 - Projektplanungs- und Steuerungssystem
- Modellbildung in PPS3 -

3.2   Verbindung der Strukturen in PPS3

Die enge Verbindung zwischen Netzplan und Projektstrukturplan macht ein Projekt überschaubar und liefert die natürliche Vedichtungsrichtung für die auf der detaillierten Vorgangsebene berechneten Termine und Kosten.

Oft ist es sinnvoll, Vorgänge selbst noch in Teilnetzpläne zu untergliedern, um Terminvorgaben wirksam in die Planung einzubringen und um in der Verdichtung nicht zu früh aussagekräftige Termingrößen zu verwischen.

Die in Abb.3 dargestellte Verknüpfung der Strukturen Baum und Netz ist somit für das Management umfangreicher Projekte wesentlich.

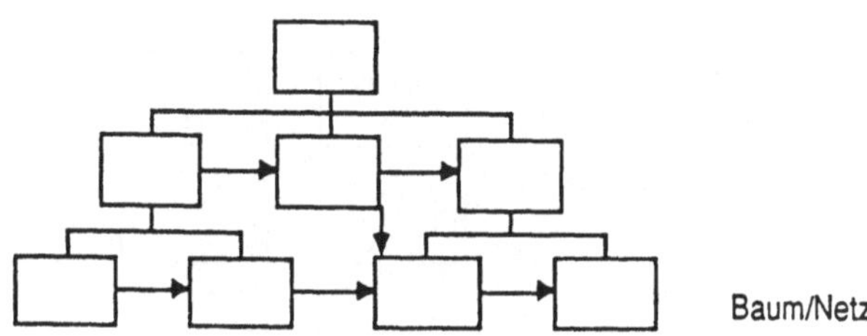

Abb. 3: Verknüpfung der Grundstrukturen

PPS3 - Projektplanungs- und Steuerungssystem
- Modellbildung in PPS3 -

Auch zwischen Baumstrukturen sind Verknüpfungen zu bilden: Die
Teilaufgaben, Arbeitspakete und Vorgänge stehen immer in Beziehung zur Organisationsstruktur. Sie können zusätzlich unterneh-
menseinheitlich standardisierten Erzeugnisstrukturen (z.B. einheitlicher Aufbau für alle Kraftfahrzeuge) oder Funktionsstruktu-
ren (z.B. einheitliches Phasenmodell) zugewiesen werden. Dies
wird durch spezielle Relationen (Kanten) zwischen den Knoten
dargestellt, siehe Abb.4.

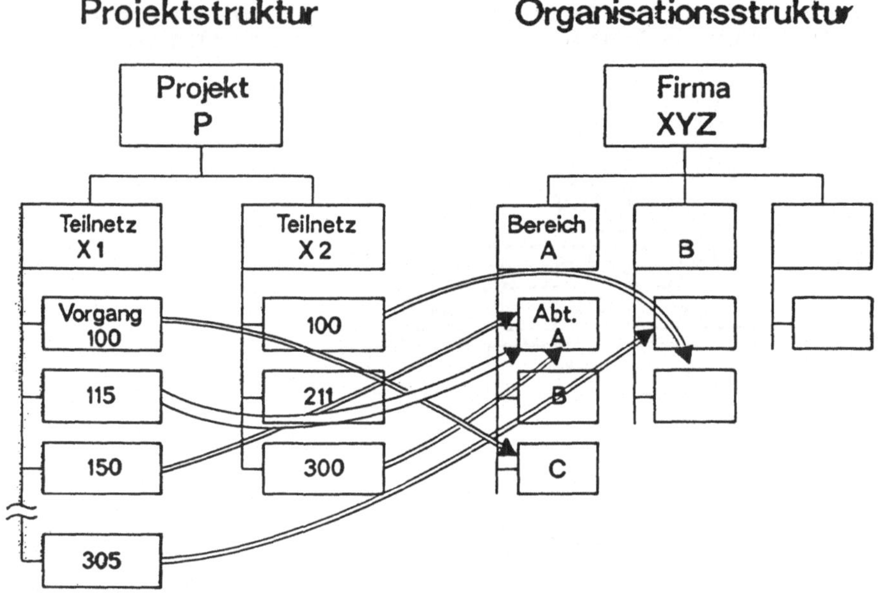

Abb. 4: Verknüpfung von Strukturen

PPS3 - Projektplanungs- und Steuerungssystem
- Modellbildung in PPS3 -

3.3 Ergänzung der Grundstruktur

Der Netzplan kann noch durch <u>Ereignisse</u> und <u>Meilensteine</u> ergänzt
werden.

Die Verwendung von Ereignissen verfeinert die Modellbildung im
Netzplan: Zu jedem Vorgang werden implizit sein Anfangs- und
Endereignis gebildet. Zusätzlich kann der Anwender Zwischenereig-
nisse eingeben, die das Ende wesentlicher Arbeitsabschnitte innerhalb eines Vorgangs darstellen. Die Knoten, welche von den
Anordnungsbeziehungen inzidiert werden, sind in diesem detaillierten Modell nicht mehr die Vorgänge, sondern die Ereignisse.
In der PPS3-Knotenhierarchie sind die Ereignisse demnach direkt
dem Vorgang untergeordnet.

Zu jedem Projekt gibt es technisch oder organisatorisch besonders
kritische Arbeitsschritte oder Zwischenergebnisse. Bei einer
guten Planung sind die zugehörigen Ereignisse im Netzplan besonders exponiert und sinnvoll in der Knotenhierarchie verteilt.
Diese Ereignisse sollten als Meilensteine ausgezeichnet werden
und so gezielten Auswertungen zugänglich gemacht werden. In der
Projektüberwachung liefert die Meilensteinplanung also eine für
die Termintreue des Vorhabens besonders aussagekräftige Verdichtung der Zeitdaten.

PPS3 - Projektplanungs- und Steuerungssystem
- Leistungsmekmale des PPS3-Systems -

---

4. Leistungsmerkmale des PPS3-Systems

4.1 Datenbasis und Datenstruktur

Sämtliche Strukturen mit allen Daten für alle bearbeiteten Projekte werden nach einem einheitlichen Konzept in <u>einer</u> Datenbasis verwaltet.
Im Falle der SQL-Version ist dies das System ORACLE.

ORACLE ist als relationales Datenbanksystem (RDBMS) besonders geeignet für Anwendungen mit zahlreichen Verweisen wie sie im Projektmanagement vorkommen. Dank seiner Flexibilität können kundenspezifische Erweiterungen der PPS3-Datenstruktur leicht vorgenommen werden. Es verfügt einerseits über flexible Vorkehrungen zur Speicher- und Laufzeitoptimierung, andererseits über eine im wesentlichen vollständige Entwicklungsumgebung mit Kommandoschale, Precompilern für 3GL's, interaktivem Menü- und Maskengenerator sowie Listengenerator.

Die normierte Datenbanksprache SQL ist die zentrale Sprache in ORACLE mit allen Werkzeugen und nicht etwa auf andersartige Datenmodelle oder Abfragemechanismen aufgesetzt. Auch durch seine hohe Portabilität und das angeschlossene Tabellenkalkulationsprogramm eignet es sich als Basis für eine integrationsfähige Standardsoftware wie PPS3.

Weitere Hilfsmittel zur Integration sind der Mehrbenutzerbetrieb und der Datenschutz des RDBMS.

Durch die Verwendung von SQL ist es grundsätzlich möglich, PPS3 auch auf andere relationale Datenbanken zu portieren.

Das für PPS charakteristische Zusammenwirken der Grundstrukturen <u>Baum</u> und <u>Netz</u> wird durch eine gemeinsame Hierarchie der Knotentypen Teilaufgabe/Arbeitspaket, Vorgang, Ereignis und Dokument dargestellt ("<u>Knotenhierarchie</u>"). Die Baumstruktur ist ein wertvolles Ordnungsmittel, beginnend mit der Unterteilung der <u>projektübergreifenden</u> PPS-Datenbank in projekteigene Zweige (s.Abb.5) über die Strukturierung der einzelnen Projekte in Teilaufgaben bis hin zur Zuordnung der Vorgänge mit ihren Zeitdaten zu den Teilaufgaben. Neben dieser Ordnungsfunktion definiert die Baumstruktur auch die von der Praxis geforderte Verdichtungsrichtung für Termin- und Kostendaten. Erst durch diese <u>Verdichtung</u> gewinnen die komplexen Netzplandaten an Informationsgehalt für das Management.

Die Knotenhierarchie liefert also die gewünschte Synthese der Grundstrukturen Baum und Netz. Auf diesem Wege werden auch Ereignisse, Meilensteine und Dokumente sowie Kosten- und Einsatzmitteldaten und organisatorische Daten auf natürliche Weise in das Informationssystem eingebunden.

Weitere wesentliche Bestandteile der PPS3-Datenstruktur sind die bereits in Kap.3 erwähnten Anordnungsbeziehungen und speziellen Relationen.

PPS3 – Projektplanungs- und Steuerungssystem
– Leistungsmerkmale des PPS3-Systems –

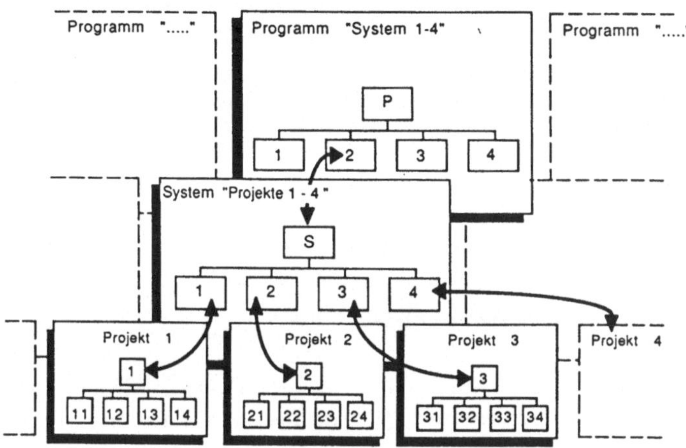

Abb. 5:   Programme/Systeme/Projekte in der PPS3-Knotenhierarchie

Diese Einheitlichkeit der physischen Datenspeicherung und der logischen Datenstruktur bieten zusammen mit PPS3-spezifischen Datenopera-
tionen eine wesentliche Hilfe für Standardisierungen und Vergleiche
der Projektverläufe.

PPS3 - Projektplanungs- und Steuerungssystem
- Leistungsmerkmale des PPS3-Systems -

4.2 Terminplanung

Der Funktionsmodul "Zeitrechnung" berechnet aus den vorgegebenen,
Fix- und Ist-Terminen und der Dauer der Vorgänge deren zeitliche
Lage und Pufferzeiten, die sich aus ihrer Verflechtung in dem aus
Vorgängen und Anordnungsbeziehungen gebildeten Netz ergibt. Die
Ergebnisse werden nach frühester und spätester Lage unterschieden
und als Kalenderdaten und relative Zeitpunkte angegeben.

Die Zeitrechnung in PPS3 bietet:

- Berechnung von Netzen mit oder ohne Berücksichtigung hierarchischer Abhängigkeiten

- Berechnung von Teilhierarchien

- Mehrprojektplanung

- Berechnung von Mischnetzen (Vorgänge als Knoten oder Kanten
  dargestellt)

- Dauern und Zeitabstände können in unterschiedlichen Kalendern
  angegeben sein

- Übertragung der Rechenergebnisse in andere Strukturen und Verdichtung entsprechend dieser Strukturen

- Bearbeitung von Vorgabe, Fix- und Ist-Terminen.

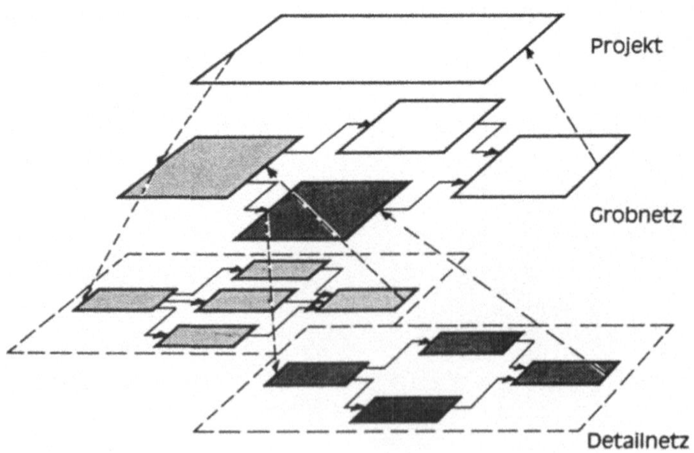

Abb. 6: Netzhierarchie

PPS3 - Projektplanungs- und Steuerungssystem
- Leistungsumfang des PPS3-Systems -

4.3 Kostenplanung und -Verfolgung

Die Kostenrechnung in PPS3 bietet:

- Zuordnung beliebig vieler Kostenpositionen zu Elementen der Projektstrukturen

- Ermittlung der Kosten für jedes kostenrelevante Strukturelement

- Summierung bzw. Verdichtung der objekt- und zeitbezogenen Kosten je Struktur

- Vergleiche der geplanten mit den aktuellen Kostengrößen

- Berücksichtigung von benutzerspezifischen Kalkulationsschemata

- Verarbeitung von Ausgabepositionen zur Planung und Überwachung des Mittelabflusses:

  Direkte Eingabe des Arbeitswertes oder Berechnung des Arbeitswertes (über den Fertigstellungsgrad im Netzplan) durch das System.

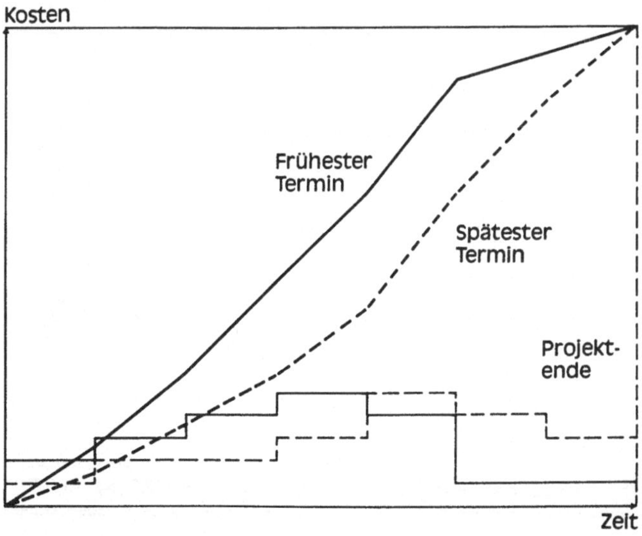

Abb. 7: Kostenplanung

PPS3 - Projektplanungs- und Steuerungssystem
- Leistungsmerkmale des PPS3-Systems -

4.4 Benutzerschnittstelle

Das Datenmanagement in PPS3 bietet:

- Eingabe, Anzeige und Änderung von Projektdaten im Dialog,
  wahlweise im Laienmodus (Masken) oder Expertenmodus (befehls-
  gesteuerter Dialog)

- Alle Daten-Operationen mit Plausibilitätskontrollen

- Massendateneingabe mit frei wählbaren Formaten

Die Ergebnisdarstellung in PPS3 bietet:

- Listenausgabe in Standard- oder frei wählbaren Formaten
  (Listengenerator)

- Graphische Ausgabe über die Standardsoftware GRANEDA der Firma
  NETRONIC

  Dargestellt werden auf Bildschirm, Drucker oder Plotter:

  - Baumstrukturen
  - Netzstrukturen
  - Balkenpläne (zeitliche Lage)
  - Diagramme (Business Graphiken)

```
┌────────────────────────────────────────────────┬──────────────────┐
│              << PPS-DIALOG >>                    │ Kalkulationsschema│
├────────────────────────────────────────────────┴──────────────────┤
│                                                                    │
│   Nummer des Kalkulationsschemas: 1                                │
│                                                   Zuschlag  Zuschlag│
│   Lfd-Nr    Sum-Ken    Bezeichn. o. Kostenart       Soll       Ist │
│   ────────────────────────────────────────────────────────────────│
│      01                 .MAT                        0.00      0.00  │
│      02         +       .FREMD                      0.00      0.00  │
│      03         +       .LOHN                       0.00      0.00  │
│      04         +       .GEH                        0.00      0.00  │
│      05         +       .SKE                        0.00      0.00  │
│      06                 HERSTELLKOSTEN              0.00      0.00  │
│      07         +       GEWINN                      5.00      5.50  │
│      08                 SELBSTKOSTEN                0.00      0.00  │
│      09         +       UST                        14.00     14.00  │
│      10                 SELBSTK. INCL. UST          0.00      0.00  │
│                                                                    │
│   Speichern des Kalkulationsschemas (J/N) : J                      │
├────────────────────────────────────────────────────────────────────┤
│ <<F1 HILFE>> <<F2 ZURUECK>> <<F3 AUSWAHL>> <<F4 VORWAERTS>> <<RETURN WEITER>>│
└────────────────────────────────────────────────────────────────────┘
```

Abb. 8: Beispiel einer Maske

Quellen:

[1]   IABG, Abteilung TDA
       PPS-Anwenderhandbuch
       Ottobrunn 1987

[2]   IABG, Abteilung TDA
       verschiedene Präsentations- und Schulungsunterlagen über PPS

Weiterführende Literatur:

[3]   GPM Gesellschaft für Projektmanagement
       (Uhdestr. 11a, 8000 München 71)

       - Schriftenreihe
       - Berichte zu den Jahrestagungen

[4]   INTERNET
       Project Management
       Butterworth & Co Publishers Ltd
       London

       z.B.: Konzeptioneller Überblicksartikel
             M. BRANTON, T. BUTLER
             Firm foundation for project management
             Heft November 1987

[5]   B. BOEHM
       Software Engineering Economics
       Prentice Hall
       Englewood Cliffs, N.J.
       1981   (insbes. Chapter 32)

Auswirkungen neuer Benutzungsoberflächen auf die Systeminfrastrukturen betrieblicher Informationsverarbeitung

Gottfried B. Bertram
ADV/ORGA F. A. Meyer AG

2940 Wilhelmshaven

Neue Benutzungsoberflächen haben Auswirkungen auf die Benutzer, auf die Anwendungssoftware und deren Gestaltung, aber auch auf die Anforderungen an Betriebssysteme, auf die Datenverarbeitungs- und Bürokommunikations-Infrastruktur sowie die Telekommunikationssysteme, die darunter liegen.

Auswirkungen auf den Benutzer

Was ändert sich für den Benutzer?

Moderne Benutzungsoberflächen bieten dem Benutzer sog. konkrete Präsentationen. D.h. auf dem Bildschirm stellt sich konkret dar, was geschieht, womit gearbeitet wird und was als Resultat entsteht. Dazu befolgt man 3 Prinzipien.

Das erste ist das sog. WYSIWYG-Prinzip. Es bedeutet: What you see is what you get. In der Gestaltung zeigt sich das durch einen Bildschirm, auf dem in mehreren Fenstern Formulare, Texte, Skizzen und Tabellen erscheinen, so wie der Benutzer das beim Arbeiten auf dem Schreibtisch gewohnt ist.

Das Stichwort Schreibtisch liefert den Hinweis auf die sog. Desk Top Publishing Systeme die genauso ermöglichen, wie auf dem Schreibtisch mit Bleistift und Papier, nun auf dem Bildschirm Texte zu komponieren. (Bild 1)

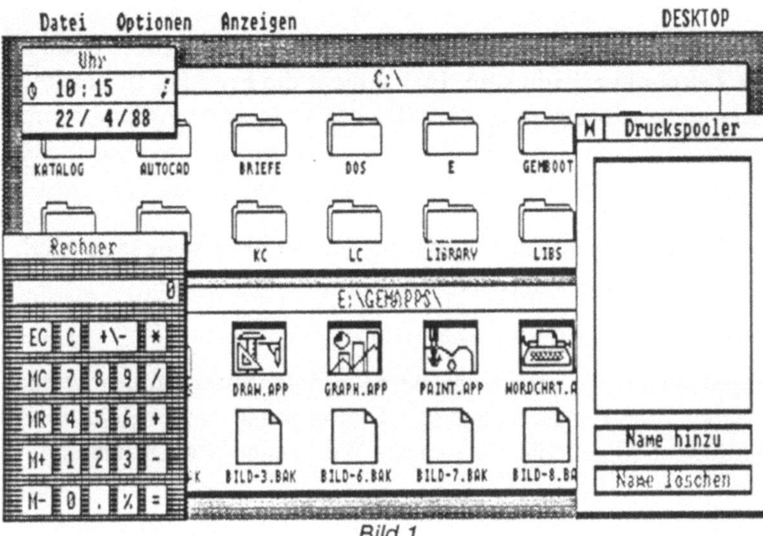

Bild 1

Das Desk Top Prinzip erlaubt die Arbeit an mehreren Arbeitsvorgängen gleichzeitig in verschiedenen Arbeitsumgebungen auf Bildschirmen, die durch Fenster dargestellt werden.

Das dritte Prinzip, das moderne Benutzungsoberflächen zu berücksichtigen hätten, ist die Dialogführung durch den Benutzer, nicht durch den Computer, nicht durch ein Programm.

Extern gesteuerte Dialoge

Heute führen die Programme Dialoge mit dem Benutzer.

Dabei gibt das jeweilige Programm vor, welche Interaktionen dem Benutzer zu einem bestimmten Zeitpunkt erlaubt sind. Er hat nicht die Freiheit, zu bestimmen, welche Aktionen zu welchen Zweck er anwählt. Da ist das Anwendungsprogramm, das dieses vorgibt.

Das führt zu Reaktionen, die durchaus schon aus der Presse bekannt sind, daß sich in vielen Fällen die Benutzer am Arbeitsplatz kontrolliert fühlen.

Demnächst jedoch werden wir über moderne Benutzerinteraktionstechniken die Möglichkeiten haben, daß der Benutzer den Dialog selber steuert, daß die Programme diesen Steuerungen folgen, daß sie sich wie Werkzeuge benutzen lassen.

Bisher hat sich noch keiner durch die technischen Hilfsmittel auf seinem Schreibtisch, z.B. den Tischrechner, die Schreibmaschine, das Telefon oder das Telexgerät, kontrolliert gefühlt. Warum sollte er das, wenn die gleichen Hilfsmittel und Werkzeuge multifunktional vom Arbeitsplatzcomputer angeboten werden. Das Gefühl des Kontrolliertseins kommt von der gebräuchlichen Präsentations- und Interaktions- d.h. Dialogtechnik, bei der das Programm, oder für den Laien eben der Computer, den Dialogablauf steuert und nicht der Benutzer. Extern, also vom Benutzer gesteuerte Dialoge, sind jetzt erst möglich. Und das aus zwei Gründen: nämlich aus neueren Erkenntnissen und Entwicklungen und eben auch durch die Verfügbarkeit immer mehr und immer preiswerterer Computerleistungen am Arbeitsplatz.

Gleichartige Gestaltung gleicher Bedienvorgänge

Zu den neueren Erkenntnissen gehört, daß in allen Dialogen, egal für welche Anwendungen, immer wieder dieselben Interaktionen vorkommen. Das sind immer dieselben Bedienungen und Anzeigen, beispielsweise zum Schreiben, Zeichnen, Positionieren, Anwählen, Auswählen, Kopieren, Rückgängig machen oder zu komplexeren Aufgaben, wie z.B. dem Ausfüllen ganzer Formulare.

Man hat gefunden, daß der anwendungsspezifische Teil der Dialoge durchaus kleiner ist, als man früher glaubte oder als man es bisher gesehen hatte.

Bisher wurden Dialoge immer wieder neu erfunden, immer wieder neu gestaltet, aus jeder neuen Anwendungssoftware heraus für im Prinzip immer dieselben Interaktionen. Das führte zu beliebig gestalteten Dialogen und zu mehrfachen Ausbildungsaufwänden für die Bedienung von z.B. unterschiedlichen Textverarbeitungssystemen.

Von den neuesten Entwicklungen ausgehend sind wir also jetzt in der Lage, die Dialoggestaltung, zumindest die vieler Dialogelemente, zu standardisieren und zu normen. Sinn jeder Normung ist es, immer viele gleichartige, aber verschiedene technische Konstruktionen für den gleichen Zweck zu vereinheitlichen. Das ergibt Austauschbarkeit und gleiches Veständnis von und gleiches Verständigen für gleiche Dinge.

Mittlerweile ist auch die technische Entwicklung der Geräte so fortgeschritten, daß bezahlbare Voraussetzungen für moderne Benutzerinteraktionssysteme möglich sind. Arbeitsplatzsysteme mit viel Computerleistung, mit Mausbedienung und Fenstertechnik auf dem Bildschirm und das Verständnis, wie die Software dafür aussehen muß, und Ideen zur genormten Dialoggestaltung liegen vor.

IBM hat dazu den Begriff des Common User Access geprägt. Er bedeutet, daß jeder Computer und jedes Programmsystem sich zukünftig mindestens im Prinzip gleichartig bedienen lassen sollten. So wie sich jeder in jedes Auto setzen kann und dort dieselbe Anordnung aller Bedienelemente vorfindet, wie das Lenkrad, die Gas-, Kupplungs-, und Bremspedale oder den Ganghebel, mit immer der gleichen Lage der Gänge, so erwartet man zum Benutzen von Programmen, und auch was die Effekte und Reaktionen dieser Benutzung angeht, zukünftig ebenfalls immer eine gleichartige oder dieselbe Gestaltung. Sicher wird es leichte Unterschiede in Dialogen geben, beispielsweise in solchen für die fotosatzfähige Textverarbeitung oder in solchen zur Auslösung einer Finanzbuchhaltungstransaktion. Trotzdem sind zwei wichtige Auswirkungen jetzt schon abzusehen.

1   In Zukunft wird sehr viel lokale Computerleistung an Arbeitsplatzcomputern oder Arbeitsplatzsystemen zur Verfügung stehen.

2   Gleiche oder gleichartige Dialoge, auch für unterschiedliche Anwendungen, erlauben, die Dialoge von der Applikation zu trennen.

Das wird einen starken Einfluß auf die Software-Architektur der Zukunft haben.

Auswirkungen auf die Anwendungssoftware-Architektur

Die letze erwähnte Tatsache der Trennung des Dialogs von der Anwendungssoftware wird sich zukünftig sehr stark auf die Struktur der Anwendungsprogramme auswirken.

Mit einer externen Dialogsteuerung, d.h. einer solchen, die beim Benutzer liegt und nicht im Anwendungsprogramm, entsteht eine Situation, in der sich Dialogprogrammierung und Anwendungsprogrammierung trennen lassen. Das eine realisiert die Benutzerinteraktion und das andere die Anwendungsfunktionalität. Beispiele dafür sind Dialoge, in denen man ein Formular ausfüllt, korrigiert, überprüft und freigibt. Alle Vorgänge zum Ausfüllen eines solchen Formulars haben im allgemeinen sehr wenig mit einer nachgeschalteten Anwendung zu tun, mit der die im Formular erfaßten Daten beispielsweise irgendwo verbucht werden. Der Dialog und der Benutzer der Anwendung sind frei davon, wie das Anwendungsprogramm funktioniert. Sicher wird der Dialogteil einige applikationsspezifische Prüfungen und Reaktionen auf Fehleinträge aufweisen, zu 90 % aber unabhängig von der Anwendungsfunktionalität sein. Der Dialog gibt irgendwann einmal auf die Freigabe des Benutzers hin einen Datensatz in Form einer Botschaft an das Anwendungsprogramm ab, das seinerseits die so gewonnenen Daten verbucht.

Trennung von Dialog und Anwendung

Plastisches Bespiel dafür ist die Elektronische Post. In naher Zukunft werden die Fernmeldedienste der Postverwaltungen derartiges anbieten. Das funktioniert konkret so, daß man auf dem Bildschirm eines Arbeitsplatzsystems einen Brief mit Addressaten und Absender schreibt, dafür gibt es selbstverständlich einen Dialog, der, wenn der Brief fertig ist, ihn elektronisch an einen Postrechner weiterleitet, wo er anhand der Adresse wiederum weitergeleitet wird, bis er über evtl. mehrere Computer das Arbeitsplatzsystem des Empfängers erreicht.

Den Dialog, solche Briefe elektronisch zu erzeugen und zu versenden, nennt man in der jetzt schon für diesen Zweck erstellten Norm den User Agent.

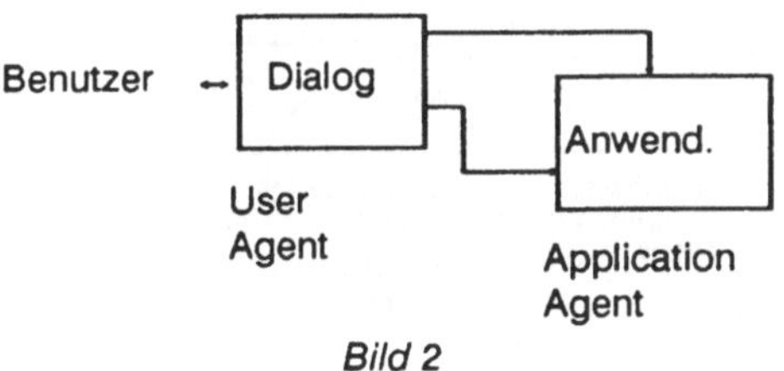

Bild 2

Die Anwendungs-Software aber, die die Briefe sortiert und weiterleitet bis zum elektronischen Briefkasten des Empfängers, heißt Message Transfer Agent und führt nie einen Dialog mit einem Benutzer (Bild 2).

Diese Programme realisieren nur die Funktionen der Anwendung, nämlich die, die Post weiterzuleiten.

Eine solche Trennung von Dialog und Anwendung ist nicht nur wünschenswert, um allgemein verständliche, immer gleichartige und mit modernen Hilfsmitteln gestaltbare Benutzungsoberflächen zu erzeugen, sondern sie ist auch für andere Zwecke und Situationen nützlich und sinnvoll. Man kann eben den Dialogteil, der den losgelösten Anwendungsteil mit einem Strom von Daten und Botschaften versorgt wegnehmen und bei gleicher Anwendungssoftware durch ein Gerät ersetzen, das dieselben Daten automatisch erfaßt und an die Applikationen weiterleitet. Man kann z. B. Ein- und Ausgangszeiten von Mitarbeitern von der Stempelkarte über einen Bildschirmdialog erfassen oder aber ein Zeiterfassungsgerät direkt die Daten an die Anwendungsprogramme liefern lassen.

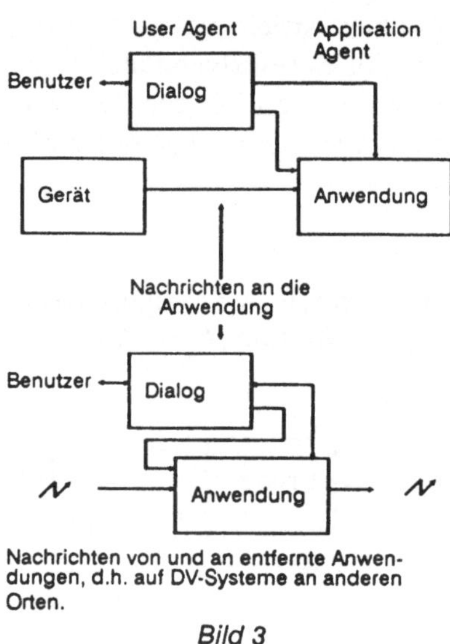

Nachrichten von und an entfernte Anwendungen, d.h. auf DV-Systeme an anderen Orten.

Bild 3

Noch interessanter wird eine Lösung in dieser getrennten Form von User Agent und Application Agent, wenn man daran denkt, daß heute große Mengen von Daten, normale Geschäftsvorfälle betreffend, von Computern gedruckt und auf Papier von der Post zum Empfänger transportiert werden, wo sie wieder über irgendeinen Bildschirm einzugeben sein werden. Ist dagegen eine Anwendung vom Bediendialog getrennt, dann könnte sie ihre Eingaben zur Verbuchung von Geschäftsvorfällen auch direkt über die Fernmeldeleitung von einer anderen Anwendung entgegennehmen. Das bedarf lediglich einer Absprache und einer Norm, wie z. B. eine Rechnung auf der Fernmeldeleitung elektronisch aussieht (Bild 3).

Direkter, dialogfreier Datenaustausch zwischen Anwendungen

In der Zukunft werden Logistiksysteme wie das System ILAS von ADV/ORGA direkt Daten an beispielsweise Finanzbuchhaltungssysteme wie IFAS als Empfänger versenden können.

Geschäftsverkehr Heute - Morgen

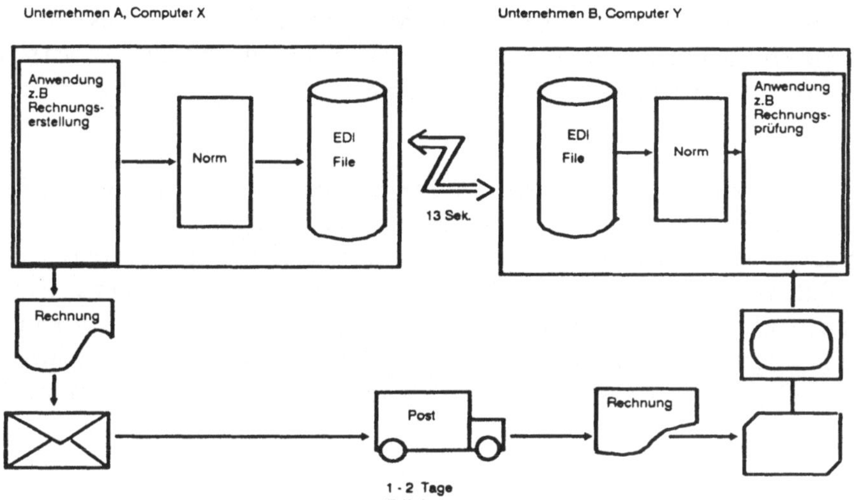

Bild 4

Normen für einige der benötigten, elektronisch darzustellenden Dokumente für den weltweiten Geschäftsdatenaustausch wurden im Dezember 1987 schon beschlossen. Es handelt sich dabei um die EDIFACT Nachrichtentypen für den Electronic Data Interchange For Finance Automation Commerce and Transport. Die direkte Abwicklung von Geschäftsvorfällen zwischen zwei Applikationssystemen über die Fernmel-

deleitung wird stark zunehmen, da sie doch viel unnötige menschliche Benutzerinteraktion und den damit verbundenen Arbeitsaufwand ersetzt (Bild 4). Technisch gesehen
bedeutet diese Trennung von DV-Anwendungen in Dialog und Anwendungsfunktionalität, daß die Dialogkomponente Nachrichten an die Verarbeitungskomponenten
senden, die in etwa immer denselben generellen Aufbau haben. Sie beschreiben, um
was es sich handelt in der Form von Aussagen darüber, was die Applikation tun soll
(Aufträge). Und sie beschreiben Daten, die von der Anwendung für den Auftrag benötigt werden.

Diese Nachrichten enthalten zusätzlich einen Verständigungsbereich, der sicherstellt,
daß das Zusammenspiel korrekt abgewickelt wird. Für eine Anwendung zur Führung
von Sparkonten ergäben sich beispielsweise die Aufträge: Kontoeröffnen, Einzahlen
und Verbuchen, Auszahlungen prüfen und verbuchen und das Konto ggfls. wieder
schließen. Dazu gehören jeweils die Daten, die Kontonummern und die Beträge. Das
Protokoll zur Verständigung zwischen dem Dialogteil und der Anwendungsfunktion
enthält dann noch Nachrichten, ob das Konto genug Deckung für Auszahlungen auf-
weist und ob Abhebungen im Sinne der gesetzlichen Bindung nicht zu hoch sind. Letz-
teres wäre im Verständigungsteil auszutauschen.

Die Technik, Software so zu bauen, daß ihre einzelnen Teile über Nachrichten miteinander in Verbindung stehen und darüber Objekte austauschen, die logische Sachver-
halte darstellen anstelle konkreter Software-technischer Implementierungen, nennt
man mittlerweile objektorientierte Programmierung für in verschiedenen Zusammen-
hängen mehrfach zu benutzende Programmkomponenten. Die objektorientierte Programmierung erlaubt, das ist ein weiterer Vorteil, die leichte Austauschbarkeit von
Teilen z. B. im Änderungsfalle, ohne daß jeweils das gesamte Softwaresystem betroffen wäre.

User-Interface-Management-Systeme (UIMS)

Bisher zeigten sich die Auswirkungen neuer Benutzungsoberflächen von Dialog und Interaktionstechniken bzw. die Ergebnisse der Forschung hierzu auf die Software-Architektur und sogar auf die Programmiertechnik.

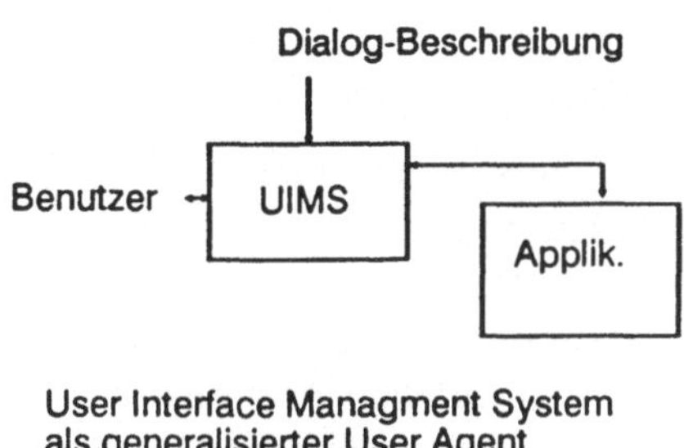

User Interface Managment System
als generalisierter User Agent
Bild 5

Zusammenfassend ist festzuhalten, daß Dialoge zukünftig mit mehr oder weniger gleichartigen Gestaltungselementen gebaut werden, und zwar nicht durch individuelle Programmierung, sondern durch einfache Spezifikation dessen, was der Benutzer in einem Dialog tun darf und nicht was er tun soll. Dialoge werden von speziellen Software-Teilsystemen abgewickelt werden, die man UIMS User Interface Management Systeme nennt und die meist lokal in Arbeitsplatzcomputern ablaufen (Bild 5). Man erhält damit ein weiteres, generalisiertes Systemsoftware-Teilsystem ähnlich dem DBMS Datenbanksystem für die Datenhaltung. Ein UIMS erzeugt die Dialogreaktionen auf Benutzerinteraktionen entlang einer Dialogbeschreibung, die nicht den Ablauf starr festlegt, sondern nur gewisse Reaktionen für gewisse Aktionen anbietet, darunter natürlich solche, die im Dialog gewonnene Daten an die abgetrennten Applikationsprogramme weitergeben. Die Möglichkeit, Dialoge lediglich zu spezifizieren und nicht mehr zu programmieren, erlaubt zusätzlich zu einer stark vereinfachten Entwicklung mit weniger Aufwand eine leichte Änderbarkeit und Anpassbarkeit der Dialoge an Benutzerwünsche, an nationale Sprachen, was Textelemente betrifft, und an sich manchmal doch ändernde Applikationsfunktion.

Das PPD-Modell moderner Systemarchitektur

Aus den aufgezeigten Entwicklungen, die Benutzerinteraktion von Anwendungssoftware zu trennen und beide über Nachrichtenaustausch miteinander zu verbinden, ergeben sich Möglichkeiten, Konsequenzen und Fragen, wo z. B. das User Interface Management-System ablaufen kann oder soll, und wo die Applikation als Programm ausgeführt werden sollte.

Seit einigen Jahren schon kennen wir analog zu den User-Interface-Management-Systemen die Möglichkeit, daß Anwendungen Datenbanksysteme über Nachrichtenaustausch auf anderen Computersystemen benutzen, auf anderen als auf denen die Programme selber ablaufen. Darauf beruhen die Mehrbenutzersysteme in der Form von Netzwerk. Jedes Programm hat in solchen Architekturen seinen eigenen Computer und teilt sich nicht mehr im Zeitscheibenverfahren die Rechnerleistung mit anderen.

Computernetze als Mehrbenutzersysteme

Es muß aber über ein geeignetes und schnelles Netzwerk zentral gemeinsam benutzte Daten im Datenbanksystem erreichen können. Wir haben es hier mit Shared Information Resource Systemen zu tun, in denen die zentrale Datenbankfunktion nicht im gleichen Rechner angesiedelt ist wie die Anwendungsprogramme.

Bild 6

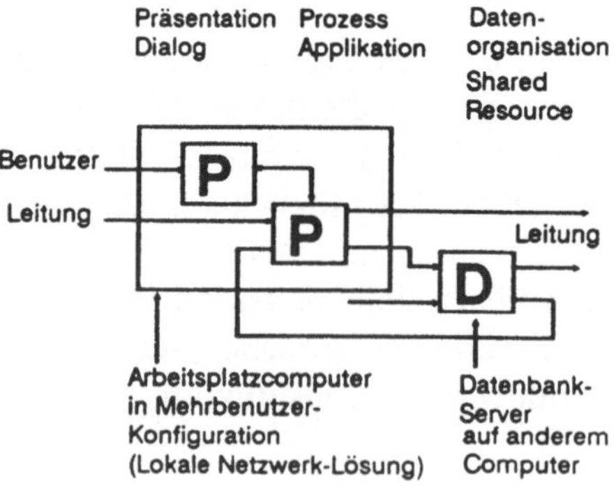

Man sieht auch, die Datenorganisation und der Datenbankbetrieb lassen sich, analog zu den Dialogen, vonden Anwendungsprozessen trennen. Diese Möglichkeiten führen zur Zergliederung zukünftiger Softwaresysteme in eigene Programmbereiche für die Präsentation und den Dialog, für den Prozess als Ablauf der Anwendung und für die Datenorganisation als gemeinsam benutzten Datenbankbetrieb. Diese PPD Architektur moderner Anwendungssysteme kann unter Umständen auf einem einzigen Computer koexistieren.

Das ist auch der Fall bei als Einplatzsystem genutzten Arbeitsplatzcomputern oder in klassischen Großrechnersystemen mit mehreren Benutzern an dummen Terminals. In letzterem Fall gibt es jedoch einige Probleme, da moderne Präsentations- und Dialogtechniken mit graphischen Gestaltungselementen sehr viel Rechenleistung für jeweils einen Benutzer erfordern und schnell Bildänderungen aufbauen müssen. Dem können weder die klassischen Großrechnersysteme entsprechen noch die Übertragungsgeschwindigkeiten, die von Terminalnetzen angeboten werden. Deshalb erfand man schon Anfang der 80er Jahre verteilte Lösungen, in denen Dialoge von User Interface Management Systemen in lokalen, am Arbeitsplatz angesiedelten Computern ausgeführt wurden, um einen schnellen Bildaufbau und eine schnelle Reaktion zu gewährleisten (Bild 7).

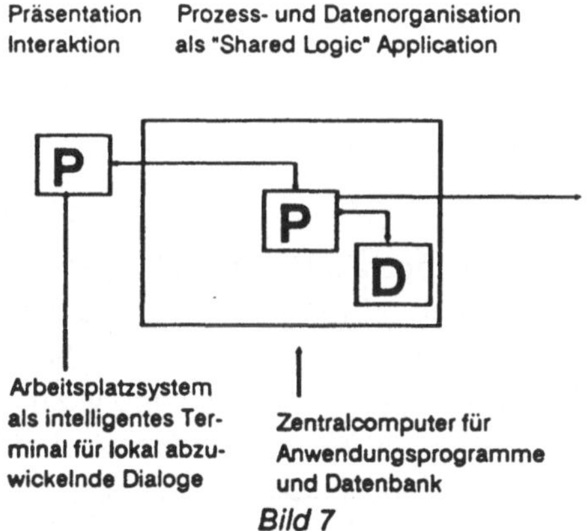

Bild 7

Wenn ein Computer einem Benutzer allein zur Verfügung steht, gibt es eben keine Probleme mit den sog. Antwortzeiten. Die so oft als intelligente Endgeräte bezeichneten Arbeitsplatzcomputer liefern nur noch Datenpakete an die Applikationen in den zentralen Großrechnern und entlasten sie so von allen Leistungen für die Präsentation, den Bildaufbau und die Benutzerinteraktionen. Mit fallenden Preisen für Computer, für Rechenleistung und für den Speicherausbau, bei dem hohen Bedarf, den User-Interface Management Systeme an Speicher haben, ca. 1 - 2 MB, stellte man fest, daß viele Applikationsfunktionen und ihre Programme oft klein im Vergleich dazu sind und packte sie konsequenter Weise in das Arbeitsplatzcomputersystem zusammen mit den Dialogteilen (siehe Bild 6).

Nur der Betrieb der Datenbank verbleibt in solch einer Architektur auf einem Zentralsystem, das evtl. nur noch diese Funktion erfüllt und deshalb je nach Größe nicht mehr ein klassischer Großrechner zu sein braucht.

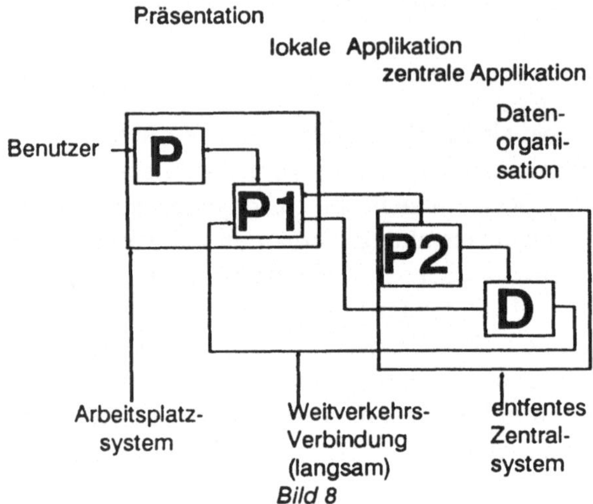

Bild 8

Verteilte DV-Lösungen für Weitverkehrsverbindungen

Will man in dieser Situation die zentrale Datenbank über die Leitung erreichen, muß dies in Geschwindigkeiten möglich sein, die der eines lokalen Plattenzugriffes gleicht. Das bieten nur lokale Netze. Die aber dürfen sich nicht über öffentliches Gelände erstrecken, denn dort gilt Posthoheit und Hochgeschwindigkeits-Datennetze gibt es noch nicht. Auch die ISDN Dienste mit 64 KB/sec. an Geschwindigkeit sind nur ca. 8 mal schneller als heutige Terminal-Leitungsnetze und damit zu langsam für umfangreichen Datenaustausch. Deshalb werden wir immer dann, wenn Weitverkehrsverbindungen zu benutzen sind, eine verteilte Datenverarbeitungslösung nach dem PPD Modell finden, in der einige Anwendungsprozesse auf der Dialogstation laufen, andere aber, z.B. solche zur Aufbereitung großer Datenmengen, in Zentralsystemen verbleiben. Das vermeidet den Transport größerer Datenmengen über vergleichsweise langsame Weitverkehrsverbindungen (Bild 8).

Auswirkungen auf die System-Infrastruktur

Da Arbeitsplatzsysteme, wie PC's und Workstations, heute schon in Preiskategorien gefallen sind, die denen dummer Terminals entsprechen, und weil Arbeitsplatzsysteme multifunktional nicht nur das Terminal ersetzen, sondern gleichzeitig noch das Schreibsystem, den Tischrechner und das Telexgerät, werden sie bald reine Bildschirmterminals verdrängen.

Das wird zwangsläufig PPD Architekturen für moderne Anwendungen fördern, genauso wie der Wunsch nach immer gleichartig gestalteten Benutzerinteraktionen.

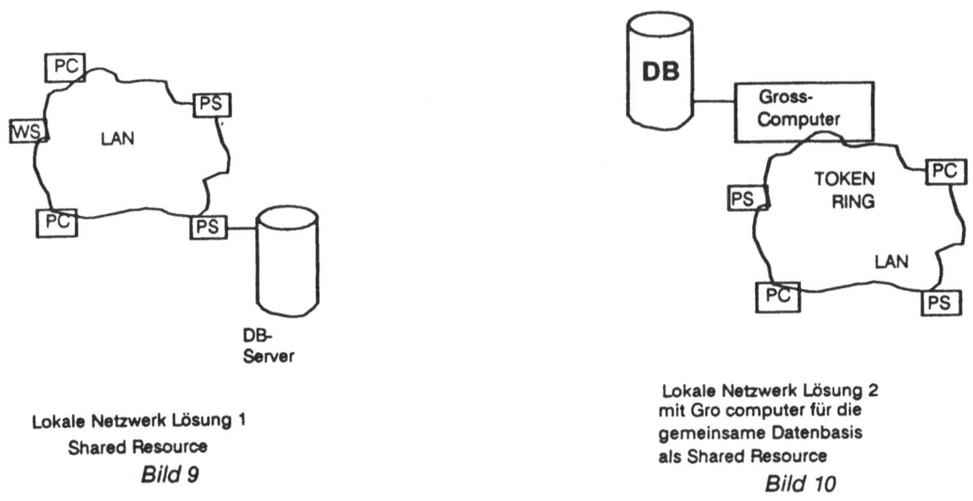

Lokale Netzwerk Lösung 1
Shared Resource
Bild 9

Lokale Netzwerk Lösung 2
mit Gro computer für die
gemeinsame Datenbasis
als Shared Resource
Bild 10

Mehrbenutzersysteme in Netzwerkform (Shared Resource Systeme, Bild 9) in denen sich Programme auf verschiedenen Arbeitsplatzcomputern eine gemeinsame Datenbank teilen, im Gegensatz zu Shared Logic Architecturen, die erzwingen, daß Programme sich einen Computer teilen, werden zukünftig ebenfalls vermehrt anzutreffen sein. Sie bieten mehrbenutzerfähige DV Anwendungssysteme auf der selben Systeminfrastruktur, die man für die Büroautomation und Kommunikation benötigt. Auch hier wird der multifunktionale Aspekt Markt und Möglichkeiten fördern. Das Endgerätenetz der Zukunft ist das schnelle lokale Netz LAN (Bild 10). Es erlaubt Datenverkehr zwischen Programmen, d.h. Computern, mit Geschwindigkeiten, die diesem Zweck angemessen sind. Der hochleistungsfähige Computer am einzelnen Arbeitsplatz erlaubt lokale Dialoge mit allen Vorteilen, die moderne Benutzungsoberflächen bieten können. Auf dieser Basis wird die Zukunft der Datenverarbeitung stärker verteilt sein als heute und zunehmend weniger große Zentralsysteme aufweisen. Das geht einher mit zunehmender Ausfallsicherheit durch Dezentralisierung.

Typische Systeminfrastrukturen die sich herausbilden sind das lokale Netz in zentral nutzbaren Informations-Resourcen auf Serverstationen oder das lokale Netz mit Großcomputern für eben diese Aufgabe. Daneben existieren klassische Zentralsysteme mit Bildschirmterminals zur Benutzerinteraktion und Mischformen. Letztere bieten lokale Netze von Arbeitsplatzsystemen mit sog. Gateways als Weitverkehrsverbindungen zu zentralen Großrechnern (Bild 11). Solche Mischformen lassen erkennen, daß es eine allmähliche Migration in moderne Systemarchitekturen geben wird, so daß existierende Investitionen in DV-Anlagen geschützt bleiben.

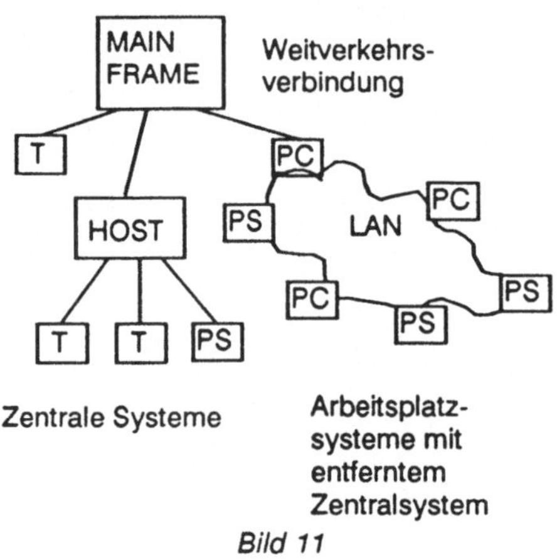

Bild 11

Forschungs- und Entwicklungsaktivitäten der ADV/ORGA

ADV/ORGA arbeitet aktiv in Forschung und Entwicklung sowohl an Systemen als auch an Anwendungssoftware-Produkten, die diesen Entwicklungen Rechnung tragen. Zusammen mit dem Zentrum für graphische Datenverarbeitung ZGDV in Darmstadt, dem Institut von Professor Encarnacao, wird bei ADV/ORGA der User-interface-

Manager Theseus, eine Entwicklung des ZGDV, zur Produktreife weiterentwickel
und für alle wichtigen System-Infrastrukturen bereitgestellt. Er wird portabel verfüg
bar sein für PC's unter MS-DOS und MS-Windows, für Personalsystems unter OS/.
und Presentation Manager, für Workstations unter UNIX und X-Windows.

Seit nunmehr 4 Jahren bietet ADV/ORGA verschiedenste Datenaustauschsysteme fü
Datenbankzugriffe, für Dateiübertragungen und für den Dokumentenaustausch. Si
funktionieren zwischen Computern jeder Größe über alle verfügbaren Leitungsnetze
Ein System zum Zugang zu Datenbanken auf zentralen Großrechnern ist mittlerwei
le hundertfach installiert. Ein weiteres System zur Mitbenutzung entfernter Datenban
ken durch lokale Programme über Leitungsnetze wird zur Zeit benutzt, ein einfaches
aber sehr effizientes elektronisches Postsystem zu bauen, eines für den privaten Ge
brauch auf existierenden Großcomputerinstallationen und deren Terminalnetzen mi
PC's als Fremdgerät. Mehrere Forschungsaktivitäten befassen sich zur Zeit mit den
elektronischen Austausch von Geschäftsdaten über OSI Netze. D. h. über Verbindun
gen und Protokolle nach internationalen Normen, damit Anwendungen mit Compu
tern beliebiger Hersteller und beliebiger Architektur miteinander kommunizierer
können.

Literatur

(1)　Hübner,W. Lux-Mülders,G. Muth,M.
　　　THESEUS
　　　Die Benuzungsoberfläche der UNIBASE Software-Entwicklungs-Umgebung
　　　Springer-Verlag, Berlin Heidelberg New York 1987

(2)　Lokale Netze mit IBM-Systemen
　　　IBM Deutschland GmbH 1987
　　　Form Nr M-125021

(3)　Ullrich,K.
　　　CUA Common User Access und der Presentation Manager,
　　　IBM's strategische Benutzungsoberfläche
　　　IBM Deutschland GmbH (intern) 1988

(4)　Pfaff,G. (ed.)
　　　User Interface Management Systems
　　　Proceedings of the Workshop on User Interface Mangement Systems
　　　held in Seeheim, FRG, November 1-3, 1983
　　　Springer-Verlag, Berlin Heidelberg New York Tokyo